ALL POLITICS IS LOCAL

ALL
POLITICS
IS LOCAL

Family, Friends, and Provincial

Interests in the Creation of the Constitution

Christopher Collier

University Press of New England
HANOVER AND LONDON

University Press of New England, 37 Lafayette St., Lebanon, NH 03766
Printed in the United States of America.

5 4 3 2 1

Library of Congress Cataloging-in-Publication Data
Collier, Christopher, 1930–
All politics is local : family, friends, and provincial interests in
the creation of the Constitution / Christopher Collier.
p. cm.
Includes bibliographical references and index.
ISBN 1-58465-290-X (cloth : alk. paper)
1. Connecticut—Politics and government—1775–1865.
2. Political culture—Connecticut—History—18th century.   3. Local
government—Connecticut—History—18th century.   4. State rights—
History—18th century.   5. United States. Constitutional Convention
(1787)   6. Constitutional history—United States.   I. Title.
F99 .C65 2003
973.3'18—dc22
2003016930

Maps by Northern Cartographic of Burlington, Vermont.

FOR MY BROTHER

Contents

Illustrations

Acknowledgments

In the course of writing a scholarly monograph the author builds on the work of other scholars. My great debt to three dissertation writers is manifest in my citations. They are John Gaspare Saladino, Harvey Milton Wachtell, and Philip H. Jordan. I am happy to have this opportunity to thank John K. White of Catholic University, who offered support and encouragement at a timely moment. John P. Kaminski and Jere Daniel, readers for the University Press of New England, provided many useful suggestions and corrections and priceless encouragement as well. I very much appreciate their interest and assistance. Richard D. Brown and R. Kent Newmyer, colleagues at the University of Connecticut, read an earlier version of this study, and I appreciate the time they took to do so.

The formulation, "dual localism," first came to my attention by way of a 1974 doctoral dissertation by Thomas Jodziewicz. I thank him.

To the editors and staff at the University Press of New England, I extend heartiest thanks for their encouragement, support, technical know-how, and cheerful good works.

Everything I do benefits from the participation of my wife, Bonnie, who over a generation and more has morphed from my student to my teacher, a colleague of everyday intellectual surprises.

ALL POLITICS IS LOCAL

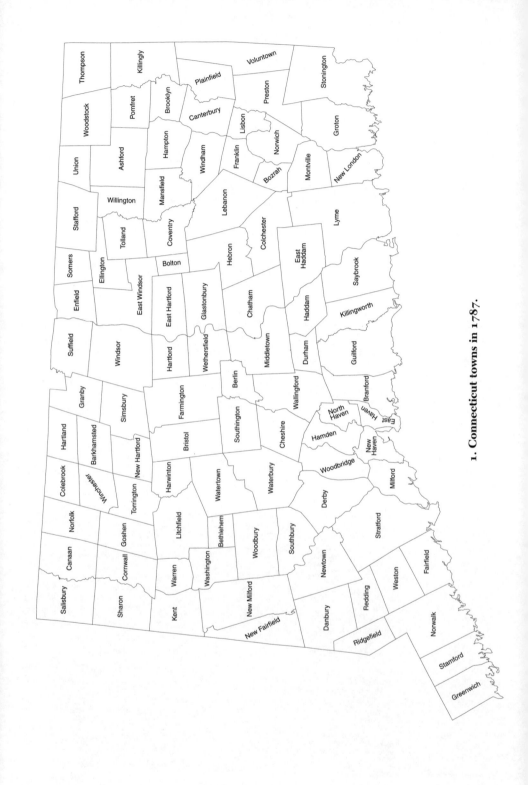

1. Connecticut towns in 1787.

Introduction

The great political prognosticator of the mid-twentieth century, Samuel Lubell, attributed his success in predicting elections to his survey method. He identified bellwether families in bellwether counties in bellwether states. He would stay in close touch with those families—visiting, staying for dinner, even spending the night. During the 1960 Wisconsin primary campaign between Hubert Humphrey and John F. Kennedy, one such family was on his lists of visits; but he considered skipping it because it was an unquestioned Kennedy vote—Catholic, urban, working class, socially conservative. His professional conscience, however, finally propelled him to their modest 1920s bungalow in a Milwaukee urban fringe development. Lubell had hardly settled in for a Sunday chicken dinner when to his startled ears came word that this archetypical Kennedy family would vote for Hubert Humphrey in the next week's primary. "Why, for goodness sake," the amazed pollster sputtered, "why are you doing that?" "Because," came the emphatic and certain response from the man of the house, "he once gave my brother-in-law a shopping bag."[1] So also in the eighteenth century, politics was personal.

Everyday political experience supports this analysis, and so do the conclusions of historians surveying the American political scene in a variety of eras. The urban analyst Robert Wiebe has shown that despite the heavy overlay of industrial urbanism in the late nineteenth century, modern cities were still moved by the face-to-face relationships that had dominated what he called "island communities" in preindustrial society.[2] In the earlier era such relationships were even more determinative. David Fischer writes about the early nineteenth century that "family connections and conflicts in a society which was still strongly familial" were the "more pervasive, more generally operative"; and, he adds, "The 'Family Compact of Connecticut' is much the most famous example."[3] Indeed, in that state, a representative yeoman farmer explained his loyalism during Connecticut's most divisive era: "Entirely unacquainted with Politics, [he] did as almost every ignorant man generally does, swim with the tide or current near him."[4] The family, the neighborhood, and other face-to-face relationships affect all people, not just the ignorant, but the well educated, the high and mighty, as well.

As long as there have been professional politicians, they have lived by the knowledge that the run-of-the-mill voter was moved by narrow local and personal factors. Samuel Lubell was not the first observer to note this truth nor was Tip O'Neil, who built his enormously successful political career on the conviction that all politics is local: The Tammany ward boss George Washington Plunket comes to mind, and so does Alexis de Tocqueville, for that matter, who observed about representatives in American state and national legislatures that "[t]he seeds of his own fortune . . . are sown in his own neighborhood." And in the very decade this study embraces, a Virginia politician wrote to James Madison that, "[i]ndividual and local considerations appear to me to be too general and so fixed as to afford but small consolation to those who wish the policy of the State to be governed by more enlarged and liberal principles."[5] The twin theses of this study are that very specific state needs shaped many clauses of the U.S. Constitution written in Philadelphia, and that local and personal concerns often determined the vote of members of state ratifying conventions. At minimum, this "dual localism" provides additional perspectives from which to view the Constitution's many original meanings.

In the United States in the late eighteenth century, every state had a unique colonial history, unique in part because each had closer, more active, and better articulated relations with England than among themselves. These separate histories created political cultures no two of which were the same. In the revolutionary and Confederation era, efforts to unify the thirteen revolutionary colonies were impeded by these differences. This primary commitment to their states' political culture and commercial prospects reduced the Congress under the Articles of Confederation to hardly more than an empty gesture, a leftover symbol of the wartime need for unity. Days and weeks passed without so much as a quorum. No business could be done, and few political leaders seemed to care. As one member commented despairingly, the Congress was reduced to a "caput mortuum of vitriol."[6] But there were a few political leaders who did care.

Led by James Madison and Alexander Hamilton, supported by George Washington, and urged on by great commercial potentates like Robert Morris and Jeremiah Wadsworth, this cadre of nationalists called a convention to meet at Annapolis in September 1786. Only twelve people representing five states showed up. But the energetic young Hamilton persuaded the gathering to issue a new call to meet in Philadelphia in the succeeding May. That one fared better.

The assembly that we have come to call the constitutional, or federal, convention formally convened on May 14, 1787, but a lack of members delayed the beginning of debate until May 24, when thirty delegates representing nine states were in attendance.

In all, the states chose seventy-four men to go to the convention; fifty-five actually did. Of those, many came late and left early, so that at any given moment there were only about thirty debaters on the floor. Forty-two of them had done service in Congress; half were lawyers; three were governors; eight had signed the Declaration of Independence—the document that gave each of the states the sovereignty that would now face its severest test since Cornwallis laid down his sword at Yorktown.[7] The delegates most determined to protect that sovereignty won the first round. Sovereignty was served in principle and practice by the adoption of the rule that each state delegation would cast one vote.[8]

The nationalists wanted to revolutionize the general government by basing it on the people directly—a system that implied proportional voting by population. It would revolutionize state governments as well. Ultimately the nationalists won the war, but not without heavy casualties inflicted by delegates determined to protect and even promote their states' interests. Those casualties would have been heavier had not a number of presumed stalwarts of state sovereignty declined to attend the convention. Patrick Henry, for instance, "smelled a rat," and Erastus Wolcott told the Connecticut General Assembly that he was afraid of contracting smallpox in Philadelphia.[9]

The draft Constitution seemed to bespeak a unity—indeed, near unanimity—among the participants in the convention debates. But that was the public face presented at the conclusion of what had seen at times profound and bitter disagreement among the delegates. The differences arose because the men came from different parts of a widely spread confederation. Each reflected his local culture—its social structure, economic base, and legal and political and, perhaps most significantly, commercial relationships with neighboring states and foreign nations. The spatial and demographic size in relation to other states and unsettled western lands also figured prominently in shaping each delegate's views.

The special requirements of the several states abounded. Georgia needed protection against Indians; New York feared loss of its import duties; and beyond that, Madison opined, "politics [there] are directed by individual interests and plans"; Maryland leaders wanted to be sure that they were not cut out of the income from the sale of western lands; New Jersey wanted to neutralize the economic dominance of Pennsylvania and New York, who were tapping its trade at the north and south ends; in South Carolina the protection of the institution of slavery and the foreign slave trade was of first concern; in New Hampshire and Massachusetts, those protections were an embarrassment to the federalists; in Rhode Island, the mere prospect of a new constitution threatened the state's radical fiscal reform. No delegate to the convention could face his constituents if he could not say that the new system was good for them. Ratification in every state depended on that. The progress of ratification in each state reflected its own combination of internal and external needs; thus the narrative of ratification in each is unique.[10]

Indeed, in surveying the thirteen experiences of ratification, one is struck more by their great diversity than their commonalities. Lance Banning, after conning the situation in Virginia, writes that every state "had a separate history, a unique position in the Union, and a separate set of state and regional concerns." These arose, wrote William Pierce at the time, out of "a variety of local circumstances, and the dissonant interests of the different parts of the Union." John Kaminski, summarizing the historiography of antifederalism, wrote in 1989, "the debate over the Constitution must be analyzed as thirteen separate debates conducted within each state with the internal politics of each state playing the predominant role." Indeed, writes Forrest McDonald, "the story [of ratification] is one of labyrinthine complexity. . . . Each state made its own rules about the number [which ranged from twenty-six to 355], apportionment, and manner of choosing delegates, the result being that approximately 1,750 men who sat in the several conventions were selected in hundreds of largely uncoordinated elections. . . . Moreover, the process unfolded over a period of almost three years."[11]

It is not even accurate to say that there was a contest over ratification in every state. Three of the first four states to ratify did so unanimously. Georgia's need for help in an impending war with the Creeks impelled rapid and unanimous ratification. New Jersey and Delaware saw great benefit in protection from commercially dominating neighbors; they ratified quickly and unanimously. Connecticut joined Maryland and South Carolina in producing, relative to some states, easily engineered lopsided votes in favor.

These more or less consensual outcomes contrast starkly with the bitterly contested campaigns in Virginia, Massachusetts, and New York, where proponents of the Constitution won by margins of only 8, 9, and 10 percent. New Yorkers found it hard to believe that surrendering their power to tax the commerce of neighboring states was worth the price of union. The Pennsylvania delegates tried to incorporate the principles of bicameralism and separation of powers in the national Constitution in part to undermine the state's unicameral majoritarian system and hasten reform there. These federalists had to resort to physical intimidation and kidnapping, enlisting the aid of street mobs along the way, to rush through ratification by December 12. In New Hampshire, federalist power brokers were forced to postpone a vote until they could be sure of a favorable outcome at a second session of their convention. North Carolinians refused to ratify until November 1789, when they were assured of a bill of rights; and Rhode Island, where the dominating antinationalists had refused to send delegates to Philadelphia, held off ratification until threatened by the new Congress with economic isolation, and did not come into the Union until a year after the new government was up and running. And so it went, one set of unique circumstances after another. A very influential subtext to the nationalism that ultimately infused the spirit of the convention did not die in Philadelphia in 1787; it just went underground, but not very deep and only temporarily.

The unique circumstances of each state's participation in writing and ratifying the Constitution can be identified and described only by studying each state in depth and detail. That is what this essay does for Connecticut, a stalwart defender of provincial prerogative.

Throughout its century and a half of colonial history, Connecticut's leaders stoutly maintained the principle of provincial autonomy. The colony's government, in the shadows of imperial insignificance and obscurity, was able to practice that principle. A culturally homogeneous population relative, for instance, to Rhode Island, New York, New Jersey, and Pennsylvania, and a solidly homogeneous leadership, were able to present a unified front to imperial pressures—slight as they were—only excepting a few scattered episodes over fourteen decades and two biblical lifetimes. Whole generations of Connecticuters grew to maturity without ever experiencing an imperial contretemps. Thus their "darling liberty" flourished in the context of a developing republicanism defined as an autonomous representative government. The first tier of the state's "dual localism" is manifest in her delegates' unbreakable persistence in protecting certain quite concrete interests of a strictly provincial nature.

In assessing Connecticut's role in writing and ratifying the U.S. Constitution, the first question that has to be answered is one that was asked at the time: Why would a people so jealous of their local autonomy willingly and overwhelmingly surrender so much so quickly?

There was, first, a whole set of rational economic and security concerns that were satisfied by the new federal arrangement. No one would be hurt, and everyone would be helped. Second, the principal pro-Constitution leaders interpreted—and often misinterpreted—the document so as to minimize its effects on the state's citizens and their political institutions. In this phase of the process, ratification was, despite the anguished cries of a handful of prostrated antifederalists, a seduction, not a rape.

Whether deliberately deceptive or deeply self-deluded, the federalist spokesmen described a skeleton that bore little relation to the pregnant potential for a truly national government. Thus between September 1787 and January 1788, a profoundly skeptical citizenry was persuaded that a federal government under the new Constitution—even without a bill of rights—would bring great benefits and no liabilities.

In view of this rapid and broad shift in consensus, then, a new question arises, the mirror image of the first one: Why would any rational person in Connecticut want to block ratification and prevent the implementation of such a beneficent national system, or stay out of one that might be constructed? The short answer is, of course, that man at base is not rational. Very large numbers of usually fiercely localist voters were swept up in the new consensus because of the enthusiasm of their family, friends, and neighbors. But the federalist leadership provided real reasons as well as rationalizations to support these enthusiasms. The more evident irrationality was expressed by those who opposed joining the new nation.

In all outward respects, Connecticut's forty nay voters were cut from the same cloth as the 128 aye voters. The antagonists shared virtually all identifiable characteristics; their commonalities far outweighed their differences.[12] Connecticut's antifederalist delegates in the state's convention opposed ratification each for his own local and personal reasons. Some, like those in the former Massachusetts towns, shared an antigovernment view shaped by a generation of struggle against that colony; others, like those in eastern New Haven County, fulfilled expectations emanating from membership in a network of militia and family connections of many decades' duration. Still others, like those in Litchfield County, were moved by local political and personal squabbles having nothing whatever to do with the U.S. Constitution. While the federalist majority—certainly the leadership—seems to have held a certain ideological coherence, the antifederalists did not. For them, it turns out, all politics was local and personal.

For over a hundred years American historians have been trying to rationalize these divisions over the ratification of the Constitution of 1787. For about half that time, the line between pro-Constitution federalists and anti-

Constitution antifederalists was cast in economic and geographic terms. Agrarian localists far from port cities and commercial centers were juxtaposed against mercantile men of national vision. Families whose wealth lay entirely in farms were set up as opposed to those who owned commercial wealth, paper notes, slaves, and speculative land holdings: debtors and creditors; U.S. bond holders and state bond holders; inland dwellers and coastal residents.[13]

Beginning about the middle of the twentieth century, historians turned to ideological differences and to the social and cultural bases that underlay these differences. These historians made strenuous efforts to articulate a cohesive federal ideology and to identify the subconscious social attitudes that brought forth the rhetorical expression of those attitudes. At the same time, a smaller number attempted to discover commonalities among the antifederalists. Some saw a common economic interest and a common residence pattern. Others tried to find commonalities in the rhetoric of antifederalists, expressions that would add up to an ideology. Other historians of antifederalism were content to generalize about the common social attitudes as inferred from the rhetoric of published polemical essays, as well as informal private meetings.[14]

These efforts have largely failed. The best and most complete of them wisely abandons a search for ideological commonalities and characterizes antifederal thought as diverse, often disconnected, and sometimes contradictory.[15] In Connecticut the agrarian and localist spokesmen, whose written works should form the basis of our understanding of antifederalism there, ended up voting to ratify the Constitution. Those voting against ratification left virtually no literary remains; their ideology remains a blank. But that probably reflects reality.

In Connecticut what seems to explain the behavior of antifederal delegates is not class, interest, or ideology. It is the powerful pull of personal networks—familial, militia—and the circumstances of very local village politics. Thus the leading antinationalists, with one exception, voted to ratify the Constitution. Those who voted against ratification represent a broad spectrum with no universal or even dominant commonalities. What tied the core nay voters together lies in some very local—often familial—relationships. In Connecticut, I contend, then as now, all politics was local.

This, then, is a study of "dual localism": Provincial concerns carried to Philadelphia by three politicians whose objectives and perceptions were shaped largely by the Connecticut context in which they had flourished for fifteen to forty years; and the effects of town and parish politics, and family and militia connections on the men delegated locally to go to Hartford and vote ratification, up or down.

My study is of Connecticut, but I intend to suggest that what was the case there was the case in the other twelve states—all politics, to one degree or another, is local.

1

Geography, Politics, and Society

The creation of the United States Constitution in the summer of 1787 is the subject of a huge scholarly and popular literature. Overwhelmingly, writers have described the work of the framers as nationalizing: The new system located much more authority and power in the central government and restricted the authority of the state governments much more than had the Articles of Confederation, in force since 1781. This conclusion is certainly correct. Nevertheless, the thoroughgoing nationalists, James Madison, Alexander Hamilton, Charles Pinckney, James Wilson, and others, came away profoundly dissatisfied. As the document went off to the states for ratification, Madison believed that the proposed system would "neither effectually answer its national object nor prevent the local mischiefs which every where excite disgusts agst state governments."[1] The nationalists had been forced to compromise too deeply with men who saw in the creation of the Constitution an opportunity not only to strengthen the central government, but to use it to fulfill certain specific needs of their state that had not been protected by the government under the Articles.

With only two or three exceptions, all the delegates to the Philadelphia convention were nationalizers in the spectra of their states' politics. They all wanted to strengthen the central government's ability to deal successfully with certain security, fiscal, and commercial problems that became evident during the old Continental Congresses and under the Articles of Confederation. Every state would benefit from these reforms; but some states would have to give up more than others to bring them about. In some states these negative outcomes caused majorities or near majorities of voters to oppose ratification of the new system.

Political leaders in other states saw not only the general advantages of nationalization, but also gains for their states in specific provisions of the new

9

Constitution. Indeed, some delegates went to Philadelphia intending to write these gains into the document. Other delegations feared that the convention might do harm to local institutions and either stayed away, left early, or remained principally to protect local needs. Thus Georgia looked for protection against the Indians and the Spanish; New Jersey wanted to neutralize the commercial dominance of New York and Philadelphia, who were tapping its trade and collecting duties at each end; Maryland, without any western lands, wanted to be sure to receive the benefits of the sale of the national domain. South Carolina delegates were there to protect slavery and its export trade; New Yorkers (with the notable exception of Alexander Hamilton) didn't want to give up their state's huge advantage in collecting duties and left early when they saw what was coming. Rhode Island, fearful that its fiscal liberalism might be undone, stayed away entirely. Every state additionally had an interest in fashioning whatever system of representation would replace state equality in the unicameral Confederation Congress. And this list only scratches the surface of specific individual objectives of the state delegations.

In many cases, what was good for a state was also good for the country. Every state but New York and Pennsylvania benefited from nationalizing the collection of import duties, for instance. But in many cases the desires of one or two states clashed with the needs of all the rest. Sometimes individual state delegations were overridden as was New York's. Sometimes state needs were accommodated when compatible with national objectives. But more often compromises were struck, compromises that frequently left both sides dissatisfied. Thus the high nationalists disliked many elements of the proposed system such as equal state representation in the Senate, the absence of mandatory federal inferior courts, and the lack of a congressional veto of state legislation. Most states' righters at the convention were less unhappy.

The greatest loss was suffered by Delaware and Maryland, who lost the equal suffrage they enjoyed under the Articles. South Carolina and Georgia faced the prospect of losing control over the foreign slave trade. But the small states, being small, needed military and commercial protection badly. The advantages to them of the new system were great and obvious. They ratified quickly and unanimously: Delaware ratified unanimously after two or three days of debate in early December; the tallies in New Jersey ten days later and in Georgia on January 2 were also unanimously federalist. But everywhere where there was a struggle over ratification, the paramount question was, is this good for our state? Had the delegates brought home the bacon?

The state of Connecticut exhibits this provincial outlook as well as any. Its delegates to the convention were products of a very republican system. Deference in this egalitarian society had to be earned; even men born into leading families after an initial push, had to earn higher office. Frequent elections meant that ambitious politicians had to be reelected frequently; long-term officeholding was the only route to high position in the state. Legislative success went to those who were good at deal-making. Connecticut's three delegates to the constitutional convention were all supreme politicians, and they used their skills in Philadelphia to get what Connecticut citizens wanted. Fortunately, they were also statesmen: They could see that what was good for the states collectively was often good for Connecticut as well.

The Connecticut delegates wanted to give the central government more energy; but they were also determined to protect the state's "darling liberty" as reflected in its very republican political system and a century and a half of autonomous government. They had three very specific local objectives: balance national authority with at least equal power in the state governments; protect the state's jurisdiction and rights to soil in the Western Reserve; and make sure that their trade-based economy was not restricted—especially by national export duties. The delegates successfully fulfilled all of these local objectives. They were less successful in carrying Connecticut republicanism into the Constitution. Nevertheless, Connecticut delegates were central to bringing about the two major compromises of the convention—one involving representation and another involving foreign commerce and the slave trade—and both satisfied the needs not only of national unity, but of Connecticut's special circumstances.

We must try to see Connecticut's objectives at the constitutional convention of 1787 as its delegates saw them. What follows is a description of the state's society, economy, and political structure during the Confederation era. It illuminates the context from which the delegates operated and shows what they were sent to get and why their constituents wanted it.

Roger Sherman, at Philadelphia as a delegate to the First Continental Congress in 1774, was asked one day by Patrick Henry "why the people of Connecticut were more zealous in the cause of liberty than the people of other states?" Sherman is reported to have answered, "Because we have more to lose than any of them."[2] Sherman was referring specifically to the Royal Charter of 1662, which gave the colony virtually full local self-government. Thirteen years later, despite the intervention of a successful war for independence from the Crown, Connecticut was still ruled by its charter of 1662, and Sherman still thought the colony, now a state, had more to lose than any of the others.

Connecticut's Darling Liberty

And indeed it did. Connecticut was a minor backwater of the British Empire, economically insignificant and demographically and spatially small. "[W]e live in a corner of the world," declared one resident in 1737, "and none will concern themselves with us."[3] That was a hope, not a complaint, however, for Connecticut had benefitted greatly, not only from her own obscurity, but also from the imperial neglect resulting from England's internal and external wars of the seventeenth and eighteenth centuries. Royal disallowance by which the King could nullify colonial legislation was not countenanced in Connecticut—a unique circumstance and one that was a matter of provincial practice rather than of any law that the British would recognize.[4]

Writing in 1692 in the wake of the reassertion of local government after the Restoration, Gershom Bulkeley, the nearest thing to a royalist in Connecticut, described what he characterized as a usurped autonomy. The locals "think that, the king having incorporated them by a charter, &c, they are invested with a summum imperium, and are become a free state." Indeed, "they have assumed and exercised all supreme power . . . in all matters ecclesiastic, civil and military, capital, criminal, and common." The General Court had abolished all English statutes and substituted only "the forgeries of our own rustical shop." The Board of Trade disgustedly reported to Parliament in 1741 that the Connecticut settlers "think themselves by their charters little dependent on the Crown, and seldom pay obedience to royal orders." "Virtually the only line from London to the colonies," writes the historian Richard Bushman, "was the set of instructions issued to the governor with his commission and subsequently supplemented as needed." Of course, Connecticut never had a royal governor and, of course, no commissions with accompanying instructions were ever issued. "The laws of England," wrote a Connecticut jurist about colonial Connecticuters, "had no authority over them."[5] The colony, said another lawyer in 1794, "always exercised legislation respecting all internal concerns of the community, to the exclusion of all authority, and controul from the king and parliament, as much as an independent state."[6] That, at least was the view from the American side of the Atlantic, and the success of arms ratified in 1783, turned Connecticut's legal fiction into a legal fact.

A major concern in Connecticut on the eve of the federal constitutional convention of 1787, then, was the protection of local autonomy and republican institutions. As one local patriot said, by revising the Articles of Confederation, "the liberties of the people would be endangered . . . the constitution of this state [is] already sufficient for every purpose."[7] Not, then, to be taken for granted by the delegates who went to Philadelphia was the protection of Connecticut's darling liberty.

Connecticut-Style Republicanism

The society of Connecticut, opined Benjamin Franklin at about the time its delegates convened at Philadelphia to reorganize the United States government, was one where extremes neither of wealth nor poverty would be found but rather a "general mediocracy of fortune prevailed." Recent scholarship supports Franklin's description. Indeed, the most sophisticated analysis reveals considerable upward—and some downward—mobility in eighteenth-century Connecticut. There were very few permanent poor, and an uncommonly small gap existed between the well-to-do and the hoi polloi.[8] This economic leveling bred an egalitarian ethos virtually unparalleled in the British American colonies.

Connecticut society had grown up around a political system that, in its basic design, had been put in place exactly a century and a half before the inauguration of George Washington as president of the United States. It was a very democratic state—or republican, they would have said in the revolutionary era. Town meeting suffrage was almost universally available to adult males, though few took advantage of it during politically quiet times; and freeman status, which conferred the right to vote in colonywide elections, was not hard to gain for adult, white men who owned even very small amounts of property. The political structure was founded on the most homogeneous society in any of the British American colonies. Unlike states with large port cities like Newport, Providence, Boston, and New York, where poor foreigners and unsettled seamen could be exploited by unscrupulous politicians, Connecticut's population was static and steady. Noah Webster explained in 1787 that in Connecticut "there is no conflux of foreigners, no introduction of seamen, servants, &c., and scarcely an hundred persons in the state who are not natives, and very few whose education and connexions do not attach them to the government; at the same time few men have property to furnish the means of corruption, very little danger could spring from admitting every man of age and descretion [sic] to the priviledge of voting for rulers."[9]

Throughout the whole period of 1774–90, the average and median size of Connecticut towns hovered at about 2,250. This allowed for a maximum town meeting of about 450 voters and a very equitable representation in the

General Assembly on a town basis. In Rhode Island during the revolutionary era about a quarter of the whole population lived in only two of the state's twenty-nine towns, but Charter stipulations dating from 1663 left these urban voters vastly underrepresented. In Massachusetts, of course, one town dominated the legislative activities of the state.[10]

Until the rise of mill villages in the 1820s and 1830s the General Assembly made an effort to keep the towns—the basic electoral districts—relatively equal in population by routinely dividing the largest of them (see Appendix B, pages 144–48). Overall, preindustrial Connecticut evinced a high degree of economic and political equality—at least in its institutional arrangements.

This demographic leveling was reflected in Connecticut's political culture and institutions. As a general rule, each town sent two representatives to the General Assembly, who were paid by the colony/state. Thus absenteeism hardly existed; customarily about 98 percent of the elected deputies attended. In contrast, Rhode Island legislators were not paid, but sought office for its potential for graft, special legislation, and manipulation of taxes to benefit themselves. In Massachusetts each town had to finance its own representatives. As a result, many small towns there chose to go unrepresented. Thus in the crucial Assembly session of June 1787, only twenty-one of 125 eligible deputies from the western counties of Berkshire, Hampshire, and Worcester were present.[11]

Property qualifications for the freeman status required for voting in statewide elections were virtually the same as for inhabitancy required for voting in town meetings (in some eras actually a bit lower), so there were no legal restraints preventing every male head of household from voting for deputies, lieutenant governors, and governors. Most servants, apprentices, and impoverished tenants were left out of the electorate, as were some adult sons of poor farmers. In a few towns these classes may have amounted to as much as half the adult, white males, but statewide the suffrage was uncommonly inclusive compared to other states.[12]

Unlike the practice in any other colony but faction-ridden and tumultuous Rhode Island, Connecticut's governor was elected annually by the freemen, as were the members of the upper house, called the Council of Assistants. Small, local clavens of opposition were rendered impotent since the councilors were elected at large, an unusual arrangement; the only other state to share it being Maryland.[13] Freemen elected deputies to the lower house, the House of Representatives, twice a year. Beyond those controls, a highly effective tradition of deference caused voters year after year to return incumbents to the executive office and the upper house. There was considerable turnover in the lower house, but the ability to hold a seat there for a period of years was a necessary prerequisite to promotion by the electorate to the Council.[14]

Reelection to high office was commonly granted to those with wealth enough to provide leisure to play the politician and who were persevering enough to serve a long apprenticeship in lower offices. Frequent elections and small electoral districts forced the deputies in the lower house to reflect their constituencies accurately. Though they didn't vote much, the yeomen could if they wanted to.

A broad suffrage, frequent elections, equal representation in the lower house, and a popularly elected upper house and governor characterized Connecticut's eighteenth-century political structure. But that is only half the story. In fact, this constitutional architecture supported a de facto oligarchy.

The Familial Oligarchy

From the start, Connecticut had been an oligarchy. During most of the seventeenth century the rulers were drawn from the nonprofessional church hierarchy: the elders and the elect. After two or three generations, when traditions of family leadership had become established and family wealth was solidified through large land grants, the rulers were drawn mostly from a score or so of those families who for the most part had arrived among the earliest settlers of their towns and had been able to make their fortunes land jobbing in the wilderness.[15]

The domination of Connecticut politics by a few families, or what one close investigator has called clans, has often been noted. David Daggett's approving description of prewar Connecticut is no doubt accurate. "The minister, with two or three principal characters were supreme in each town. Hence the body of the clergy, with a few families of distinction, between whom there was ever a most intimate connection, in effect, ruled the whole state."[16] These families are easy to identify. Perhaps a couple of examples will suffice. Take the Griswold-Wolcott-Pitkin tribe, for instance.

Roger Wolcott was governor 1750 to 1754. He was colonel of the 1st Regiment in the 1740s; his major was his first cousin William Pitkin; Pitkin was governor 1766 to 1769. Pitkin's granddaughter, Ursula Wolcott, was Roger Wolcott's daughter. She married Matthew Griswold, who was governor 1784 to 1786. Their son Roger was governor 1811 to 1812. Ursula's brother, Oliver, served as governor 1796 to 1797 and another brother, Erastus, was a justice of the state's highest court, a member of the Council, and a brigadier general. Her nephew was governor from 1817 to 1827.[17]

In New London County it was the huge Huntington family that ran things. The nineteenth-century historian of Norwich found them so ubiquitous in her account of that city that after about sixty index entries she just gave up listing page numbers for them and simply noted, "This name appears on about 180 pages."[18] One branch of the family made its way up the militia hierarchy. Two brothers, Jabez and Jedediah, gained the top military appointment of major general in the 1770s and 1780s. Jedediah, who was briefly married to Governor Jonathan Trumbull's daughter, was appointed high sheriff of New London County and later state treasurer in 1788. He was U.S. customs collector from 1789 to his death in 1819. Their brother, Joshua, who became a colonel during the war, was a frequent deputy from Norwich and a business associate of the principal Continental quartermaster and war profiteer, Jeremiah Wadsworth. A fourth brother, Ebenezer, became a colonel during the war and in 1792 was appointed chief military officer of the state, a position he held for thirty years.[19]

Benjamin Huntington, married to his cousin, the daughter of Jabez, was a longtime deputy from Norwich ultimately a member of the Council and the first mayor of Norwich when it became a city in 1784, a position he held for twelve years. He was a member of Congress under the Articles of Confederation, where his cousin Samuel was president, and in 1789 a congressman under the new Constitution.[20] Samuel Huntington was a chief justice and governor in Connecticut and president of the old Congress under the Articles of Confederation. His scholarly biographer notes that the "Huntington bloodline merged with those of such prominent families as Coit, Davenport, Ellsworth, Fitch, Griswold, Hosmer, Lathrop, and Wolcott. Kinsmen, lineal and collateral, would eventually play an important role in furthering Samuel's career."[21]

Another such family web, which overlapped the New London network, was that linking Huntingtons with Davenports and Burrs in Fairfield County. The Davenport brothers, James and John, of Stamford were sons of Abraham, descendant of the founder of New Haven and the major political figure of lower Fairfield County. The sons' paternal grandmother was a sister of Jonathan Edwards. That made them first cousins of Pierpont Edwards, Timothy Dwight, and numerous other influential figures. Their maternal grandfather was Jabez Huntington, the influential commercial and military figure and second cousin to Governor Samuel Huntington. The Davenports were connected by both marriage and blood to the Fitch and Burr families of Fairfield. This, then, was another of the family networks that constituted the Connecticut oligarchy.[22]

Though new men could gain access to the levers of power in Connecticut without family connections—Roger Sherman is an example—it was a lot easier to do so by being born into a reigning family or—like Oliver Ellsworth—marrying into one. At any event, there is ample evidence to support John Adams' oft-quoted and perhaps only somewhat exaggerated statement, "The state of Connecticut has always been governed by an aristocracy. . . . Half a dozen families, or at the most a dozen, have controlled that country when a colony, as well as since it has become a state." Thomas Jefferson wrote Adams that his own observation confirmed the impression that in Massachusetts and Connecticut "a traditionary reverance for certain families . . . has rendered the offices of government nearly heriditary in those families."[23] Connecticut was, in reality, an oligarchic republic; a theoretical republic, but a working oligarchy based on voluntary deference encouraged by family exclusivity, multiple officeholding, and economic leverage.[24]

The oligarchy dominated colony politics by monopolizing positions in the upper house where they could veto appointments to all offices and all legislation coming from the deputies. They were not above appointing themselves to the most prestigious and lucrative positions; indeed, they did it routinely. One perennial outsider wrote in 1782 that "we have been . . . loading some with so many places of honor, trust and authority, they can hardly stagger under the weight of them." Plural officeholding was part of the system. The Council of Assistants constituted the supreme court; general officers in the militia were almost always assistants; congressmen under the Articles and later under the Constitution were usually members of the Council at the time of their appointment.[25] In 1783, of the twelve assistants, eight sat on the Council of Safety, four served as county court justices, four were judges of the superior court, three were judges of the very lucrative probate court, and five had been elected delegates to the Continental Congress. Oliver Wolcott was all of the above at the same time and was also a major general in the Connecticut militia. The assistants each also held one or more local offices such as justice of the peace, moderator of the town meeting, etc.

Assistants had no hesitation about voting themselves financial rewards as well as positions of power. They began by exempting themselves from paying the poll tax, and continued by assigning themselves certain commercial and industrial monopolies, and giving themselves and their families the most lucrative contracts to supply the government and the army.[26] William Pitkin, for instance, got the contract to produce the state's gunpowder in 1775, and Jabez Huntington filled many military contracts—both while they were high military officers sitting on the Council of Assistants and the Council of Safety.

Governor Trumbull's son, Joseph, was appointed commissary general.[27] There were, especially during wartime, more plums than there were councilors, so many went to family and friends.

Traditional eighteenth-century deference played a part in keeping the oligarchy in office. But deference was not so powerful in Connecticut as it was in other American colonies where the classes were more sharply articulated, spread wider apart, and maintained by a highly qualified suffrage. When John Adams declared on the eve of the Declaration of Independence that all the states should set up "Governments of our own, like that of Connecticutt,"[28] the stability that deference provided to members of the government appealed to Adams' aristocratic side; the relatively open and mobile political system appealed to his republican side. But the conventional wisdom in late eighteenth-century Connecticut held that it was the republicanism, not the deference, that engendered the state's steady habits. As Noah Webster pointed out at the moment that Adams' Massachusetts was recovering from Shays' Rebellion, Connecticut's stability lay in the fact that the lower house of the legislature—elected every six months—"wear the complexion of the people."[29] Deputies to the General Assembly were elected by the freeman, and significant numbers of yeomen did not bother to become freemen and significant numbers of freemen did not bother to vote. Probably distance from the meetinghouse and the state of a farmer's planting and harvesting schedule played the most significant part in determining his level of political participation. Really ambitious men moved closer to the town center.[30] The body more representative of yeomen's views was the town meeting, but again distance from farm to meetinghouse played a major role in determining who would influence local politics there.

The Militia

A potent instrumentality of the oligarchs' power was the militia. Since it will play a significant part in our story later, a close look now is necessary. The militia in eighteenth-century Connecticut was a highly political institution. Military, like civil, rank in this republican society was ardently sought. Military expertise was not essential; leadership ability was. Thus men who had demonstrated leadership through election to local office were preferred candidates for military commissions.[31] Most officers began their careers as sergeants elected by their companies and moved into the commissioned ranks to ensign, lieutenant, and captain through elections that customarily followed seniority, occasionally disrupted by a lack of popularity.

An analysis of eighty-four militia elections from 1764 to 1766 shows that 69 percent followed seniority; in Groton between 1692 and 1780, 87 percent of 154 known militia elections held strictly to seniority.[32] In virtually all cases, ensigns were elected from among sergeants, corporals, and company clerks, and when available, from among those with wartime experience.[33] Thus the nineteen-year-old lieutenant was a distinct rarity in the Connecticut militia, the exception being sons of high-level civil and military officers. During the French and Indian War, for instance, ensigns and lieutenants averaged about thirty years of age and captains nearly forty.[34] They were responsible, well-respected men in their towns and societies. Indeed, there is a clear pattern of temporal proximity of election to civil and military offices. It was very common for selectmen to be militia captains, justices of the peace, or deputies—that is, members of the General Assembly.[35] Since field and general officers were appointed from among the company commanders, they, too, began their careers on waves of popularity and owed their early promotions to their ability to earn and hold their men's confidence and loyalty. During the war decade 1775 to 1784, 3,541 men received their first militia commissions, so there was very great mobility and turnover among them.[36]

During eras of peace, militia training and readiness fell into decline—indeed, it often degenerated into debauch. Training days became festive occasions marked by athletic contests, target shoots, and lots of drinking. Company elections, held on these days, were often influenced by liquor supplied by contending candidates for higher rank, a practice that became so blatant and obviously disruptive of the good order of the army that in 1772 a General Assembly committee recommended it be made illegal, which it was. But so strong was the tradition that only a much watered-down law was passed.[37] In the meantime the General Assembly felt compelled to step in and void elections of men obviously not suited to military command even under peacetime conditions.[38]

Indeed, civil and regimental officers—majors, lieutenant colonels, and colonels—were nominated to the General Assembly by the deputies who met in county caucuses at separate private homes during Assembly sessions. Normally, the caucuses rubber-stamped the men chosen by the local bodies; and normally the General Assembly approved the nominees. Local elections of obviously inappropriate men—men who may have relied on numerous family members or wide-scale treating for their election—were undone by the General Assembly, which appointed more malleable figures, not infrequently their colleague deputies.[39]

Militia elections were generally respected in part because all eligible voters could participate. Men over fifty were excused from training in 1736, and a long list of other categories was also excused.[40] But all of these exempted men, among the most respected in town, could vote in militia elections. And, of course, large numbers of those legally exempted from militia duty—such as constables, sheriffs, etc.—chose to accept commissions. A lieutenant or captain who sat in the General Assembly when field grade commissions were being given out was in a nice position to give his own promotion a little lift, and there is a clear pattern of rapid rise among men who combined service in the militia with service in the legislature.[41]

Indeed, the monopoly of general and field grade commissions held by members of the General Assembly became a matter of public disgruntlement. "Are there general officers to be appointed for the militia?" wrote one sarcastic newspaper correspondent; "The chief recommendation is a seat in the assembly. Or field officers for the established army? The being members of assembly, in a wonderful manner communicates both courage and military skill."[42] The reason for selecting local political figures for military command was quite rational, however. Officers were frequently appointed for particular engagements and authorized to enlist their own regiments. They would recommend their colleagues as subalterns. Thus companies were raised from parishes and towns, and regiments from wider areas. When the General Assembly or the Council of Safety tried to go around this system and, for instance, appoint a New London man to raise forces in Litchfield County, potential officers in Litchfield would object and the likelihood of enlisting men from their towns would evaporate.[43]

High military rank was reserved for the gentry who—in most cases—had proven their leadership by local election. This is to be expected since, as one close student has written, "the almost universal nature of military obligation, plus colonial ideas concerning class and duty, demanded an impregnable social position for officers who were responsible for impressing their neighbors and their neighbors' property."[44] Christopher Leffingwell articulated the prevailing wisdom when in 1774 he said, "The superior or commissioned Officers to be appointed by the General Assemblys . . . [should] be such as are possessed of Real Estate worth contending for."[45]

Appointment to the field grade ranks and brigadier and major generals was made by the General Assembly. This was necessary because these officers commanded units that included companies from several towns. Caucuses of the deputies from the towns made the nominations. It was difficult—though not impossible—to gain one of these ranks without the requisite seniority in the next lower rank and considerable political influence. In 1739 the structure of the militia went through a reorganization that would last till the Revolution. Regiments were introduced for the first time and a whole new batch of high officers was authorized. Of the twelve Assistants, ten were among the thirty-nine field grade officers appointed at this time, and twenty-three more were deputies. Only three officers were appointed from outside the body that appointed them. Political influence was a major factor. It is no coincidence that the only man commissioned colonel without prior civil or military experience was the thirty-one-year-old Gurdon Saltonstall, Jr., son of the former governor.[46]

Long-term militia officers who combined their military service with repeated terms in the General Assembly might cap their careers with appointment as a regimental colonel or even a brigade general. There was one senior and one second major general, and by the 1770s it had become almost a tradition to appoint to those positions colonels who were also members of the Council of Assistants. This was the case with Jabez Huntington, Erastus and Oliver Wolcott, and James Wadsworth, for instance. It was quite possible, then, to carve out a successful political career that coupled elective office with lucrative appointive office by building on a base of popularity and fame as a militia officer.[47]

Republicanism Asserted

With the creation of the Continental army, a great range of opportunity was opened for the martially ambitious. But since the new army operated under an entirely different set of assumptions, procedures, and even objectives, major differences developed between militia officers and Continental officers. Continentals were enlisted for terms of one year, three years, or the duration of the war. They were appointed by Congress on nomination by George Washington and his subordinates, and their objective was a Continental victory. Most significantly, Continental officers tended to see themselves as part of a great national campaign directed and financed by Congress. Militia units, on the other hand, were called up for short periods ranging from two or three days to six or seven months for a particular piece of work or seasonal campaign. Since militia officers depended on the goodwill of their men for their position, discipline was lax and training was not rigorous. Militia units were agents of their states and even when incorporated into the Continental command, Connecticut units continued as companies drawn from towns and parishes and from regiments that roughly followed county lines.

As the war continued, the differences between militiamen and Continentals became greater and cooperation became more difficult. Says Harold

Selesky, "An officer corps dominated by men from outside the traditional leadership groups was one reason why the Connecticut Continental regiments developed a sense of corporate identity separate from the rest of Connecticut society." The Continental officers no doubt agreed with George Washington that the militia were often worse than useless: They "consume your Provisions, exhaust your stores, and leave you at last at a critical moment."[48]

The militia was a local organization under local control. The Continental army was something else and, as we shall see, there was a good deal of unfriendly rivalry between them. When former Continental officers joined together to form an exclusive and privileged class, Connecticuters were outraged.

Fear of the concentration of wealth and power in the hands of a small coterie also underlay the uproar that greeted proposals to establish an hereditary association of Continental army officers. Titled the Society of the Cincinnati, this was a national organization, one of whose founders was David Humphreys of Derby. Connecticut's yeomen, expressing themselves at town meetings, saw the Cincinnati as "a clique of placemen and pensioners." They feared that the Society was a "combination to distress them and establish an Aristocracy."[49] The popular outcry forced the Society to alter its constitution to eliminate the hereditary element and the secrecy of its meetings, but its association with the merchants and nationalists in Connecticut kept it under a dark cloud all through the 1780s.[50]

What particularly distressed Connecticut farmers and artisans was that the Cincinnati had come along just in time to act as a political force behind the payment of substantial cash bonuses to the very officers who would constitute its membership. In 1778 Congress had passed an act providing officers holding Continental commissions with a pension of half pay for seven years if they would continue to serve to the end of the war and fulfill several other requirements. Enlisted men who stayed to the end of the war would get eighty dollars.[51] Because of the dilapidated condition of the Continental treasury and for other reasons, the plan was not carried out. Variations of it were proposed from time to time, and when Congress began to disband the army in 1781 and 1782 a new plan was put forward. This would "commute" the seven years' half pay—later increased to five years' full pay—to a one-time lump sum.[52]

Only Continental officers would receive the payments; Continental soldiers and militia officers and men would receive nothing from Congress nor would the men of the Connecticut Line, regiments enlisted for three years or the duration who fought as part of the Continental army. Indeed, since

only those officers holding commissions under Congress on or after the date
the pension bill was passed in 1780 would receive the money, very few of the
old militia officers who served in the Continental regiments before 1780
would benefit.

Connecticut antifederalists were correct to perceive the effort to grant
cash payments to the officers as linked to a nationalist plot to increase the fiscal independence and power of Congress. General Alexander McDougall,
the officers' spokesman, suggested to General Henry Knox—soon to be secretary of war and at the moment the chief organizer of the Cincinnati—the
desirability of uniting "the influence of Congress with that of the Army and
the public creditors to obtain permanent funds for the United States."[53] The
public creditors referred to included men who held IOU's from Congress,
and they included also Generals McDougall, Knox, and all their subalterns.
Pensions, Connecticut yeomen feared, would help the Cincinnati become
the engine of that much-dreaded hereditary aristocracy so many farmers and
their sons had fought against so recently at so much bloody cost. But in Congress, Oliver Wolcott, among Connecticut's staunchest nationalists, voted for
the commutation. And, under the most excruciating political pressure, so finally did Eliphalet Dyer.[54] They would pay a price back home.

Continental Pensions and the Commutation

Connecticut citizens, about 20,000 of whom had done militia service and suffered from it, also paid taxes to pay Continental officers' wages.[55] They were
not pleased to think that they would be subject to additional taxation to support a class of pensioners. The commuted pensions, recall, were to be given
to Continental officers who were in service when the commutation bill was
passed or who had accepted commissions subsequently. A bloc of militia officers, elected by the most democratic suffrage available anywhere in America, now stood challenged by their peers who had served in the Continental
army, many of whom had spent years away from local politics but whose influence and esteem could threaten the local civil power of the militia officers.

The whole idea of granting such a bonus to a small group of men was
anathema to New Englanders generally and Connecticuters in particular.
Jesse Root, a member and usually a strong supporter of Congress, wrote a
friend that the character of Connecticut's "people would not brook the paying of annual pensions, that they could not bear to see men strutting about
their streets in the port of masters who had a right to demand of the people

a part of their annual labor and toil to support them in idleness." And Samuel Huntington agreed that he was "much more concerned on account of [the commutation's] consequences among the people."[56]

Huntington's concern was well advised. The issue of commutation riled the state's populace more than any other of the Confederation era. Town after town passed resolutions decrying it. The Farmington town meeting, for instance, feared that "an excessive Power, the constant attendant of property," would be thrown "into the Hands of a Few . . . and finally . . . dissolve our present Happy and Benevolent Constitution & . . . erect on the Ruins a proper Aristocracy: wherein . . . the Direction & management of the state is committed to the Great & Powerful alone." When the General Assembly—due to upper house intransigence—failed to submit a protest to Congress, a majority of the towns sent delegates to an extralegal convention at Middletown.[57]

Not only was the very concept of a popularly elected convention a threat to constituted government in a state without a constitution, but the meeting inspired by the commutation grant represented the most democratic interpretation of the libertarian and egalitarian rhetoric of the early war years.[58] Fear of concentrated power infused every line of the plea sent forth by the Middletown convention. All men "are fond of power, and too often too fond of exercising it," the conventioneers declared, and everyone must at all times be ready to protect "their natural, civil, religious and constitutional rights and privileges . . . against that lust for power and spirit of domination, which prevails the whole human race." In particular, no man, no state, should ever give up the taxing power, for that would permit Congress to establish "an arbitrary sovereign and despotic power over the States."[59]

Connecticut's eighteenth-century citizens were deeply engaged in the affairs of their parishes and road surveys, and would even dabble in town meeting politics, especially when taxes were an issue. Much less attention would they give to interstate or national affairs. Yet, when Confederation policy seemed to threaten their liberty or pocketbook, they would muster the political will to attempt to maintain control. Deputies were not elected by town meetings, but by the freemen, nevertheless town meeting voters took it upon themselves to instruct their deputies as to how to conduct themselves in the Assembly. The new lower house ordered its speaker, the popular provincialist William Williams, to send the remonstrance directly to Congress without again referring it to the Council.[60]

The commutation split militia officers from Continental officers and nationalists from localists. The issue brought support to such men as Williams, Erastus Wolcott, and James Wadsworth.[61] Indeed, Wadsworth, formerly major general, the member of the civil government with the highest militia rank, came out the big winner when elected to the newly created office of comptroller, a job that paid £150 a year; only the governor got more. An effort by James Wadsworth to replicate his victory in 1786 in the struggle the next year to ratify the new Constitution would turn out differently.

The Western Reserve

Connecticut yeomen would not tolerate taxes to support a class of military pensioners, but they did think that veterans should be rewarded in some way. That could be done without cost because the vast western lands the state claimed were theirs to give away. By 1786 Connecticut was the only state still holding lands in the Northwest Territory that had been ceded to the United States by the Treaty of Paris of 1783. Thus an objective of very high priority of the Connecticut delegates to the convention of 1787 was the preservation of Connecticut's Western Reserve granted by Congress the year before. Underlying this cession was an old issue, passionately reasserted in Connecticut, and roiling Congress in the spring of 1786: the state's claim to lands in Pennsylvania and points west. Connecticut's Charter of 1662 granted all the land lying in a strip about seventy miles wide (the distance from the Massachusetts boundary south to Long Island Sound) all the way to the Pacific Ocean. Connecticut never asserted any claim to lands west of the Mississippi, and the affected area in New York had been settled before Connecticut farmers began to be pressed for land.

Then in 1754 a group of speculators from eastern Connecticut organized a land company to buy from the Indians some territory running 120 miles westward from a line ten miles east of the east branch of the Susquehanna River—land claimed by Pennsylvania, much of which had fallen into the hands of speculators in that colony. Eventually, but only after a long and extremely acrimonious political battle, the Susquehannah Company got the Connecticut General Assembly to adopt the claim. A town, later a county, was established and deputies from it were sent to the General Assembly.

Pennsylvanians did not let these events go unnoticed, and before, during, and after the Revolution disputed them—often with armed forces. There was considerable loss of blood, the dead numbering in the hundreds. At one point Connecticut militia were fighting Pennsylvania troops, and during the Revolution a combined force of Loyalists and Indians perpetrated the worst massacre of the war in the Susquehanna River Valley in an area called

Wyoming. Reviewing the debacle at the end of the era, a remnant of the injured parties said it "Occationed great Confusions . . . cost the lives of hundreds . . . Ruined thousands, and Injured the State greatly."[62]

During the Confederation era, the dispute was brought before the only judicial tribunal ever established under the provisions of the Articles of Confederation. The judges, sitting at Trenton, heard William Samuel Johnson and two colleagues argue the case for Connecticut, and James Wilson, a heavy speculator in the lands in question, and two colleagues argue for Pennsylvania. The decision at Trenton in December 1782 was a complete victory for Pennsylvania as to the jurisdiction over the area.[63] But Connecticut settlers and their partisans at home and in Congress asserted that this did not resolve the matter of rights to soil—that is, who actually owned the farms that the pioneers had been developing over, in some cases, the previous twenty years and over which buckets of blood and rivers of tears had been shed.

The issue was kept at the fore in Congress by the nature of Connecticut's cession of its claim to the area west of Pennsylvania. Connecticut reserved to itself a section of land beginning at Pennsylvania's western border and extending 120 miles into the Northwest Territory—the Western Reserve. States with no western claims were outraged because they felt that the whole Northwest Territory had been secured by the efforts of all the states equally and all the states should benefit from its sale. Virginia and New York were even more upset because they had peacefully ceded their claims to the same area.[64]

Continued bloody conflict in the Wyoming Valley, the momentary intervention of Ethan Allen then carving Vermont out of lands claimed by New York and New Hampshire, rumors of a statehood movement, and fears that the area would provide a refuge for Shaysites all kept the issue crackling. In addition, a number of Congressmen such as Wilson and Connecticut's Eliphalet Dyer were personally heavily invested in the lands.[65]

In Congress, then, a debate over the terms of Connecticut's cession, bitter at times and never less than acrimonious, continued from the moment the Articles were ratified to the very eve of the constitutional convention. Getting Congress to allow the Reserve, William Samuel Johnson and Stephen Mitchell told Governor Griswold, "requires a delecate negociation."[66] The open debate was conducted principally by Johnson and Wilson in May 1786; but the resolution of the conflict was brought about by backroom maneuvers begun by Roger Sherman during his last term in Congress two years earlier.[67] This deal had the Pennsylvania delegation agreeing to support the Reserve if the government of Connecticut and its agents would cease support of the settlers in Wyoming and the absentee speculators in Connecticut. Johnson apparently brought Wilson around to these arrangements in May 1786. But one Virginian told Madison that "some of the states particularly Pennsylvania voted for them on the same principle that powers of Europe give money to the Algerines."[68]

The cession was formally accepted by Congress, but the underlying arrangements were concluded with a wink and a nod, and thus were left open to misunderstanding at a later time. "These Things being understood rather than expressed," wrote Charles Pettit to Jeremiah Wadsworth, "may be differently conceived of by different Minds . . . In Compromises of this kind it is [fo]und dangerous to go too minutely into Explanations." William Grayson, writing to Madison, characterized the business as "nothing but a state juggle contrived by old Roger Sherman to get a side wind confirmation to a thing they had no right to."[69] Madison at the constitutional convention in June 1787 asked pointedly, "Have we not seen the public land dealt out to Cont. to bribe her acquiescence in the decree constitutionally awarded agst. her claim on the territory of Pena.?"[70] The congressmen from the landless states were not amused, and in their concern lay the potential to upset the delicate deal at first opportunity.

On the eve of the Philadelphia convention, the settlers on the Wyoming lands were being pressed to accept Pennsylvania jurisdiction and were promised that their lands would be confirmed to them without costs. Many—perhaps most—were highly skeptical. One faction among them wanted the Trenton decision overturned, or even ignored as unconstitutional. This group included owners of shares in the Susquehannah Company, many of whom, like Eliphalet Dyer, were absentee speculators.

Another faction accepted Pennsylvania jurisdiction and would abide by an act of the Pennsylvania General Assembly confirming their right to lands they had developed. But Pennsylvania would not confirm other claims in unoccupied lands away from the settlements. Hard-core Susquehannah speculators in Wyoming and in Connecticut hoped that the central government would collapse. This would permit the establishment of a new state in the Wyoming Valley and close-by western New York; or bring about chaos followed by a monarchial government before whose courts the Susquehannah Company speculators would have a better chance of winning control of the territory. But that was fantasy.[71] In the meantime, the official stance of the settlers was to acquiesce in Pennsylvania jurisdiction but call for a new trial under the Articles to try the rights to the soil.

In the spring of 1787, leading figures among the speculator faction petitioned the Connecticut General Assembly to pursue the case for rights to soil, not only of the actual settlers, but also of the absentee Susquehannah shareholders. Susquehannah settlers and their influential speculating bro-

kers still commanded the support of a majority of the lower house as late as
May 1787. This majority was willing to reopen the old Company claims in
order to obtain legal confirmation of ownership, not only of settled farms, but
also of the unsettled lands. A resolution passed by the lower house authorized Johnson, Sherman, and Ellsworth, only days earlier elected delegates to
the Philadelphia convention, to receive documents allegedly held by Pennsylvania supportive of the Company's claims and to negotiate Pennsylvania's
surrender of them. This move, of course, represented an abrogation of the
deal that Johnson and Sherman themselves had made in Congress after the
Trenton decision of 1782. The upper house rejected these belated extreme
claims.[72] No representative of the absentee land speculators or of the radical
statehood faction was among the trio sent to Philadelphia in 1787.

At that time, however, thousands of Connecticut families still lived on
farms they had laboriously established at a time when the Connecticut government was asserting the claim and encouraging its citizens to pioneer the
territory. Even as late as October 1788 Governor Huntington, who had been
president of Congress when the Trenton court was established, wrote Benjamin Franklin, then chief magistrate of Pennsylvania, that since the Wyoming
farmers had originally settled "under contenance" of Connecticut and "lived
under the exercise of the Government" of that state, "powerful connections"
remained between the pioneers and "a numerous class of Citizens in this
State in both the ties of interest and consanguinity."[73]

But the Connecticut Council would not entertain a reopening of the
arrangement made by Johnson and Sherman in the old Congress. Those two
men would have work enough just protecting that deal: holding onto the
Western Reserve and looking out for the interests of the Connecticut settlers
in Pennsylvania, a state full, still, of claimants to the lands that settlers had
been watering with sweat, blood, and tears for years. Johnson's and Wilson's
winks and nods would be tested in Philadelphia in 1787.

2

The Economic and Political Context

In the seventeenth and early eighteenth centuries, wealth and political influence were linked by land jobbing. Owning or controlling lots of land helped get men elected to colonywide office who then used their political influence to further enlarge their real estate. The heirs of these great estates had a lock on the governorship and the Council by the mid-eighteenth century, by which time all the land in the state had been taken up. Many of the scions of these great land jobbers continued the family tradition of public officeholding. They turned to commerce and again were able to manipulate government so as to monopolize its gifts by way of contracts, special charters, and the like. As we have seen, they also passed around among themselves lucrative public offices.

The reciprocal link between commercial wealth and political influence was strong during the 1780s; it was also obvious and thus the focus of attack. Connecticut society was characterized by gradations of wealth and power, not a sharp division between a small aristocracy and everyone else as was found in neighboring states. The forces to resist commercial domination were strong; and in the mid-1780s they were galvanized by a number of state and national issues, issues that would influence the choice of delegates to Philadelphia and the stance those men took when they got there. Under the Articles of Confederation, local profits from agricultural exports were threatened and protection from foreign nations and sister states did not exist.

The Economic Background

The Connecticut economy in 1787 was, of course, basically agricultural. About 80 percent of the families depended entirely on agriculture for their living and many of the rest at least partly. But not since the founding of the colony a century and a half earlier had they been wholly self-sufficient. There were always things that *had* to be bought—like iron goods and salt—and plenty that were desirable—like textiles, pewter, and ceramics. From the start, Connecticut farmers tried to produce at least a small surplus for sale or trade.[1] By the eighteenth century, Connecticuters had discovered that livestock and lumber along with vegetables and grains would find a good market in the southern colonies and a great one in the West Indies. What developed, then, was a commercial economy dependent upon exporting large amounts of goods. The sticky part of the arrangement was that these goods could not be exchanged for other goods, but had to be sold for cash. Why was this?

In the first place Connecticut had no major deep-sea harbor. Her only transatlantic port city was New London on Long Island Sound at the mouth of the Thames, and the inlet there was too narrow to harbor more than a few large vessels. Governor Leete reported in 1680 that "a ship of 500 tunn may go up to the Towne, and com [sic] so near the shore that they may toss a biskit ashoare," and only smaller vessels could sail past New London to Norwich.[2] The Long Island Sound bays at Stonington, New Haven, Black Rock in Fairfield, and Norwalk were all too shallow. Vessels went up rivers to Middletown, Hartford, Norwich, and Derby, but again only those with a draft of six feet or less. Aside from New London, there was no port for transatlantic ships. Connecticut exporters could not send their abundant provisions to Europe except by way of Newport, Boston, or—mostly—New York, a port closer to more of Connecticut's hinterland farmers than New London. Nor could imports come directly from Europe to Connecticut.

This was not a commercial disaster, however. The famously shrewd Connecticut Yankees had worked out a scheme that perfectly fit the market needs of the farm economy. Livestock, lumber, and foodstuffs were sent to the West Indies, where they were sold for cash. A small amount of that cash was spent there for sugar products such as cane, molasses, and rum, which were brought back in casks carried over as bundles of staves cut from the Connecticut white oak. It was not uncommon for captains to buy some Dutch or English china in the Dutch West Indies, or some French wine, and other small manufactured goods.

But the great bulk of European imports came through New York City. Lightly laden sloops and brigantines primed with West Indian cash headed for that port city where they sold off some of their rum and molasses. Here they loaded up with Irish linen, English pewter, furniture from England and France, even silver service, embroidered textiles, fiddles, spinets, and other luxuries. And here they spent their cash. In addition to the profits they left with the New York importers, they also left money in duties and excise taxes to support the New York government. Though to a much lesser extent, they also carried on the same relationship with Newport and Boston. Thus the relatively high level of living enjoyed by most Connecticut families depended on an unencumbered export trade that provided the favorable balance of payments with the West Indies to offset the unfavorable balance with neighboring colonies.[3]

Neighboring states were different. New York and Massachusetts were each dominated commercially by a single major port city. As the maps in Appendix B show, there was no such city in Connecticut. New York and Boston carried on a flourishing diversified trade, not only in the productions of their own hinterland, but also as transshipment points for other states. Rhode Island had a single cash "crop"—rum; but traded in a worldwide commerce so that the carrying trade supported its huge fleet. The fact that virtually the whole state was coastline with two-thirds of its towns on the Narragansett Bay made for a heterogeneous and dominating overseas commercial economy.[4] Connecticut's economy was dependent on the major deep-sea ports of these neighboring states; and though Connecticut shipping through New York was a significant share of that port's business, none of these three states were dependent on Connecticut's trade.

The Revolutionary War altered the direction of West Indian and coastal trade by routing it inland away from Long Island Sound and across the top of the state through Hartford and Litchfield to the Hudson River. Wartime conditions shut out European imports and provided American and French armies in place of lost West Indian customers. The demand for livestock and foodstuffs was stronger than ever, and farmers made hay while the wartime sun shone. Connecticut became "The Provisions State."

When peace broke out, however, an economic calamity was visited upon the state. The French military went home and Congress disbanded its army. The domestic market for Connecticut's flourishing provisions and meat production collapsed. And worse yet, a parliamentary order-in-council of July 1783 restricted American visits to the British West Indian ports, so Connecticut farmers and merchants lost their most important market. With these markets gone, the Connecticut economy went flat, and though merchants suffered, farmers suffered as much. To farmer Jones, who sold his six head of beef cattle to William Deming, who in turn sold those along with several dozen others to Jeremiah Wadsworth, who then shipped them with hundreds more out of the state, the external cause of the depression was obvious. Low prices and high taxes at home hit the large-scale commercial livestock producer; but even more affected was the family farmer several removes from the interstate and international causes of his plight. For all of these people, free trade among the states and an untaxed export trade were matters of great moment. The delegates at Philadelphia would work hard—and successfully—to see that they got them.

Political Divisions

Though the roots of the political transformation that took place in Connecticut in 1788 go back to the era of the Stamp Act and the Revolutionary War, the ratification of the U.S. Constitution can be explained by reference to local postwar economic and political conditions. Connecticut politics in the 1780s was dominated by issues relating to: state tax and fiscal policy; nationalism and state sovereignty; and traditional versus more open state government. There was a frequent connection among those favoring a stronger central government, maintaining a traditional tax structure that bore heaviest on the agricultural class, and keeping government in the hands of a small long-term leadership group. On the other side were those who jealously guarded the authority of the state against the central government; desired to balance the tax burden by shifting some of it onto absentee landlords, merchants, and professionals; and wished to introduce a number of democratic reforms into the state government.[5] But the personnel of these coalitions fluctuated as the membership of the lower house varied, since local conditions determined local elections.

Thus this division was not clean. Leaders supported combinations of measures drawn from each collection of issues. To make state politics even more complicated, there were struggles between ins and outs over office, often driven by those family networks and other local institutional ties that knew no logic or consistency in terms of issues anyone would mention in public.

Taxes

On a statewide basis, the most palpable condition dividing Connecticut citizens' political predilections in the 1780s was economic. On one side stood a relatively small group of merchants and commercial farmers with their professional allies in the law and ministry along with a rentier class of absentee landlords who fought to minimize taxes on unimproved lands. On the other side were the great majority made up principally of yeoman farmers. A rising class of artisan-capitalists centered principally in Norwich most often sided with the farmers but sometimes found common interest with the merchants. The economic issues that divided these two groups most clearly were tax policy, fiscal policy, and whether to support state or national import duties.

Taxes in Connecticut from the start had been laid on land. Land was the source of about 90 percent of the wealth of probably nine out of ten of the residents of the colony. It seemed only fair to tax this ubiquitous wealth at its source. Land was rated differentially according to its presumed return. Thus unimproved land held by absentee speculators was rated very low. Livestock was taxed as well, which somewhat differentiated the more from the less wealthy farmers. In addition to the basic tax on land and livestock, all males over twenty-one years old were assessed a poll tax based on a value of £18; those sixteen to twenty-one counted as a half poll, £9. This was highly regressive and became a major bone of contention. Artisans (shoemakers, tanners, smiths, and "every other Handy Craft"), merchants, tavern keepers, physicians, and lawyers were assessed a "faculty" tax "proportionable to their gains and returns" derived from their trade or practice.[6] Duties on imports were also levied as were, from time to time, taxes on sales. In 1785 taxpayers were liable for twenty-five different tax levies, of which they had to pay six in very scarce hard currency.[7] Among the six, significantly, were those for paying the salaries of legislators who passed the laws and the men who collected the taxes; and the very unpopular payment of the state's quota to the United States Congress.[8]

Under these circumstances, it is to be expected that tax reform advocates would arise among Connecticut's agrarian leaders. They became numerous and at various times between 1779 and 1786 dominated the lower house of the Assembly. Their principal leader was Erastus Wolcott of East Windsor. Erastus, the older brother of the lieutenant governor, Oliver Wolcott, was a member of one of the most influential families in the state. His father was governor in the middle of the eighteenth century and he was connected by marriage to several others of the ruling circle, as we will see.[9] Erastus Wolcott was a farmer, large landowner, absentee landlord, and an entrepreneur who ran a ferry across the Connecticut River and in 1787 bought the tavern at the ferry slip. He was the most influential figure in the parish of East Windsor and was the leader of the movement that separated the parish from Windsor in 1768. He was a regular officeholder in the new town. He was a long-term militia officer and resigned in 1781 as a brigadier general.[10]

Wolcott held many hundreds of dollars' worth of state securities, and about one hundred dollars in Continentals.[11] He was the leader of the state creditors and published several long essays proposing tax reforms that would equalize the burden by shifting some of the state debt onto merchants and wealthy personal property holders.[12] His interest led him, then, to champion the farmers' cause; shifting the tax burden would help him collect from the state. He favored a state impost and voted against a national impost.[13] He was concerned to maintain the traditional fiscal and political integrity of Connecticut, and to see that the majority class—middling farmers—were treated fairly by the oligarchic government. He was, however, firmly anchored in that oligarchy himself.

Wolcott's East Windsor, like many towns, was facing severe difficulty in collecting taxes to pay the various state levies. By 1785 it would be £10,000 behind, and its tax collectors and selectmen would be liable to imprisonment if they did not pay up. As early as 1780 Wolcott as a selectman and deputy wrestled with the problem.[14] His reforms would reduce the land, livestock, and poll tax, maintain a state import duty, increase taxes on luxury items like carriages and clocks, increase the taxes on personal property such as elaborate houses, stock in inventory, and paper securities, and raise as well the faculty tax on artisans and professionals. He would also allow taxpayers to use all state and Continental notes for tax payments.[15] By 1786 Wolcott saw nearly complete success in his reform campaign.[16]

On the other side were the large-scale merchants, a small, tight-knit group who had built up capital from profits made supplying the American and French armies during the war. These men were closely connected to the ruling circle the fulcrum of which was the "merchant magistrate," Jonathan Trumbull, governor till 1784. They were expansionists whose aim was to develop the state's commercial sector.[17] By the war's end, the central figure in the mercantilist camp was Trumbull's son-in-law, Jeremiah Wadsworth, made one of America's richest men through his public and private commissary dealings, and now hoping to become even richer by both state and congressional trade policy.[18] These merchants wished to reduce or eliminate the state import duties in favor of a national impost, do away with state excise taxes, and strengthen Congress's ability to regulate interstate and foreign commerce, and, of course, pay the national debt, much of which they held.[19]

The strength of the two major factions in the lower house of the General Assembly shifted from time to time during the 1780s, with the agrarians— aided on many votes by the artisan-capitalists—dominating in 1779–80 and 1784 through the spring of 1786. But the commercial faction lost control of the upper house only for the two sessions of 1786. In the spring of 1787, when delegates to the Philadelphia convention were chosen, the factions were in balance. Changes in the tax system, though generally favorable to farmers, were not revolutionary and were being readjusted back to favor commerce at the time the national constitutional system altered the ground rules. Tax reforms that reduced the burden on agrarian landowners and increased it on professional and commercial taxpayers no doubt mitigated unrest among the agricultural poor. It was, perhaps, fortunate for Connecticut's steady habits that the reform—modest as it was—came just as the Shaysites were rallying on the state's northern border. Thus Connecticut took a middle road between the hard-line commercial/creditor policies of Massachusetts and the fiscal libertarianism of Rhode Island.[20]

Paper Money

At the legislative sessions of fall 1785 and spring 1786 the agrarians were at their strongest. They reformed taxes to help farmers, suspended the collection of the tax to pay the civil list, refused levies to pay the congressional requisition, permitted towns to rebate 5 percent of their taxes to ease collection from the poorest citizens, granted ten major debtors acts of bankruptcy, protected fifty more from imprisonment, and began to talk of printing paper money.[21] This last was what worried the commercial class the most.

The situation was indeed frightening. Hundreds of farmers lost their farms to the tax collector and joined the thousands of unlanded young men fleeing economic oblivion for the rich and fruitful acres of New York and points west.[22] "Everyone knows that our emigrations are great and increasing," stated one newspaper polemicist, "the reasons they assign is the insupportable burden of our taxes." Indeed, the regressive system of taxation would drive "every poor landholder . . . and three fourths of our mechanics and young men" out of the state.[23]

During the 1780s paper money problems became a major issue in every state. Laws making paper and commodities legal tender—called "tendry laws"—and moratoriums and provisions for installment payments of debts—called "stay laws"—were proposed in every state. At least seven states passed one or more of these provisions. In others, one house passed them. Connecticut's New England neighbors represent the extremes. The Massachusetts General Assembly not only refused to countenance such debtor relief, but actually passed a tax measure in 1786 that required payment in hard currency. Their action brought on Shays' Rebellion. In Rhode Island the debtor majority got control of the legislature, authorized new paper emissions, and declared them legal tender. Creditors had to accept the greatly depreciated paper or never get paid at all. When shopkeepers and others refused to accept the new money, fiscal chaos took over.[24]

In Connecticut the paper money forces were spearheaded by a town meeting in Sharon at the state's northwestern corner touching Shaysland. Paper money enthusiasts may have constituted a majority of the public in 1786. In early 1787 William Samuel Johnson wrote an out-of-state friend that "we have a pretty strong party in favor" of paper money. "Hitherto happily they have been kept undr. & the misery of the other St[ate]s who have acceedd. to the measr . . . strengthens the argts. agst."[25] State emissions of paper money, its Connecticut opponents insisted, would bring about a society ridden with "idleness and wickedness among the people . . . indolence and dissipation; that would hasten the moral decay of Connecticut society."[26] Paper money advocates in the Assembly apparently represented the extreme of the economic radicals there and could not hold even those deputies usually on the side of fiscal liberalism. The delegates to the Philadelphia convention were all hard-money men, and Connecticut's Roger Sherman led the movement to ban even Congress from printing money. The movement for paper money, he said, must be "crushed."[27]

On the other hand, none of the aristocratic and nationalist extremists like Noah Webster, Jeremiah Wadsworth, and David Humphreys were sent to Philadelphia. Connecticut's delegation included no men from either the agrarian or commercial fringes.

To all the college educated, the professional, and the members of the long-standing oligarchy, however, promiscuous emission of paper money represented public immorality, violation of property rights, collapse of sacred contracts, and in general the rule of the mob. And in Philadelphia it would indeed be crushed.

The Impost

The plan to levy an impost for the benefit of the national government went way back to the bleakest days of the Revolution. First broached in 1778, it had been the focus of nationalists since at least 1781, and constituted the link that connected them with the army. Indeed, some high nationalists such as Alexander Hamilton and Robert Morris supported the commutation scheme just to get Continental army officers behind the revenue measure.[28]

The most popular plan for such an income was to permit Congress to levy a 5 percent duty on all goods imported into the American states. The effect of this would be to take from New York and other major port states their exclusive control over that money and put it to use for the benefit of all states. As Connecticut's leading merchant, Jeremiah Wadsworth, pointed out succinctly, "No state has more reason to wish for an alteration of the Articles of Confederation than Connecticut. Fertile and well-cultivated, we have large exports from the produce of our land, and we consume much foreign produce—the profits of our importation go entirely to our neighboring states."[29]

Since the revenue derived from the impost was earmarked to pay the national wartime debt, many Connecticut men who owned United States notes would finally collect. As Charles Chauncey told his fellow deputies, "If Congress had power to regulate trade and establish a system of revenue we might be paid."[30] Though large numbers of Connecticut yeomen owned notes given in return for military services and sales of provisions, most of the U.S. debt held by Connecticuters was owed to the state's merchants. The sum was significant, estimated at $1,310,000 in specie value, the largest per capita of any of the states, and exceeded in total only by Massachusetts and Pennsylvania. "We are . . . assured," wrote one merchant, "that the Public Creditors are much more numerous & in greater Sums in this State than in any other in proportion to the Number & Wealth of the State."[31]

After the British restricted American access to their West Indian ports, it became clear to these same merchants that no single state could exert enough pressure on any European nation to gain advantageous commercial treaties. Massachusetts, New Hampshire, and Rhode Island restricted British entry. But the Connecticut General Assembly refused to go along in hopes of drawing that trade to New London, so the efforts of the others failed.[32] Some merchants concluded that only a national government with exclusive authority to regulate commerce and make and enforce treaties could restore prewar commercial life.

Merchants had another reason to look for a national government strong enough to limit the action of the states. During the war both the state governments and the U.S. Congress had issued large amounts of IOU's in the form of paper money, quartermaster certificates, soldiers' notes, bonds, and treasury notes. This paper lost value rapidly since the governments could not pay the principal or interest. Some states' notes retained at least partial value when their governments accepted them for payment of taxes. Some states also accepted U.S. notes and used those to pay their quotas to Congress. But generally, the depreciation of all this paper was cataclysmic, some of it circulating at 2 percent of its face value, though most would be redeemed at about twenty cents on the dollar.[33]

Creditors, public and private, wanted a national government that could stabilize the currency, perhaps by monopolizing minting and prohibiting paper emissions. Those who held U.S. government bonds wanted a federal monopoly on import duties to raise a revenue to pay them off. Those who held state bonds had cause for alarm, however. Though in Connecticut it was often the case that the major creditors held some of each, apparently a significant number of political leaders owned only state notes.[34]

Merchants and creditors wanted to strengthen the central government, then, and so might those large-scale farmers whose prosperity depended upon the robustness of foreign trade. And anyone who bought imported goods ought to have been able to respond to repeated assertions that they were paying $50,000 to $100,000 a year to the New York government and merchants in duties and profits that might be better paid into national coffers. Connecticut consumers also paid elevated prices for wheat imported from Maryland, where an export tax was levied. This was especially galling during the mid-1780s, when imports were in great measure due to Hessian fly incursions into Connecticut's own crop. Pennsylvania threatened a similar tax.[35] As Timothy Colt wrote Jeremiah Wadsworth, "as long as each State seperately claims a Sovereign Power in these matters . . . The American Trade in general must be on a bad footing and that in this State still more wretched than its neighbors."[36] National funds, in part at least, would spill into Connecticut pockets through liquidation of the U.S. debt and the establishment of an exclusive national foreign trade policy including a navy and diplomatic corps.

Less extreme nationalists also favored the 5 percent ad valorem congressional impost. All of Connecticut's congressmen present when the impost was under consideration supported it.[37] Since the Articles of Confederation did not permit Congress to tax in this way—or any other—the proposed impost was sent to the states for approval. The Connecticut General Assembly was persuaded to support the proposal in principle, but balked at certain major features of it. The authorizing act it passed in February 1781 limited its application to three years after the end of the war rather than the duration of indebtedness as the congressional act stipulated.[38] Other states encumbered the impost with their own reservations and Rhode Island rejected it outright, so it was not put into place. Another attempt by Congress in 1783 asked for a twenty-five-year grant of authority to levy and collect the impost.[39] But this time the issue became entangled in the bitterly emotional brouhaha over commutation. If Congress intended to use the income from the impost to pay pensions to officers who might then constitute an idle aristocracy, the Connecticut public wasn't going to grant it. And indeed the outcry was so great that the General Assembly again balked.[40]

The impost was seen in Connecticut as part of a scheme to centralize government; and after all, hadn't the war in which so many had sacrificed so much been over that very question? The conspiracy between the Continental army officers and congressional nationalists was suspected, and one ardent and articulate antinationalist, Benjamin Gale, spelled it out in a speech to his town meeting. Soldiers' notes—sold to speculators for a quarter of their value or less—and the commutation payments would never be paid off by either the state governments or the Congress under the Articles, Gale asserted:

> And the officers of the Army also well know that the vote of Congress for their commutation was obtained by art and intrigue, by a pretended mutiny of the army just at the conclusion of the war, and then obtained in Congress but by a single vote. . . . And they well know unless they alter our present form of government and convert into a *military government,* they must and will finally lose their prize. Again, there are others who are promised to mount up higher in the saddle by promotion. All these combining have raised a mighty outcry of the weakness of the federal government, and they have continued it so long and so loud that many honest people are made to believe it. . . . Gentlemen, this outcry of the weakness of the federal government is only a specious pretense to cover the artful schemes of *designing men* who would recover their commutation securities and the notes purchased of the soldiers.[41]

Gale was more perspicacious and prescient than others, but even the dullest yeoman could see the threat to Connecticut's sovereignty. To give up control over one source of their revenue, indeed to expand the powers of Congress in any way, went "well beyond the true spirit" of the Articles of Confederation, and would constitute "as great, or greater tyranny" than that of George III.[42]

Since other states refused to grant Congress authority to levy the impost on its own terms, the 5 percent impost of 1783 never became law.[43] This failure to give the central government an independent income and other proposals to grant some control over foreign commerce were among the principal reasons for calling the constitutional convention of 1787. For Connecticut's merchants and nationalists, these economic issues provided concrete and easily articulated responses to those local leaders who feared any kind of centralization of authority. But emotions run deeper than reason, and fears of aristocracy and loss of local power made most men in Connecticut highly skeptical of any move to strengthen the Congress.

By the spring of 1787 the agrarian tide in Connecticut had crested. The localist and militia forces had seen, though they did not yet know it, their high-water mark. But, still, most Connecticut yeomen saw the world through Connecticut eyes, and often narrowed their vision by squinting through the lens of their town, parish, or neighborhood. There were plenty who had never been fifty miles from home. Connecticut republicanism and life on the farm was their norm.

Traditional deference was cracking, however, and the fear of creeping aristocracy nearly reached the stage of paranoia. Apprehension that an aristocracy might be created from outside the state through a conspiracy of secret societies and an interstate cabal of merchants and militarists lay at the base of the antinationalism that pervaded the state. Thus on the eve of the fateful convention in Philadelphia, the nation's future would be decided by political forces that were moved by local structures and local concerns in every state. Connecticut was no exception, and in May 1787 the localists and nationalists were almost exactly evenly weighted.

The Election of Delegates

Connecticut politics on the eve of the constitutional convention was in a state of suspense, delicately balanced. It was, opined one legislator, "a time of jealousy; all men are on Tiptoe, the waters are troubled and the people are just ready to jump in and be healed." Noah Webster described the situation as he saw it in November: "There are two parties in the state—jealous of each other; *federal men and anti-federal.* The federal men suppose the anti-federal to be knaves, designing artful demagogues. The anti-federal suppose the federal to be ambitious tyrannical men, who are aiming at power and office at the expense of people at large." [44] Webster believed the antifederalists commanded a majority of the fall 1786 session of the General Assembly.

Webster's political parties were not parties in the modern sense, but there were clearly discernable factions consisting at the poles of antielitist states'-rights agrarians and aristocratic nationalist merchants. States' righters were hostile to the idea of altering the Articles for fear of congressional encroachment on local prerogatives. The localists in the General Assembly—and even some timorous nationalists—had persuaded their governor to ignore the call for delegates to the Annapolis meeting which convened in September 1786, and hoped to repeat that performance when Congress called for delegates to meet in Philadelphia in May of the following year.

Nationalists were so wary of localist strength that they, too, wished to avoid sending delegates to a constitutional convention at any time during the fall or winter of 1786–87. President Ezra Stiles of Yale "doubted the Expediency" for a number of reasons, one of which was that he did not think "the People were ripe . . . for the best one." The high nationalist, David Humphreys, a former aide to George Washington, in January wrote his erstwhile commander somewhat hysterically that there was a danger of sending to a new convention "some of the most antifederal men in the State who believe or act as if they believe that Congress is already possessed of too unlimited powers and would wish apparently to see the Union dissolved." These antifederalists, Humphreys told the General, were trying to persuade the people that they are "in danger of having their liberties stolen away by an artful designing Aristocracy."[45]

At Congress, sitting in New York, Connecticut's delegates, William Samuel Johnson and Stephen Mix Mitchell, voted against the call to the convention in part because they were afraid that it would be dominated by antinationalists. On February 21 the Connecticut congressmen cast the only negative votes against what Johnson considered "a very doubtful Measure at best." Madison reported that Johnson "considered this resolution as a deadly blow to the existing Confederation."[46] Mitchell was opposed to conventions in general because of their extraconstitutional and antinational character in Connecticut.[47]

In Connecticut, Governor Huntington refused to call a special session of the Assembly to respond to the Annapolis invitation. That invitation had been on tap at the Assembly's October session, but the provincials desired a negative response, and the nationalists thought time was on their own side. The antinational-tending Council had agreed unanimously with Huntington that a special session of the Assembly was not necessary. Action on the invitation was put off until May. In March 1787 David Humphreys, still worried, reported to Washington that he doubted the Assembly would send delegates. "And if they do," he added, "my apprehension is still greater that they will be sent on purpose to impede any salutary measures that might be proposed." Conversations with many people in New Haven, he said, gave little hope for a "successful issue of the meeting." Connecticut, in his exasperated view, was "under the influence of a few such miserable, narrow minded & I may say wicked Politicians."[48] On the other side, there were many who feared that the delicately bred might set up a regal government. But there were nearly as many who, like Noah Webster, scorned those provincials who "think as they have been bred . . . on a small scale" and were ready for a stronger confederation.[49]

Shays' Rebellion in Massachusetts raised the nationalists' fear of rampant democracy in the states. At last, their worst fears were fulfilled when Shaysism reared its ugly head in Connecticut. Activity or rumors of activity in two widely separated, but isolated communities—Sharon in the northwest corner near Massachusetts and Preston in the southeast near Rhode Island—terrified not only the high nationalists, but moderates as well. Word of the outbreak at Sharon arrived on May 15 right in the middle of the Assembly session. Two legislators and a couple of sheriffs were dispatched to quell "the Massachusetts Rebels and other Subjects of this State." In short order the threat was "happily crushed in the Head," but the excitement no doubt pushed some borderline deputies into the proconvention column.[50]

The May session of the General Assembly opened with a sermon by Elizur Goodrich of Hartford, who pointed out the "Necessity of National faith to the Happiness of a State." Governor Huntington suggested that the deputies get right to the election of delegates, which they did. When debate opened, the opponents of revising the Articles, and therefore the opponents of sending a delegation, based their fight on the aristocratic tendencies that such changes might bring about. They were also against giving up any more state power, especially in the area of taxation. These were the same men generally who had opposed increases in land taxes in the state and a reduction in the size of the General Assembly, and who had railed against the aristocratic Society of the Cincinnati.[51] Daniel Perkins of Enfield on the Massachusetts border feared that the "State would send men that had been delicately bred, and who were in affluent circumstances, that could not feel for the people in the day of distress." And, he added, "if we send we will be under double obligation to adopt what the convention shall recommend." Abraham Granger liked the Articles of Confederation. They were, he said, "sufficient for every purpose." Power enough was already delegated to Congress, and a strengthened constitution "would be disagreeable to his constituents," for it might tend to "produce a regal government in this country."[52]

Paper money plans, proposals to make all real property legal tender for private debts and taxes, Shays' Rebellion, and fiscal anarchy in Rhode Island alarmed not only the national-commercial sector, but also many moderate localists, especially those who held significant amounts of state notes. It is likely that Shays' Rebellion tipped the scales against the agrarians. Indeed, in the spring of 1787 a bill to make goods legal tender for private debts was rejected 124 to 22, and the paper money sponsor exercised his discretion rather than his interest and didn't even reintroduce his bill.[53]

Though extremist proposals were easily defeated, the Assembly did not vaporize in the hands of the mercantilist nationalists who tried to put the democratic genie back into the bottle. Antidemocratic efforts to streamline the legislature by limiting every town to one deputy and to repeal the measure permitting annual—instead of good behavior—appointment of judges, were also easily repelled. On issues of nationalism, too, the localists held their ground when they defeated the commutation, refused to pay the state's congressional requisitions, and encumbered the proposed national impost.[54]

Nevertheless, with unexpected ease—though last among the states to do so—the Assembly agreed to send delegates to Philadelphia. The provincials were down, but not out, however, so the delegation reflected a compromise. No radical states'-rights advocates were sent; but neither were any high-flown federalists. Instead, among the three delegates was Erastus Wolcott, brother of the lieutenant governor, but the leader of agrarian tax reform, a large landowner, and a major holder of state securities. Wolcott had been elected to Congress, but never attended. He had, apparently, an aversion to leaving the hearth and home he so devoutly worked to preserve.[55] And he did not disappoint himself on this occasion. He declined to go to Philadelphia, "having never had the Small Pox a Disorder to which he would be greatly exposed in the City to which he is appointed to repair, he cannot suppose it would be prudent for him to hazzard his Life without the most pressing Necessity. . . ."[56] In his place the Council, without reference to the lower house, appointed Roger Sherman. The other two delegates were William Samuel Johnson and Oliver Ellsworth.

The substitution of Sherman for Wolcott was a good thing for Connecticut and for the nation, too. Sherman, who had lived his first nineteen years in Massachusetts, was nevertheless much more experienced in Connecticut politics. Wolcott had never served in Congress and, indeed, had hardly ventured outside of his ancestral state. Sherman, on the other hand, had served more days in Congress than anyone from anywhere, and even under cover of his unfeigned provincialism showed glimpses of statesmanship. His extraordinary ability to negotiate deals got some exercise in the old Congress. It would find a wide field to play on and a great measure of success in the convention where Wolcott would have been a cipher.

3

National Objectives, Local Concerns
at the Constitutional Convention

Part 1. Protecting State Governments

The part played by Connecticut's delegates to the Convention of 1787 was shaped not only by the constituents who sent them and the political and economic needs of their state, but also by the character and personality of each of the three men. These had been formed by their families and by their political biographies—the latter in Roger Sherman's case extending over a period of forty-three years. Who were these men?

The Delegates

The most experienced of the three delegates was Roger Sherman. He became the state's first mayor in 1784, when New Haven became the state's first city. Sherman had been a local and state officeholder since 1745 and was one of the members of Connecticut's initial delegation to the First Continental Congress in 1774. By 1787 he had spent more time in the national Congresses than any man in America. At sixty-six, he was the oldest of the fifty-five men at the convention, with the exception of eighty-one year-old Ben Franklin.[1]

Sherman was an old-fashioned Calvinist, a characteristic that infuriated his more enlightened and urbane colleagues. Once, on his way with other Connecticut delegates to the old Congress, his refusal to take a ferry on Sunday was condemned by an enraged companion as "superstitious neglect." When during the Revolution Washington requested to increase the number of lashes of the whip allowed for desertion to five hundred, Sherman invoked the authority of Deuteronomy to stay the executioner's hand at forty. This behavior, one of Washington's generals wrote him, "will Convince you of the incompetence of some members [of Congress] as well as the absurdity of some parts of the Confederation." On the other hand, Thomas Jefferson once pointed him out to a visitor, saying, "That is Mr. Sherman of Connecticut, a man who never said a foolish thing in his life." This was a man who was hard to love; but he was respected. Patrick Henry thought the three "first men" in the old Congress were Washington, George Mason, and Sherman. John Adams called him "one of the soundest and strongest pillars of the Revolution." Nathaniel Macon of North Carolina, who served with him in the U.S. Senate, remarked that Sherman "had more common sense than any man he ever knew."[2]

Sherman was a self-taught lawyer who had been inspired to enter the profession by the younger William Samuel Johnson, the leader of the Connecticut bar. Johnson was a product of the best legal education available in the English-speaking world, but Sherman always thought that riding the circuit was a better way to learn the rights of the people "than by staying at home and reading British and other foreign laws."[3] At the time of Sherman's death, the president of Yale College said, "*Law* & *Politics* were peculiarly adapted to his Genius. . . . He was calm sedate & ever discerning & judicious. . . . He went thro' all the Grades of public Life, & grew in them all, & filled every Office with Propriety, Ability, & tho' not with showy Brillancy, yet with that Dignity which arises from doing every Thing perfectly right." At the convention, William Pierce of Georgia wrote of Sherman, "He is an able politician, and extremely artful in accomplishing any particular object;—it is remarked that he seldom fails."[4]

Though the facts show Sherman's successes did not have the inevitability that his reputation claimed, the perception that he was invincible provided an early advantage in any conflict. Sherman's high success rate at the convention was the result of his extraordinary political finesse (and perhaps because he spoke more often than anyone other than Madison).[5] In his relations with his constituents, he was so sensitive to the movement of political opinion that he always found a position at the leading edge not of new ideas, but of majority acceptance of them. Such tactical positioning was less a conscious calculation on his part than a subtle litmuslike quality emanating from his common origins and lack of guile or pretension. High nationalist Jeremiah Wadsworth of Hartford was afraid Sherman would promote states' rights at the convention and told his friends "he is cunning as the Devil, and if you attack him you ought to know him well; he is not easily managed, but if he suspects you are trying to take him in, you may as well catch an Eel by the tail."[6]

Sherman had practiced provincial politics in Connecticut for forty years and national politics in Congress for over a decade by the time he arrived at the Philadelphia convention. "He had," said his New Haven pastor, "a happy talent of judging what was feasible, or what men would bear; and what they would not bear in government. And he had a rare talent of prudence, or of timing and adapting his measures to the attainment of his end."[7] At Philadelphia Roger Sherman would exercise his talent with a practiced prudence and skillful timing to win all his major battles; but as a defender of state prerogatives, time would tell that he lost the war.

Compared to Sherman, William Samuel Johnson of Stratford did not play a major part at Philadelphia in 1787. In a way, this cosmopolitan background and reticence at the convention combined to make an exception to prove the rule of Connecticut chauvinism established by Sherman's and Ellsworth's constituency-driven posture. Johnson, the least "Connecticut bound" of the three—indeed, he was at the moment in the process of moving to New York—was also the least active and influential at Philadelphia in 1787. He spoke infrequently, but he and James Wilson of Pennsylvania were the most respected lawyers at a convention where thirty-one of fifty-five delegates were members of their states' bar. Johnson grew up in a well-to-do family connected to New York wealth through his mother. It was as urbane a set of connections as one could find in Connecticut, and Johnson augmented his social polish by a long stay in England.[8]

As a politically ambitious Anglican in an officially Congregational colony, Johnson spent his early career learning how to walk a tightrope. He mastered that art well enough to become, as a result of the political upset growing out of the Stamp Act crisis of 1765, the first Anglican ever elected to the Connecticut upper house.[9] He was both by temperament and design a compromiser. The Connecticut political context only made expedient what came naturally anyway. "I must live in Peace or I cannot live at all," he once told his father. "Dinner of herbs earned by the sweat of humble Industry is better with love & quietness than the Table of Dainties accompanied by either domestick or Public Discord."[10] His father, when president of King's College in New York, once asked his son's help in waging a sectarian polemical battle. The younger Johnson replied, "You know I am generally averse to disputes of this kind as tending more to irritate the passions than to convince the understanding of people." It was the older man who then admonished his son that "[e]ven caution may be carried too far."[11]

When the outbreak of war threatened, Johnson resigned his lieutenant colonel's commission in the Connecticut militia, claiming that he was too old (at forty-seven), was ignorant of military affairs, had no taste for glory, and could not take time from his law business. Perhaps some of this was true; but he revealed his real motives privately when chosen to go to the First Continental Congress. In fact, he wrote a political intimate in England, he refused to become a delegate, because *"inter nous,* I did not think it advisable either on my own account or on account of the Colony to make one of that Assembly."* Ultimately, his attempt to remain neutral during the war failed in the face of extreme public pressure and threatened physical abuse, and in 1779 he finally swore an oath to the revolutionary cause.[12]

In 1787 Johnson's political standing in Connecticut had recently been bolstered by his largely successful work on behalf of Connecticut's acquisition of the Western Reserve. He was elected to Congress and was a member sitting in New York, like fifteen other convention delegates, when he was chosen to represent Connecticut in Philadelphia.

Johnson's congressional experience gave him a wide acquaintance among national politicians, some of whom he had first met at the Stamp Act Congress of 1765. His urbanity, Episcopalianism, and New York connections made him popular among non-New Englanders, and the fact that he owned slaves gave him credibility among southern delegates, who were, one observer reported in 1785, "vastly fond of him." Hugh Williamson of North Carolina and William Grayson of Virginia both paid considerable compliments to him during their time in Congress together just before the convention.[13] Johnson would prove to be a bridge between New England and the South at crucial moments during the convention. But in fact, he did not speak publicly at the convention without having "first, as was usual in every case committed the matter to my colleagues."[14] His was a typically Connecticut political style of which the off-camera deal was the hallmark.

The junior member of Connecticut's Philadelphia trio was Oliver Ellsworth.[15] Twenty-four years younger than Sherman, Ellsworth had come of political age during the Revolution accustomed to "thinking continentally," and thus was more likely to acquiesce in nationalist measures. After a rapid rise in Connecticut government, aided by a good legal mind and marriage into the formidable Wolcott family, Ellsworth was sent to Congress in 1778. At the convention he would find his old Princeton friends, Luther Martin and William Paterson. Princetonian James Madison, whom he had known less well at college was there also. Of course he knew many of the other delegates through his congressional service.

Ellsworth, like his two Connecticut colleagues, a pragmatic politician capable of tempering his principles when his objectives required it, was nonetheless not as conciliating as his older, more experienced colleagues. In the Connecticut context he represented the commercial-nationalist perspective, but among the true nationalists in the constitutional convention, he was decidedly provincial.

Ellsworth worked in the shadow of Roger Sherman, whose tutelage he enjoyed in the old Congress, voting as the old man did in 78 percent of the roll call votes during the times they served together. Ellsworth admitted having taken Sherman as his model, upon which John Adams is said to have remarked that that was "praise enough for both men."[16]

In Philadelphia, the trio worked in close harmony, though sour notes were not entirely absent. Johnson explained many years later that it "was usual in every case" for him to discuss matters with his colleagues before raising questions on the floor.[17] These three men—all six feet tall—came from the most republican state represented at the convention. They had been trained in the school of elective politics in a faction-prone setting. They were practicing politicians skilled in consensus building and knew how to shape compromises that would undergird the consensus. The principal contribution of Connecticut to the constitutional convention was this delegation of compromise makers.[18]

With Sherman replacing Erastus Wolcott, the delegation's antinationalism was much diminished, but they were still guarded in their approach to strengthening the central government. However, Ellsworth had worked with other young continentally minded congressmen such as Madison and Hamilton, and as early as 1783 he spoke of Congress' need for an independent revenue, and feared "disunion and anarchy" if its powers were not increased. Sherman had also supported efforts to give Congress an independent income through the impost and to permit it to regulate foreign trade. Johnson, typically, had not tipped his hand publicly. In the Confederation Congress, however, he favored granting the central government control over not only foreign trade, but commerce among the states as well. In Connecticut he was known as a cautious conservative.[19] Of the three, only Sherman created anxiety among the high nationalists. "I am satisfied with the appointment," wrote Jeremiah Wadsworth—who was owed more money by Congress than anyone else in the state—"except Sherman who, I am told, is disposed to patch up the old scheme of Government." If Sherman "is stubborn he will influence too many others," Wadsworth warned Henry Knox.[20]

The delegates would not have a completely free hand, however. The General Assembly sent them off with instructions that echoed the call from Congress for a convention "for the sole and express purpose of revising the

Articles of Confederation and reporting . . . such alterations and provisions . . . as shall . . . render the federal constitution adequate to the exigencies of Government & the preservation of the Union." The Connecticut instructions added that any suggested changes must be "Agreeable to the General Principles of Republican Government. . . ." Any one of the three delegates was authorized to act for the state in the absence of others.[21]

Basic Assumptions of the Delegates

The Connecticut delegates carried to Philadelphia in their intellectual baggage a foundation stone of their provincial constitutional culture heavier than any of their state's immediate economic and security needs. That was their concept of republican government. The other states had evolved during the years since 1765 or 1776 into contractual polities based on the idea that the governed and the governors were natural competitors for power whose relations had to be regulated by constitutions—Locke's political contract. Connecticut's political culture had not evolved as far. It was still dominated by the idea that society was an organic whole based on natural and voluntary hierarchies where everyone put the collective welfare ahead of individual needs or desires. The common man's principal virtue was in recognizing a natural aristocracy of talent and elevating them to temporary office—on good behavior till the next election, as it were. This was more in the tradition of Edward Coke of the early seventeenth century than of Locke seventy-five years later.[22] They carried this conception of society and government to Philadelphia, where it surfaced on a number of occasions.

The hierarchal mode should be carried into the federal system. The Constitution should be ratified by the state legislators, Oliver Ellsworth insisted, not only to protect the federal principle, but also because conventions of the people would disrupt the natural hierarchy as they had in Connecticut in the commutation furor of 1783. Roger Sherman supported him. "The people he said (immediately) [i.e., directly] should have as little to do as may be about the [national] Government. They want information and are constantly liable to be mislead."[23] Conventions were to be mistrusted; the people's judgment on public policy was to be mistrusted. These views reflected a century and a half of legislative supremacy in Connecticut, the most democratic colony in the empire with its elected governor and semiannual Assembly elections. It was, as we have noted, in the words of its leading jurist, not a constitutional state, but "a representative republic."[24]

In Connecticut, unlike those states that had recently been under the domination of royal and proprietary governors and appointed upper houses, limited government was taken for granted. Calvinist theory limited civil government, the Fundamental Orders of 1639 proclaimed it, the Charter of 1662 established it, common law enforced it, tradition demanded it, and frequent elections guaranteed it. Connecticut's Declaration of Rights of 1650 was altered from time to time by the legislature and was interpreted on a continuing basis by the courts. In Connecticut, people did not have rights because they were written on paper, but because they were part of God's system; a declaration of rights merely announced what all knew to be true.

Thus Oliver Ellsworth reflected the Connecticut tradition when he said there was no necessity to outlaw ex post facto laws in the Constitution because everyone—lawyer and civilian alike—would "say that ex post facto laws were void of themselves." Indeed, said William Samuel Johnson, Connecticut's leading legal mind, congressional prohibitions implied "an improper suspicion of the National Legislature." Frequent elections—with common law, the bulwark of Connecticut republicanism—Roger Sherman wrote a few months later, were "a much greater security than a declaration of rights or restraining clauses on paper."[25]

In Connecticut the courts, together with frequent elections, protected fundamental rights and righted wrongs committed by one private individual against another. The same courts administered law and adjudicated equity claims, where most other states had chancery courts for equity cases. Despite objections that the two functions ought not to be combined in federal courts, William Samuel Johnson managed to work the Connecticut mode into Article III of the Constitution. The delegates were unable, however, to impose upon the federal courts the requirement of juries in civil cases, a system that operated in a number of states.[26] On other, larger, issues they were more successful.

The Constitution has often been called a bundle of compromises, but that description thoughtlessly trivializes the creative work of the framers.[27] The seminal intellectual conceptions of Madison and Hamilton were too radical for most men at the convention, but the patchwork plans of Paterson and Pinckney offered enough for only a few of them. The finished document itself, in overall substance and structure, represents a mix of Madisonian nationalism and Patersonian federalism. It was, as Oliver Ellsworth so aptly put it, "partly national; partly federal."[28]

Of course the Connecticut delegates carried to Philadelphia the same concerns that all the Confederation leadership had. They wanted a central government strong enough to make and enforce international commercial treaties, to regulate commerce among the states, to raise an independent income through duties on imports, to maintain an army and navy, to survey, sell, and protect the western lands, to regulate coinage, to protect the personal property and contract rights of their constituents, and to safeguard the small states against their larger neighbors.[29]

For some delegates such as the high nationalists Madison, James Wilson, and Charles Pinckney, these were the minimal needs of a reformed government. But for the Connecticut delegates, they probably represented the maximum desirable extension of U.S. authority. Sherman in fact declared that "the objects of the Union were . . . few. 1. defence agst. foreign danger. 2. agst. internal disputes & a resort to force. 3. Treaties with foreign nations 4. regulating foreign commerce, & drawing revenue from it. These & perhaps a few lesser objects alone rendered a Confederation of the States necessary. All other matters civil & criminal would be much better in the hands of the States."[30] Johnson and Ellsworth were less states' rights in their leanings and on occasion outvoted Sherman, but never on matters of great policy or principle.

Once at Philadelphia, it soon became clear that there was a strong consensus on nationalism and the protection of personal and speculative property—government securities and investment real estate. On the other hand, Benjamin Franklin pointed out the dangers inherent in bringing together any group of people no matter how great their characters and minds: "For when you assemble a number of men to have the joint wisdom. You inevitably assemble with those men, all their prejudices, their passions, their errors of opinion, their local interests and their selfish views."[31]

And, indeed, there were some "local interests" that worried the Connecticut delegates in particular. The most significant area of damage control lay in the field of states' rights. It is unlikely that the Connecticut delegates anticipated the assault on state autonomy that was laid out in the Virginia Plan. In Philadelphia, however, they found that for the first six weeks they had to exercise their best efforts in beating back attempts by the high nationalists to subsume the state governments into a centralized system. Their major accomplishment at the convention was to institute protection for the state governments by way of an equal vote in the Senate.

The Connecticut Compromise

Without question the best-known contribution of the Connecticut delegation to the American system of government is the famous compromise that established the system of voting in the two houses of the legislature. Known variously as the Federal Compromise and the Great Compromise, it is most commonly referred to as the Connecticut Compromise, a term that the dean of historians of the convention, Max Farrand, wrote in 1904 had become "almost universal."[32]

Roger Sherman had proposed something very similar to what is found in the finished Constitution when he was sitting in the old Continental Congress in 1776. [33] When the method of voting was under discussion then, Sherman had suggested that "[t]he vote should be taken two ways: call the Colonies, and call the individuals, and have a majority of both."[34] The delegates at the Congress represented states, Sherman said, and not people. It was an idea whose time had not come in 1776, when American politicians were more interested in decentralizing an empire rather than centralizing a nation. Thus the Articles of Confederation was built on the concept of sovereign state governments joined together as equals.

Now, at Philadelphia in 1787, the question of voting in the two legislative houses renewed the debate of a decade earlier. The Virginia Plan, which formed the basis of discussion, called for a two-house legislature with voting in both houses proportional either to contributions to the national treasury or "the number of free inhabitants, as the one or the other rule may seem best in different cases."[35] Suffrage weighted according to taxes was not given prominence in debate; the real fight was between those who wanted to keep an equal state vote and those who wanted a fundamental change that would make states' votes proportional to population.

The debate over the basis of representation in Congress is usually discussed in terms of "large states" and "small states," using the terms in reference to relative populations. But it should not be seen this way because the vote rarely split by populations, and protecting small states was not the principal point of Sherman's proposal. He said explicitly that he wished for an equal vote for each state in the Senate "not so much as a security for the small States; as for the State Govts."[36] True, the three largest states—Virginia, Pennsylvania, and Massachusetts—voted consistently together for representation based on population; and three of the five smallest states—Delaware, New Jersey, and Maryland—voted together consistently for equal votes; nevertheless, three of the states with the smallest populations, South Carolina, Georgia, and New Hampshire, regularly voted with the "large states," and New York, with the fifth or sixth largest population, regularly voted with the "small states."

Population figures were not precise, and in 1787 it was believed that Connecticut, New York, Maryland, North Carolina, and South Carolina were all about the same size demographically speaking. The clue to understanding the coalitions is that the Carolinas and Georgia, which were large in territory, expected to fill up relatively soon, while Delaware, Maryland, and New Jersey were small, had no western lands, and were already full. New York's antinationalist delegates, Lansing and Yates, outvoted the extreme nationalist Hamilton to protect the prerogatives of their state government, not as representatives of a small state. The New Hampshire delegates did not arrive until July 23, and then, despite the expectations of the small states, voted on most issues with the nationalists from the large states. The smallest state in size, but not population, Rhode Island, did not send delegates to the convention at all.[37] Thus, dividing states into those with large and small populations does not provide a consistent guide to delegates' behavior.

Delegates from New Jersey, Delaware, and Maryland were fearful, however, that the destinies of their state governments and the people of their states would be subject to the voting power of the "large states." Though many of the delegates from these "small states" wished to grant ample new authority to the central government, they would insist on protecting themselves first. They proposed to do this through the New Jersey—or Paterson—Plan that would have kept in place the system of one state/one vote as practiced in Congress under the Articles of Confederation.

On one hand, then, stood nationalists like James Madison and James Wilson; and on the other stood men like William Paterson of New Jersey, Gunning Bedford of Delaware, and Luther Martin of Maryland. For Madison and Wilson, proportional voting in both houses was not only the only fair system, but was also a logical imperative. Their objective was a new government that was to be national, resting on the consent of the whole people (acting through the eligible voters) and passing laws enforceable against individuals, rather than a mere federation with a congress representing state governments and acting only on them. The nationalists reasoned that if congressmen were to be representatives of the people, each one should represent roughly the same number of people.

At the convention in the early days of debate, what appeared to be hard, inflexible lines were drawn, and positions were stated in unambiguous terms. Any system other than proportional representation, declared Madison, was "inadmissible, being evidently unjust." "[W]hatever reason might have existed for the equality of suffrage when the Union was a *federal* one among sovereign States," he insisted, "it must cease when a *national* Governt. should be put into the place." Said Wilson, "Representatives of different districts ought clearly to hold the same proportion to each other, as their respective constituents hold to each other. If the small States will not confederate on this plan, Pena. & he presumed some other States, would not confederate on any other."[38]

On the other side, the Delaware delegates had been forbidden by their state legislature to consent "to any change of the rule of suffrage, and in case such a change should be fixed on," George Read declared, "it might become their duty to retire from the Convention." The youthful Gunning Bedford heatedly asked, "will not these large States crush the small ones whenever they stand in the way of their ambitions or interested views. This shows the impossibility of adopting such a system as that on the table, or any other founded on a change in the prinple [sic] of representation." And Paterson "considered the proposition for a proportional representation as striking at the existence of the lesser States."[39]

Roger Sherman had grown up in New England and lived there all his life. He knew stone walls when he saw them, and he was always looking for ways around, over, or through them. His political style, learned in the popular politics of eighteenth-century Connecticut, was to cut deals, give and take, make compromises. In the states'-rights/nationalist confrontation of early June, he thought he saw a way through. On Monday, June 11, after canvassing the possibilities among some small-state delegates on Sunday, Sherman proposed what would become the Connecticut Compromise. Rising at the opening of the debate, Madison reports, "Mr. Sharman [sic] proposed that the proportion of suffrage in the 1st branch should be according to the respective numbers of free inhabitants; and that in the second branch or Senate, each State should have one vote and no more."[40]

But at that point the large states held onto their allies, the potentially large states—Georgia and the Carolinas. Connecticut also supported, as part of a deal, a change to proportional voting in the lower house, presumably on the assumption that in the upper house equal votes would prevail. Sherman then moved an equal vote in the upper house. "Every thing he said depended on this. The smaller States would never agree to the plan on any other principle (than an equality of suffrage in this branch)." Oliver Ellsworth seconded the motion. Only Connecticut switched its vote, so the three most populous states with the three states largest in area (Georgia and the Carolinas) stuck together and defeated Sherman's motion six to five.[41] But the battle was far from over.

The Connecticut delegates continued to promote the compromise. They were determined to protect their local autonomy, that "darling liberty" established by the Charter of 1662. As Madison noted, Connecticuters were "habitually disinclined to abridge[ments of] her State prerogatives." [42] On

June 20 Sherman again said "he would agree to have two branches, and a proportional representation in one of them, provided each State had an equal voice in the other. . . . Each state like each individual had its peculiar habits usages and manners, which constituted its happiness." The next day Johnson urged on behalf of the small states, equal voting in one house "for the purpose of defending themselves in the general Councils." On June 25 Ellsworth argued against proportional representation in the Senate. "Every state," he said, "has its particular views & prejudices, which will find their way into the general councils, through whatever channel they may flow. . . . He urged the necessity of maintaining the existence & agency of the States. . . . The only chance of supporting a Genl. Govt. lies in engrafting it on that of the individual States." [43]

Sherman spoke up for equal protection for the state governments again on June 28, and the next day Madison reported Johnson's summary of the Connecticut position: "The controversy must be endless whilst Gentlemen differ in the grounds of their arguments; Those on one side considering the States as districts of people [collectively] composing one political Society," that is, the people collectively incorporated into one government; "those on the other considering them as so many [individual] political societies." [44]

Johnson then articulated the new American basis for a second house. The generally accepted reason for an upper house was that it was to represent the aristocratic interest in a government made up of a monarch, nobility, and commoners. The men at the convention qualified that assumption to view the Senate as a body, not necessarily of the wealthy—though this was implicit in many of their statements—but as "respectable for its wisdom & virtue," as Madison characterized it. Johnson shifted the basis. "The fact is," he pointed out,

> that the States do exist as [distinct] political Societies, and a Govt. is to be formed for them in their political capacity, as well as for the individuals composing them. Does it not seem to follow, that if the States as such are to exist they must be armed with some power of self-defence. . . . Besides the Aristocratic and other interests, which ought to have the means of defending themselves, the States have their interests as such, and are equally entitled to like means. On the whole he thought that as in some respects the States are to be considered in their political capacity, and in others as districts of individual citizens, the two ideas embraced on different sides, instead of being opposed to each other, ought to be combined; that in *one* branch the *people,* ought to be represented; in the *other,* the *States.* [45]

And then, on June 29, when, by a vote of six to four (with Maryland divided), the Committee of the Whole determined on proportional representation in the lower house, Johnson and Ellsworth moved to postpone other considerations and go directly to the question of representation in the Senate. Ellsworth, Madison reports,

> moved that the rule of suffrage in the 2d branch be the same with that established by the articles of confederation. He was not sorry on the whole he said that the vote just passed, had determined against this rule in the first branch. He hoped it would become a ground of compromise with regard to the 2d branch. We were partly national; partly federal. The proportional representation in the first branch was conformable to the national principle & would secure the large States agst. the small. An equality of voices was conformable to the federal principle and was necessary to secure the Small States agst. the large. He trusted that on this middle ground a compromise would take place. He did not see that it could on any other. And if no compromise should take place, our meeting would not only be in vain but worse than in vain.[46]

No one wanted the meeting to be in vain—or worse—and so the debate over representation ground on. Ellsworth made the case for equality again on June 30, citing, interestingly, both the British system, where the few in the House of Lords could "have a check on the many," and confederacies in general, all of which incorporated "an equality of voices." By instituting proportional representation in both houses, he said, "[w]e are razing the foundations of the building. When we need only repair the roof." Significantly, Ellsworth did not mention Connecticut as a model confederacy or the General Assembly as a model legislature. He did say, however, that his "remarks were not the result of partial or local views. The State he represented . . . held a middle rank."[47]

What he wanted, said Ellsworth, was "domestic happiness. The Natl. Govt. would not descend to the local objects on which this depended. It could only embrace objects of a general nature. He turned his eyes therefore for the preservation of his rights to the State Govts. From these alone he could derive the greatest happiness he expects in this life."[48] An equal vote, thus, was needed to protect the interests of state governments as corporate entities retaining such powers as those to tax, to raise a militia, to legislate for the health, welfare, and morality of the people. But beyond that, even more local in its concern, was the necessity to preserve states' ability to protect the rights of individuals. Unlike Virginia, for instance, where slavery and a class structure made Mason's and Madison's concern for individual rights something of an abstraction, in Connecticut these rights were palpable and nearly universal. (About 1 percent of the population were still slaves—many to become free at age twenty-one.)

Ellsworth's motion for equal representation in the Senate came to a vote on July 2, and the count showed five states on each side, with Georgia divided because Connecticut-born-and-bred Abraham Baldwin switched sides and voted with his old compatriots. "We are now at a full stop," Sherman declared, but "nobody he supposed meant that we shd. break up without doing something." He suggested a committee, one member from each state, which was established. Sherman sat for Connecticut. The Committee reported on July 5 with a proposal that conformed to the Connecticut delegation's formula—proportional representation in the House and equal representation in the Senate.[49]

The compromise was not acceptable to the large states and debate continued through two hot July days. The delegates were at loggerheads and moved no faster than they had a week earlier, when Sherman had declared that they were at a full stop. Now on July 7 he

Supposed that it was the wish of every one that some Genl. Govt. should be established. An equal vote in the 2d. branch would, he thought, be most likely to give it the necessary vigor. . . . If they vote by States in the 2d. branch, and each State has an equal vote, there must be always a majority of States as well as a majority of the people on the side of public measures, & the Govt. will have decision and efficacy. If this be not the case in the 2d. branch there may be a majority of the States agst. public measures, and the difficulty of compelling them to abide by the public determination, will render the Government feebler than it has ever yet been.

Of course, when he speaks of the states, Sherman means the state governments.[50] He is pointing out that the support and cooperation of the several governments—or at least a majority of them—would be necessary for any national legislation to be effectuated at the local level. At this point in the debate, the supremacy clause had not been adopted, the judicial system had not been articulated, and judicial review of state actions was only an inference yet hardly discerned. Sherman, as we shall see, did not envision federal trial courts, and completely missed the significance of the supremacy clause.

Another week of debate had the hard-core nationalists on the ropes but still desperately fighting for proportional representation in both houses. After a compromise arrangement put forward by Charles Pinckney was defeated on Saturday, July 14, the states'-rights forces thought they could press their point.[51] It was the moment for that old fox Sherman to apply the second phase of his principal political maxim that "minorities talk; majorities vote." The first thing Monday morning the entire committee report, including the Connecticut formula, was called up for a vote. This was the climax of the debate that had begun in cooler times toward the end of May. Certainly if the states'-rights faction failed this time to gain its point, the convention would be again "at a full stop" as Sherman had said it was on July 2, and its meeting would have been in vain as Ellsworth had worried a few days earlier.

And indeed the vote was close. The states'-rights delegations held together and Connecticut, New Jersey, Delaware, and Maryland voted aye; but that was only four of ten. Pennsylvania and Virginia, along with Georgia and South Carolina, voted no. But the old nationalist coalition failed to cohere. There were wise men in the Massachusetts and North Carolina delegations who saw that this was the last chance to hold the convention to its task. A defeat for the states' righters at this point might well cause those delegations to go home. And so Elbridge Gerry and Caleb Strong voted aye, dividing the Massachusetts delegation; and North Carolina deserted its nationalist position to support equality in the Senate. The Connecticut Compromise, to the stunned consternation of Madison, Wilson, and their nationalist supporters was written into the draft to stay.[52]

The decision to aim for a legislature in which both houses were based on proportional representation was Madison's from the start. It found complete acceptance in the Virginia delegation and became part of the Virginia Plan. It was accepted by the Committee of the Whole House in the early days of the convention. For Madison, Wilson, Charles Pinckney, and others it was a sine qua non of good government and fair play. But the states'-rights delegates never swallowed it, and indeed considered a great sacrifice any deviation from the system by which Congress was organized under the Articles of Confederation.

Thus, from the states'-rights point of view, the real compromise was not equality in the Senate but rather that which provided proportional representation in the lower house. But since such a change was virtually a foregone conclusion, most historians have seen the willingness—however reluctant— of some delegates from the large states to accept equality in the Senate as the major compromise.[53] The combination of the two different systems—that so outraged the doctrinaire Madison's logical mind—was the perfect solution, and an obvious one to the pragmatic Sherman and his fellow delegates accustomed to the give and take of the popular politics that characterized Connecticut republicanism.

Sherman's system, then, strengthened the states'-rights focus of bicameralism described by Johnson a few days earlier. But despite the explanations of Johnson and Sherman most discussion of the upper house focused on its function as a "cooling" mechanism to temper the potentially unrestrained democracy of the lower house. Even after several articulate rejections of the British model, many delegates continued to think of the Senate as the safeguard of the property rights of the wealthy minority.[54] That perception gave rise to one of the principal objections to the Constitution put forward by the antifederalists during the debate over ratification—that it tended to establish an aristocratic government. To deflect these attacks during the ratification debate, the federalists tended to emphasize the states' rights basis of the Senate.[55]

A second function performed by the state basis of the Senate was to strengthen separation of powers. Though fairly well articulated in theory and accepted by most delegates, separation of powers had not been implemented with any precision in any of the state constitutions. Thus, the men at Philadelphia in 1787 continued to struggle to work out its mechanics. Obviously, the tripartite system that separates the national government into legislative, executive, and judicial branches; and the federal system that divides governmental power between the states and the United States constitute the major checks against the concentration of power. But the delegates also rejected a two-house legislature in which both houses were elected directly by the voters or in which the upper house was elected by the lower. They turned instead to a Senate, in which the members were appointed by the state legislatures, thus establishing two houses with two different constituencies that, they believed, would be divided against each other on many issues.

As we have seen, equal voting in the Senate was, as Sherman insisted, "not so much as a security for the small States; as for the State Govts. which could not be preserved unless they were represented & had a negative in the Genl. Government." As archnationalist Hamilton recognized, the people of the states as distinguished from their representatives in state governments would have different "feelings & views." The members of state governments because of "personal interest & official inducements" would be "unfriendly to the Genl. Govt."[56] Hamilton's erstwhile colleagues, Lansing and Yates, had proved that point to him when they walked out of the convention. The view of the Connecticut delegates was that by integrating representatives of the state governments—senators—into the general government, the two would be made to work in harmony. The repository of most power, then, would include an internal division, an extra check on potential tyranny. This, too, was emphasized by the federalists to disarm their opponents during the ratification debate.[57]

An equal vote in the Senate secured protection for the state governments in their corporate capacity (which in reality protected the power of the men who held it under state constitutions), and established a counterbalance to a potential combination of the large states against all the others. Among the delegates were a number of small-state nationalists, men like William Paterson of New Jersey who wanted to enlarge the powers of the central government, but demanded first that protection of the states with small populations be built into the constitutional edifice.[58] The vote of July 16 providing for equality among the states in the Senate seemed to guarantee this protection, and Paterson and other like-minded men were now willing to expand the powers of the United States. But not so the Connecticut delegation.

Sherman, in particular, was concerned about ensuring that both the people and the governments in the states retain their full internal sovereignty. The day after the fateful vote on equality in the Senate that he had done so much to secure, Sherman rose and, reading from a paper he held in his hand, moved to alter the grant of power to Congress in order to make more definite the line between state and national affairs.[59]

The relevant section of the resolution under discussion assigned to the new national legislature all those powers currently held by Congress under the Articles and gave it authority "to legislate in all cases to which the separate States are incompetent: or in which the harmony of the United States may be interrupted by the exercise of individual legislation." Sherman presciently noted that "it would be difficult to draw the line between the powers" of the national and state governments and moved to drop "of individual legislation" and insert instead "to make laws binding on the People of the (United) States in all cases (which may concern the common interests of the Union); but not to interfere with (the Government of the individual States in any matters of internal police which respect the Govt. of such States only, and wherein the general) welfare of the U. States is not concerned."[60] It is hard to see, however, that these words obviate the problem of dividing power that Sherman was so concerned about, but he ultimately persuaded himself that the powers of the federal government were well defined.

Sherman and his Connecticut colleagues were not doctrinaire states'-rights advocates like Luther Martin, or "small-state nationalists" like William Paterson. They were stalwart in their support of economic nationalism as manifest in establishing a federal monopoly of the power over interstate and foreign commerce, the minting of coin, and engaging in relations with foreign nations. They would even accept that hallmark of nationalism, a government emanating from the people and acting directly on them. In the context of Connecticut politics, this stance put them clearly in the nationalist camp. But they wanted division of state and national powers clearly defined, and despite Sherman's reservations about that problem in Philadelphia, he would go home and tell his constituents that they had nothing to fear on that score: "The powers vested in the federal government," he promised, "are particularly defined, so that each state retains Its sovereignty in what concerns its own internal government and a right to exercise every power not particularly delegated to the government of the United States."[61] Sherman was not a states'-rights man because he came from a "small" state—which he didn't—but because he, like his colleagues Johnson and Ellsworth, treasured Connecticut's century and a half tradition of provincial autonomy.

Sherman seemed satisfied by the compromise, but he remained alert to opportunities to strengthen the states' control over the central government. Very late in the convention, during the discussion of the amending process on September 10, he reverted to the primitive states' rightism of the Articles and urged that any changes to the Constitution must be unanimous among the states.[62] Five days later, fully recognizing perhaps for the first (and only) time the full potential of the amending process he "expressed his fears that three fourths of the States might be brought to do things fatal to particular States, as abolishing them altogether or depriving them of their equality in the Senate." He moved "that no State shall without its consent be affected in it's internal police, or deprived of its equal suffrage in the Senate." Only Delaware and New Jersey supported Sherman and his Connecticut colleagues on the motion at this time, but the last phrase found its way into the finished Constitution as the final clause of Article Five.[63]

It was Sherman's efforts to protect the sovereignty of the states that earned him the praise of antifederal Patrick Henry in the 1780s and brought the great nineteenth-century champion of states' rights, John C. Calhoun, to remark "that it is owing mainly to the States of Connecticut and New Jersey that we had a federal instead of a national government"; and he named Sherman, Ellsworth, and Paterson as the leaders in that cause.[64]

Sherman's effort to limit the scope of the national government is clear in another episode, a minor event of major implication. Perhaps of only historical interest in view of constitutional developments of the past century and a half, it sheds light on the Connecticut perspective of the 1780s. The Articles of Confederation included the clause, "All charges of war, and all other expenses that shall be incurred for the common defence or general welfare, . . . shall be defrayed out of a common treasury." In the draft of the Constitution as completed by the Committee of the Whole House, these words were rendered: "The legislature shall have power to lay and collect taxes duties imposts and excises, to pay the debts and provide for the common defence and general welfare of the U.S." When the clause was rewritten by high nationalist Gouverneur Morris for the Committee of Style, not only did he insert commas between the items in series, he placed a semicolon after "excises" thus disassociating the power to tax from the responsibility to pay the debts; and more significantly, making Congress' authority to provide for the general welfare of the United States an independent power. The suspicious and canny Sherman detected the ploy and the semicolon was replaced by a comma, the obvious intent of most convention delegates. In light of constitutional developments culminating in—but not concluding with—John Marshall's opinion in *McCulloch v. Maryland* (1819) authorizing Congress to act under the broadest interpretation of the "necessary and proper clause," Sherman's efforts were ultimately for naught. But during the first several decades of government under the Constitution, the reinsertion of a comma for a semicolon was of considerable significance.[65]

4

National Objectives, Local Concerns at the Constitutional Convention

Part 2. Protecting the Local Economy

Provincial political autonomy was the treasure nearest and dearest to Connecticut hearts. The state's delegates to the convention thought they had secured the closest approximation to that autonomy that would be compatible with national authority along with particular restrictions on the states designed to affect certain quite specific Connecticut objectives. These objectives relate to the economics of land and sea: protection of the Western Reserve and navigation acts that would support the state's essential triangle trade. We'll begin with matters of commerce.

The Slave Trade Compromise

There are historians who do not agree that the Connecticut Compromise was the central element of constitution making in 1787. They see, rather, the economics of commerce—the slave trade and the carrying trade—as the dispute that nearly wrecked the convention. The deal that saved the convention in this case helped to bring on the Civil War, with all its horrors, and left a legacy of racial strife and bitterness that has not been dissipated more than two centuries later. It has been justly characterized as a "dirty compromise."[1]

As we have seen, a point of great importance to Connecticut farmers and merchants was the protection of their export trade to the West Indies. Their delegates at Philadelphia would insist that the authority to levy duties on exports be denied the central government, and if possible, made illegal throughout the union. In this respect they were successful, and one of the most fascinating puzzles of the convention is how New Englanders and South Carolinians put together a deal to insert in the Constitution prohibitions against export duties—which in most eighteenth-century national systems were a major source of income.[2]

Section 8 of Article I of the Constitution in its final form authorizes Congress "to lay and collect Taxes, Duties, Imposts and Excises" in the same way that it passes any other legislation—by simple majority. Southerners were afraid that northerners, who would constitute a majority in both houses of the First Congress, would pass laws monopolizing the carrying trade and in other ways inhibit southern commerce with England and European markets. It was of fundamental importance to southerners also that no restrictions or duties be placed on their exports. Even more essential to them was the protection of the importation of Africans. In addition, they wanted a provision that would guarantee their right to cross state lines in pursuit of fugitive slaves. Some members of the convention were repelled by these demands, and virtually all northern delegates objected to the southern demands that super majorities—two-thirds or three-quarters—be required for commercial regulations.

The bargain that gave southerners protection for the slave trade and northerners protection for their foreign commerce was tremendously significant. Roger Sherman, politically neutral on the issue of the slave trade (though morally repelled by it) and in full agreement with South Carolinians in their demands for a prohibition on export duties, became with John Rutledge of South Carolina—a congressional colleague since 1774—an architect of this unfortunate arrangement. It was a bargain that saddled the nation with a continuation of slave importation that had to be settled with deadly dividends seven decades later.

As the period from the end of May to the climactic day of July 16 was dominated by a division of "large" states against "small," so the weeks between the middle of July and late August were dominated by a division apparently between northern and southern states. Each had a vested economic interest that was opposed by the other: commerce and slavery, the two horns of America's eighteenth-century capitalism. James Madison had called attention to this economic division as early as June 30 when he pointed out that "the States were divided into different interests not by their difference of size, but by other circumstances; the most material of which resulted partly from climate, but principally from (the effects of) their having or not having slaves."[3]

Of course, residents in all of the states except Massachusetts owned slaves. New Hampshire, Rhode Island, New Jersey, and Pennsylvania had all

enacted gradual abolition laws between 1780 and 1786.[4] Connecticut enacted its in 1784.[5] But slaves and masters inhabited all those states in 1787.
At the moment a general belief prevailed that Delaware was about to enact
abolition statutes as well.[6] It was customary to calculate eight northern and
five southern states. But Rhode Island sent no delegates to the convention,
and the New York delegates left on July 10, while the New Hampshire delegation did not arrive until July 23. Thus, there were never more than six
northern delegations present at any given moment, while there were always
five from the South—though the actual balance shifts to six southern and
five northern when Delaware is classed with the other slave-dependent
states.

Yet the division on the slavery questions as they came before the convention was not a simple North-South split. In Maryland and Virginia, where the
tobacco lands were rapidly becoming depleted and slaves lived longer and
had larger families than those in the rice and sugar swamps of the Deep
South, there was a surplus of slaves. Their owners found a ready market for
them in Georgia and the Carolinas.[7] It also happens that two of the members
of the convention most opposed to continuing the foreign slave trade were
Virginians, George Mason and James Madison. The strongest spokesmen
against the institution of slavery itself, both slave owners, were Gouverneur
Morris of New York and Pennsylvania, who inherited slaves but manumitted
them, and Rufus King of Massachusetts.[8] It was only from the delegates of
the deep south that vehement proslavery sentiments were heard.

The question before the convention was most distinctly not the abolition
of slavery, however. That issue was never seriously discussed, and any sug-
gestion that it might be was quickly squelched by men from Georgia and the
Carolinas. The central issue for the debaters in Philadelphia was whether the
importation of blacks from Africa and the West Indies should be allowed to
continue. This concern was assailed by Morris, who castigated "the inhabi-
tant of Georgia and S[outh] C[arolina] who goes to the Coast of Africa, and
in defiance of the most sacred laws of humanity tears away his fellow crea-
tures from their dearest connections & dam(n)s them to the most cruel
bondages."[9]

Traditional wisdom has it that New Englanders were less than enthusiastic about limiting the Atlantic slave trade because they were the principal
financial beneficiaries of it.[10] The facts, however, profoundly qualify those
impressions. Central to the New England states' economy was commerce:
exporting, importing, and the carrying trade. The carrying trade alone probably earned more money for New Englanders than their export of American
goods.[11] While a portion of this trade consisted of slaves carried from Africa

to the West Indies and the American South, and from the West Indies to the South, the economic significance to New England of the slave trade was not great and in Connecticut in particular virtually zero.

Indeed, Rhode Island in 1787 and Connecticut and Massachusetts in 1788 forbade their citizens from engaging in the foreign slave trade.[12] In addition, a sharp increase in American slave imports in the 1780s depressed prices and caused even South Carolina to impose a temporary ban on importations in 1787.[13] It bears repeating that for New Englanders the combined value of exports to the West Indies, to American and Canadian coastal ports, and across the Atlantic probably did not equal the profit made from merely carrying other people's goods.[14] Thus both shipborne commerce and the carrying trade—but not the slave trade—were vital interests to New Englanders in 1787. The one New England state where the slave trade was economically significant, Rhode Island, was not represented at the convention.

Virtually no slave traders left from Connecticut ports. Indeed, very little transatlantic trade at all sailed in or out of Connecticut. Beyond that, Connecticut's proximity to Newport, the heart of New England slaving until 1788, resulted in unchallengeable transatlantic competition in the slave business. Therefore, the Connecticut trade in general consisted almost entirely of coastal and West Indian exchange, virtually none of it in slaves.[15] The bone and sinew of the New England economy lay in the production of its fields, forests, and fisheries. But these commodities had little monetary value without access to West Indian and North American coastal markets. The relatively high level of living enjoyed by New Englanders could not have been supported without the external trade and the associated business of carrying other people's goods from port to port. The clusters of wealthy families in New England port towns outside of Connecticut owed their great comfort entirely to trade.[16] All the delegates to the convention from Massachusetts and New Hampshire represented that social class. Nathaniel Gorham spoke for these interests when he said that the New England states "had no motive to Union but a commercial one."[17]

The situation in Connecticut differed. In the first place, as has been pointed out, the state's merchants carried on almost no transatlantic trade, and thus very few large fortunes such as existed in Boston and Newport were accumulated in her port cities. Second, and most important in explaining the delegates' position at the convention, Connecticut merchants exported Connecticut produce directly to West Indian ports but imported European goods indirectly through Boston and New York, principally the latter.[18] Duties for the support of the New York government were collected there, and thus Connecticut citizens paid not only their own civil list but also made a significant contribution to that of their western neighbor. In addition, though many Connecticut merchants maintained their own import agencies in New York, most goods came through New York importers, so mercantile profits were paid by Connecticut consumers to New York merchants. Estimates of the annual cost of duties and profits left in New York by Connecticut traders ranged from $50,000 up to twice that figure.[19] As Madison pointed out, Connecticut with New Jersey and North Carolina "not being commercial States [i.e., not engaged in transatlantic trade] were contributing to the wealth of the commercial ones." In addition, Connecticut consumers were paying inflated prices for wheat from Maryland, where an export tax was collected.[20]

These factors informed the concerns of Sherman, Ellsworth, and Johnson at Philadelphia. A failure to accomplish their commercial objectives would disappoint their principal supporters at home. Thus they sought: a uniform national impost that would benefit all the states equally; an absolute prohibition on national and state export duties; a ban on interstate duties—effectively a nationwide free-trade area; and control over trade acts lodged exclusively in a national government that would guarantee evenhanded treatment of all the nation's ports. Through some clever wheeling and dealing—the kind of politics of which the trio were acknowledged masters—they got them all.

On the first there was no disagreement. A national import duty as a revenue-raising measure had been the first item on the nationalists' agenda since the early 1780s.[21] With the exception of Yates and Lansing of New York, it is unlikely that there was a man at the convention who did not desire one. On the second—prohibiting export duties—there was a fundamental conflict. Strong nationalists like Madison and Gouverneur Morris thought of a national export tax as an essential instrument of national fiscal policy. Such a tax was customary in the eighteenth century and was favored by most nations because foreigners paid it while consumers at home paid only import duties. As James Wilson pointed out, "To deny this power is to take from the Common Govt. half the regulation of trade," and Morris declared that prohibiting export taxes "was so radically objectionable that it might cost the whole system the support of some members." Others insisted that the authority to tax exports be given to Congress on grounds that it was a necessary revenue source, that it could be used to encourage domestic manufacturing, and even that it would help wrest equitable commercial agreements from other nations.[22]

The Connecticut delegates, however, had important allies in the contest. South Carolina in particular shared an abhorrence of export taxes. That state was by far the largest exporter of all thirteen. Its vast crop of rice, and lesser amounts of naval stores and indigo, were taken to England and the Continent—and taken largely in English and other non-American ships.[23] Export duties appropriated to the use of the United States would put South Carolina as well as North Carolina and Georgia at a great competitive disadvantage with certain West Indian islands. The southern states, in fact, were always alarmed by any measures that might permit northerners to gain control of national commercial policy. They had at least three fears. One was that an early Congress, temporarily dominated by northerners, might enact legislation monopolizing the carrying trade for American ships—particularly those of Massachusetts, Rhode Island, New York, and Pennsylvania. A second concern of southerners, of course, was protection of the slave trade; a third related to the navigation of the Mississippi River, controlled at the time by Spain.

Only months before the meeting at Philadelphia, southerners had received a major shock when a temporary northern majority in Congress voted to give up, in a treaty negotiated by John Jay of New York, the right to navigate the mouth of the Mississippi in exchange for an open trade with Spain.[24] Such an arrangement would not only prevent exports from the vast hinterlands of Virginia, North Carolina, and Georgia (which became the states of Kentucky, Tennessee, Alabama, and Mississippi), but radically depress the prices of speculative landholdings in the area. Southerners had good reason to fear northern domination of the national government. Rufus King, a Massachusetts congressman, in June 1786 wrote privately to Elbridge Gerry—both now sitting in Philadelphia—"I have ever been opposed to the encouragements of western emigrants. The States situated on the Atlantic are not sufficiently populous, and losing our men, is losing our greatest Source of Wealth." Encouraging settlements west of the mountains would divide the nation into two regions and "the pursuits and interests of the people on the two sides, will be so different, and probably so opposite, that an entire separation must eventually ensue."[25]

Southerners were quite aware of this sectional bid for power. James Monroe of Virginia, also a congressman, wrote his governor, Patrick Henry, that easterners intended to "break up . . . the settlements on the western waters, prevent any in future, and thereby keep the [southern] States . . . as they are now. . . . To throw the weight of population eastward & keep it there, to appreciate the vacant lands of New York and Massachusetts." Monroe accused Jay of "a long train of intrigue and management seducing the representatives" of the northern states.[26] Southern congressmen, under the leadership of James Madison, eventually fought off efforts in Congress to sacrifice the Mississippi navigation. But it was a close call. To guard against the possibil-

ity of such damaging public policy under a new government southern delegates at the convention wished for a provision requiring a two-thirds majority for all navigation acts.

Most important to delegates from the Deep South was their fear that a
Congress dominated by northerners would interfere with the slave trade.
South Carolinians in particular were looking for allies to help them protect
their interest in the importation of slaves and in preventing the imposition
of export duties. John Rutledge, a backroom conniver the equal of Sherman
or Johnson, thought he saw an opportunity in Connecticut's similar antipa-
thy to taxing exports.

These two states were very odd bedfellows. South Carolina, the leader of
the Deep South group, was the most aristocratic of the states; Connecticut
was the most republican. Connecticut had already provided for the gradual
abolition of slavery. Over a hundred thousand of the people in South Carolina were slaves and another hundred thousand were determined to keep
them that way. South Carolina, the wealthiest of all the states, was dominated
by great plantations and a two-crop economy; Connecticut was a land of
small family farms and diversified agriculture. But despite these differences,
the two states held in common one very important, if less obvious, interest. For
both, the export trade was a critical part of their economies. South Carolina
lived by exporting its huge crops of rice and indigo. Connecticut families
maintained a relatively high standard of living by exporting large surpluses
of livestock, lumber, and foodstuffs to the West Indies. Indeed, at this time,
Connecticut had about three hundred vessels in foreign trade and exported
more to the West Indies than Boston did, and about the same as did New
York—about three-quarters of a million dollars' worth of local goods.[27]

The major trading states of Massachusetts, New York, Pennsylvania, and
Virginia exported in their own ships large quantities of produce from other
states as well as their own goods. New Jersey and Delaware exported and imported through Philadelphia and New York. Connecticut exported directly
to the West Indies, but imported European goods through New York and
Boston. South Carolina also exported directly—though not in its own ships.
Thus only South Carolina and Connecticut were entirely dependent upon
the *direct* export of their *own* produce. This common interest in the export
trade bridged the deep division between the two states. Moreover, the slave
owning Episcopalian William Samuel Johnson had many friends among the
southerners. That a deal had been made becomes clear from the debate on
the convention floor.

The Virginia Plan authorized the new legislature "To regulate commerce
with foreign nations, and among the several States." As it came from the

Committee of Detail on August 6, the proviso was added, "No navigation act shall be passed without the assent of two thirds of the members present in each House." The report of August 6 also would have prohibited any interference *ever* with the importation of slaves. Northerners wanted to delete both of those provisions. The report also prohibited export duties absolutely.[28]

During the course of the ensuing debate, on August 8, antislavery men such as Rufus King and Gouverneur Morris castigated slavery and the slave trade as a "nefarious institution," "the curse of heaven," and in "defiance of the most sacred laws of humanity."[29] Southerners responded with like vehemence. When the debate resumed two weeks later, John Rutledge insisted that "[r]eligion & humanity had nothing to do with this question," and Charles Pinckney stated flatly that South Carolina could "never receive the plan if it prohibits the slave trade." To Abraham Baldwin, importing slaves was one of Georgia's "favorite prerogatives."[30]

At this point the compromising Connecticut delegation stepped in to soften the sectional antagonism and break a potential deadlock. Ellsworth, who had been on the Committee of Detail that brought in the largely prosouthern report, declared that he thought "[t]he morality or wisdom of slavery are considerations belonging to the States themselves." Sherman, who regarded "the slave-trade as iniquitous," hewed to his states'-rights stance saying, "as the States were now possessed of the right to import slaves, as the public good did not require it to be taken from them . . . it [was] best to leave the matter as we find it" in order to avoid objections to the whole scheme of government.[31] When Mason—who to his dying day owned scores of slaves—then launched an attack on "this infernal traffic," the Connecticut men rose to support the South Carolinians.[32] Ellsworth snidely responded to Mason, "As he had never owned a slave [he], could not judge of the effects of slavery on character," and pointed out that Virginia could well oppose the slave trade as it would only make its citizens' surplus blacks more valuable. "Let us not intermeddle," he said. "Slavery in time will not be a speck in our Country." Sherman, too, spoke in favor of allowing the Deep South to continue to import slaves. He said that "it was better to let the S. States import slaves than to part with them, if they made that a sine qua non," which they certainly did. George Read of Delaware suggested that the question ought to be handed over to another committee. Sherman responded—with uncharacteristic procedural rigidity—that the clause guaranteeing no interference ever with the slave trade and providing for a two-thirds majority for navigation acts "had been agreed to & therefore could not be committed."[33]

Nevertheless, the South Carolinians were able to see that some delegates would not support a constitution that left the slave trade completely unfettered, so C. C. Pinckney and John Rutledge suggested that a committee be elected to resolve the issue. Gouverneur Morris "wished the whole subject to be committed including the clauses relating to taxes on exports & to a navigation act. These things may form a bargain among the Northern & Southern states." Ellsworth spoke against the idea of a committee, saying that he was "for taking the plan as it is. This widening of opinions has a threatening aspect. If we do not agree on this middle & moderate ground," Ellsworth "was afraid we should lose two States, with such others as may be disposed to stand aloof, should fly into a variety of shapes & directions, and most probably into several confederations" and, he added somewhat apocalyptically, "not without bloodshed." Despite his plea, the convention voted solidly in favor of appointing a committee.[34]

The committee consisted of some strong antislavery men such as Madison and King; the North Carolina member was the generally conciliatory Hugh Williamson, who said that "both in opinion & practice he was, against slavery." From South Carolina came Charles Cotesworth Pinckney, who had indicated a willingness to give a little, and from Georgia, the Connecticut-born-and-bred Abraham Baldwin. Connecticut's delegate was William Samuel Johnson, a slaveholder, and an inveterate compromiser.[35]

It was clear that this committee would remove some of the advantages the Committee of Detail had given the southerners. Two days later the new committee reported a bundle of provisions relating to foreign trade that constituted a rather complex compromise. The southerners got a promise that Congress would be prohibited from interfering with the importation of slaves before 1800—later changed to 1808—and a prohibition on export taxes. In return, northerners got authority to levy taxes on imported slaves and to enact navigation acts by a simple majority.[36] This proposal was appealing to southerners because they expected to dominate both houses of Congress, if not by 1800, certainly by 1808.[37] On all of these votes the three New England states and the three Deep South states joined forces against the middle Atlantic states of New Jersey, Pennsylvania, Delaware, Maryland and Virginia—often in votes of six to five.

The authority to tax imported slaves was a sop to the antislavery delegates. King and John Langdon, both of whom sat on the compromise committee, said the tax was the price for letting the trade go on, and Charles Cotesworth Pinckney, holding up his end of the bargain—agreed.[38] That the tax was limited to a nominal ten dollars was indication enough that the faction interested in stopping the slave trade was small and without much influence at this point despite its inclusion of Madison, Mason, Morris, and King.

Further evidence that a deal had been struck came several days later when Charles Pinckney attempted to break up the package by reinserting the two-thirds majority required for navigation acts. His unfriendly cousin, Charles Cotesworth Pinckney, rose to protect the deal and defend the New Englanders:

> [I]t was the true interest of the S. States to have no regulation of commerce; but considering the loss brought on the commerce of the Eastern States [i.e., New England] by the revolution, their liberal conduct towards the views of South Carolina, and the interest the weak South[ern] States had in being united with the strong Eastern States, he thought it proper that no fetters should be imposed on the power of making commercial regulations; and that his constituents though prejudiced against the Eastern States, would be reconciled to this liberality—He had himself, he said, prejudices agst the Eastern States before he came here, but would acknowledge that he had found them as liberal and candid as any men whatever.

Madison explained Pinckney's characterization of the New Englanders' conduct as "liberal" as a reference to their agreeing not to close off the slave trade right away. "An understanding on the two subjects of *navigation* and *slavery*," Madison wrote, "had taken place between those parts of the Union, which explains the vote on the Motion depending [to reject a two-thirds majority for navigation acts], as well as the language of Genl. Pinckney & others."[39]

On the vote, only South Carolina among the southern states voted with northerners against changing the simple majority to two-thirds. Just before the vote, Pierce Butler of South Carolina, who had said that he "considered the interests of [the southern] and of the Eastern States, to be as different as the interests of Russia and Turkey," explained that he would vote against the two-thirds provision because he was "desirous of conciliating the affections of the East." But he extracted a price: a fugitive slave provision abhorrent to slavery opponents such as King and Morris. His proposal read, "If any person bound to service or labor in any of the U—— States shall escape into another State, he or she . . . shall be delivered up to the person justly claiming their service or labor."[40] This provision was really obnoxious to King and others, but it was agreed to without debate, all of the states voting aye. The deal was sealed and the dirty deed was done.

The machinery constructed in early July by the Connecticut and South Carolina delegates—probably Sherman and Rutledge—worked without a hitch. George Mason later described it with disgust when he told the Virginia ratifying convention that "a compromise took place between the north-

ern and southern states; the northern states agreeing to the temporary importation of slaves, and the southern states conceding, in return, that navigation and commercial laws" should be treated like any other legislation,
subject to simple majorities in Congress. The North Carolina delegates
wrote their governor that granting authority over commerce to the national
legislature had been "given in Exchange" for the fugitive slave clause and
other advantages.[41]

In no small measure was the catastrophe visited upon the United States
in 1861 an outgrowth of these concessions to the slave-dependent states. The
Connecticut delegates were most imprescient about the rise of slavery—a
labor system that was expanding even before the invention of the cotton gin
six years after the convention. Perhaps they cannot be blamed for failing to
see the consequences of their blindness. But they were willing, in a way that
others present were not, to bargain away any chance there might have been
to shorten the life of the slave trade or curtail the expansion of slavery. We
might not expect Johnson, a slaveholder and special friend of southerners, to
view blacks with any kind of humanity. But Sherman and Ellsworth both ab-
horred slavery, and had they used their very considerable political skills
against the expansion of slavery instead of for it, the federal union might have
been built somewhat differently in 1787.

The Connecticut delegates got everything their constituents desired in
the way of interstate and international commerce on the seas. Claims on the
land presented a different challenge, but in most respects their job was to cement deals already made rather than to build new ones. Their concern was
to fend off bitter and persistent challenges by landless states to the congressional cession of Connecticut's precious Western Reserve.

The Western Reserve

The Virginia Plan included no specific remedy for the Connecticut presence
in Pennsylvania; or for a similar contretemps in Vermont, where New York
and New Hampshire had claims; or for the disagreement between Virginia
and Pennsylvania concerning the Pittsburgh area. The Plan provided for a
"supreme tribunal" that would have jurisdiction over cases in which citizens
of different states might be parties.[42] However, the circumstances in the
Wyoming Valley required more direct attention.

The Virginia Plan did include a provision by which the United States
would guarantee the integrity of the boundaries of each state—presumably
against partition by Congress as well as attacks from other states and foreign

nations. Pennsylvania had faced such attacks from the Connecticut settlers and from Virginians around Pittsburgh as well. This provision was coupled with a section dealing with the admission of new states which could be read to permit the involuntary division of states by Congress.[43]

A Committee of Detail was appointed on July 24 to shape a number of troublesome provisions. It consisted of five members including Wilson of Pennsylvania and Ellsworth of Connecticut. Ellsworth, alone of the Connecticut delegation had not been involved in the Susquehannah imbroglio, but that matter was only one of several to be resolved by the committee. Its solution to the problem of interstate disputes was to outline a procedure for establishing a special ad hoc tribunal very similar to that which prevailed under the Articles and had been used—uniquely—in the Connecticut-Pennsylvania dispute. This tribunal, however, was limited to hearing "all Disputes and Controversies now subsisting, or that may hereafter subsist between two or more States respecting Jurisdiction or Territory." A separate paragraph was written to cover the unique circumstances of the Connecticut settlers in the area secured to Pennsylvania under the Trenton decision:

> All Controversies concerning Lands claimed under different Grants of two or more States, whose Jurisdictions, as they respect such Lands, shall have been decided or adjusted subsequent to such Grants (or any of them) shall, on Application to the Senate, be finally determined, as near as may be, in the same manner as is before prescribed for deciding Controversies between different States.[44]

When the report of the Committee of Detail was debated, Sherman and Johnson reworked the phrases so as to allow for the admission of Vermont—settled largely by Connecticuters—and to guarantee that no state could be involuntarily partitioned or joined to another. This did not put finish to the debate, however, because the delegates from the landless states bitterly resented Connecticut's "side wind juggle" that gave that state 1.2 million acres of prime farmland.

In late August as time, tension, and heat began to wear the delegates down, Daniel Carroll of Maryland tried a direct attack on Connecticut's uniquely held Western Reserve: "nothing in this Constitution," he proposed, "shall be construed to affect the claim of the U.S. to vacant lands ceded to them by the Treaty of peace." He was referring to the treaty with England ending the Revolution whereby the United States gained the Northwest Territory from which was carved Connecticut's Reserve. To make his intention perfectly clear, Carroll added that "he had in view also some of the claims of

particular states." There was only one state claiming land there: Connecticut. The wily Roger Sherman professed to be amenable to Carroll's sugges-
tion, characterizing it as harmless. Clearly, authorizing the U.S. Government
to rescind the Western Reserve was anything but harmless. But, Madison
had suggested an amendment that would undo Carroll's objective: "claims of
particular states . . . should not be affected," and Sherman's apparent com-
placence was conditioned on "the addition suggested by Mr. Madison."[45]

The wording as it appeared in the draft submitted to the convention was
shaped by the Committee of Style on which sat William Samuel Johnson, the
Reserve's most involved and articulate promoter. It included everything the
Yankee delegates could have hoped for short of transferring jurisdiction of
over a third of Pennsylvania back to Connecticut. "Nothing in this Constitution," declared the draft, "shall be so construed as to prejudice any claims of
the United States, or of any particular State." Pennsylvanians no doubt got
satisfaction from the proviso that "no new state shall be formed or erected
within the jurisdiction of any other state." And except for some changes in
capitalization, this is exactly how the sections read in the Constitution. The
Western Reserve was preserved.[46]

Connecticut's settlers in Pennsylvania's Wyoming Valley got additional
protection from unilateral state action by a phrase carefully articulated and
shepherded through committees by Johnson and Sherman. "The judicial
Power: of the Federal courts," reads Article III, "shall extend to all Cases . . .
between Citizens of the same State claiming Lands under grants of different
States." Not only the Wyoming pioneers, but also the absentee speculators
in Connecticut, thus, could take their pleas directly to the U.S. courts, by-
passing those of Pennsylvania, where they would be sure to lose.[47]

The Executive Office

Cementing the Western Reserve, protecting state powers, and staving off export duties were three major successes of the Connecticut delegation at the
Philadelphia convention. Their constituents could hardly ask for more. In
another area with a strong Connecticut heritage, weak executive authority,
they failed to make an impression. But it is this negative example that demonstrates more clearly than any other the force of local constitutional tradition on delegates to the Philadelphia convention. Here, the elderly Roger
Sherman, at least, if less so Ellsworth and Johnson, was so completely satu-
rated with the Connecticut system that he couldn't even recognize a defeat
when it hit him.

In Connecticut, the governor had been elected annually by the freemen since the 1630s. He carried tremendous prestige, but little institutional authority. He presided over meetings of the Council and was the titular commander in chief of the militia. Virtually all other power lay in the hands of the General Assembly. That body, through committees, exercised all administrative functions including oversight of the treasurer, comptroller, and other officers; made all appointments to militia, judicial, and other offices; was the supreme judicial tribunal of the state and acted as a chancery court, granted divorces, bankruptcies, corporate charters, and pardons. Since all appointments and legislation had to be approved by both houses, the governor could most effectively exercise his authority by persuading several of the councilors to join him in defeating or approving actions of the lower house. That, however, was pretty much the limit of his influence.

Connecticuters were very suspicious of power, having lived since 1662 under the ever-present threat of losing their extraordinarily liberal charter, and recently having lost lives and limbs fighting off that very threat. Ellsworth universalized the sentiment at the convention: "The Executive will be regarded by the people with a jealous eye. Every power for augmenting unnecessarily his influence will be disliked."[48] It was Roger Sherman, however, who took the most extreme position. Indeed, he didn't really want an executive department at all.

He stated his position almost as soon as he arrived on the scene. On June 1 the doughty old republican had favored no fixed executive, holding that since the legislators "were the best judges of the business which ought to be done by the Executive department . . . he wished the number [of executives] might not be fixed but that the legislature should be at liberty to appoint one or more as experience might dictate." He continued that the executive ought to be appointed by the legislature, and be "absolutely dependent on that body, as it was the will of that which was to be executed. An independence of the Executive on the supreme Legislature, was . . . the very essence of tyranny if there ever was any such thing." Certainly, he concluded, the legislature should have the power to remove the executive at pleasure. But if there were to be a single executive, he preferred short terms and reeligibility as in the Connecticut tradition.[49]

At one point in his fight to weaken the possibility of a strongman, Sherman attempted to institute an executive council without whose advice the first magistrate could not act. This was rejected, and the Connecticut delegates, two to one no doubt, voted with the majority to establish a single unencumbered executive. An executive veto was, of course, anathema to the old Connecticut sage. "No one man," he said on June 4, "could be found so far above all the rest in wisdom," and should not be permitted to "overrule the decided and cool opinions of the Legislature." He had the support of at least one of his colleagues on this account, and the delegation ranged itself against an absolute executive negative—a position Sherman reaffirmed on August 15. The delegation, however, was willing that three-fourths instead of two-thirds of the legislature be required to override such a veto.[50]

Further executive limitations were pushed during the discussion of the legislature's power to "make" war. Sherman wanted the term left as it was, thus permitting the Congress to conduct war rather than to declare it only. This was the system used in Connecticut during the Revolution, when a Council of Safety and committees of the General Assembly actually organized the logistics and commanded the exercises of the militia. Ellsworth believed that the power to conduct war was an executive function, however, and shifted his vote. Sherman was overruled, and Connecticut voted to permit Congress to "declare" war, but not to "make" it.

Sherman was also opposed to executive appointment of military officers in time of peace; he would give the president command of the militia in time of war, but held that "[i]f the Executive can model the army, he may set up an absolute government." He even wanted the power to grant pardons and reprieves—in Connecticut done by the legislature—dependent on Senate confirmation, and voted all alone on his motion to put this into effect. On the matter of presidential election, his desire to keep the executive appointment in the hands of the national legislature voting as states further emphasizes the traditional Connecticut deep distrust of strong unitary executive authority.[51]

These remarks might make it appear that Sherman had little respect for separation of powers; and indeed he did not support that principle. During the ratification debate he wrote that the idea that the legislature and executive "ought to be entirely distinct and unconnected . . . [was] a gross *error* in politics."[52] Clearly, Sherman carried certain fixed ideas about government, mostly shaped in the crucible of Connecticut republicanism, that clouded his understanding of the document he so influentially helped to form. As late as January 1788 he still had not accepted the mechanics of separation of powers as set up in the Constitution. Perhaps this misperception is why he could so ardently urge ratification of a system so at odds with his deepest constitutional convictions.

Despite Sherman's careful surveillance, the Constitution as sent to Congress and to the states for their assent was full of nationalist booby traps.[53] No one in 1787 could foresee the expansive uses to which the three explosive clauses would be put; but the supremacy, commerce, and necessary and proper clauses lay in wait to blow the states'-rights defenders off the constitutional battlefield.[54] The Connecticut delegates each had his own take on the matter, however. Johnson rejoined Congress, took no reported part in the debate over the Constitution, and returned to Connecticut to sit with the upper house—but too late to participate in the Council's discussion and debate on the document. On November 1 he resigned from that body and left Connecticut politics forever to take up the presidency of Columbia College. He left the promotion of the Constitution in his home town, Stratford, to his youngest son, who secured his father's election to the state's ratifying convention.[55]

Ellsworth, it turns out, was a closet federalist. The minute he left the convention—too soon to sign the document—he evinced an ardent nationalism that culminated in his authorship of the most nationalizing act of legislation (except that which eventuated in the Fourteenth Amendment) to have come out of Congress ever: the Judiciary Act of 1789. Ellsworth, having so much to do with the enumeraton in Article I, Section 8 as a member of the Committee of Detail, and believing in his success in protecting his state's prerogatives, threw himself into the ratification debate under the false colors of a merchant and former farmer. It is clear that he was happy with the work of the convention and his part in it.[56]

Sherman, too, could be well satisfied with the work of the delegation. He and Johnson had secured the continued safety of the Western Reserve. There would be no export duties. Connecticut would share revenues collected at New York and other major ports that would now support the national government. Finally, Sherman thought he had safeguarded the ability of his state government—and all the others—to protect their own integrity and the liberties of their citizens. (In this he was deluded. He was oblivious of the maiming—even mortal—potential effect on state sovereignty of the nationalist clauses).[57]

All three men—the detached Johnson, the deceitful Ellsworth, and the deluded Sherman—believed that the economic reforms included in the Constitution would quickly redound to the benefit of the state's farmers, artisans, shippers, and merchants. In this they certainly were right. Regardless of their stance vis-à-vis the Constitution and their constituents in the fall of 1787, what Sherman, Johnson, and Ellsworth had done in Philadelphia, as would soon become evident, was good for all the states and very good for Connecticut.[58]

5

Ratification in Connecticut

In view of Connecticut's long-standing tradition of provincial autonomy—its "darling liberty"—how can we explain the quick and overwhelming adoption of a constitution that made deep inroads into that autonomy?

Principally, the security and economic advantages were so obvious that the civil and military as well as commercial leaders of the state grasped the Constitution to their bosoms with relief and alacrity. But this was in part because Sherman and Ellsworth sold them—or at least their yeoman constituents—a bill of goods. The confused Roger Sherman and the dissembling Oliver Ellsworth bought a surrender of local autonomy far greater than those fathers of the Constitution recognized or would admit.

Once the establishment had been won over, they brought the press along and shut out dissenting voices. Other political tactics engineered by the federal majority in the General Assembly and at the ratifying convention put the antis at a great disadvantage. The outcome was not a foregone conclusion—but almost.

The real question that arises is not why the independent Yankees willingly gave up so much autonomy, but rather why anyone in Connecticut would object to the new system at all. The answer might seem to be that, coupled with the fear of an overweaning national government that would curb the states' powers, was a fear that the new system would set up an aristocracy that would curb the liberties of Connecticut's yeomen.

Indeed, these fears were proclaimed by several participants in the debate both in public and private. But those men who proclaimed these fears and were elected delegates to the ratifying convention ended up voting in favor of the Constitution. Ideology and matters of broad national concern are not sufficiently in evidence in the ratification debate in Connecticut to distinguish the opponents. We must look elsewhere for ties that bound together the several pockets of antifederal voters. We will find them in part in that old Connecticut tradition of family tribalism, and in part in the vicissitudes of town and militia politics.

In Chapters 1 and 2, I delineated the first tier of Connecticut's dual localism—state-specific issues that directed the Connecticut delegates at the federal convention; in the chapters that follow I will show that family and militia connections, town-specific orientation, and internal town politics determined forty men to vote against ratification. Ideology had no detectable effect in bringing out these votes. In New England, Connecticut was the only state where the battle was not extended, hard-fought, and close, and it was the only New England state convention that did not call for amendments. Nor was the division along any kind of economic lines. Most delegates from backcountry agrarian regions favored the Constitution; a significant number of antifederalists represented coastal secondary commercial towns. These are conditions that shall be described in detail in Chapter 6.

Connecticut's delegates to the federal convention sent the text of the Constitution to Governor Huntington on September 26, and the newspapers published it on that day and during the following week. The word was out, or as one Litchfield observer put it, "the eggshell is broke," but there was no published public debate at the moment.[1] By the fall of 1787 men who passed for nationalists in Connecticut's states'-rights context so dominated politics that every newspaper in the state came out strongly in favor of a speedy ratification of the document. What had happened over the past year to diminish the number of agrarian provincials and seduce or silence most of their leadership, leaving the few stalwart antinationalists swinging, as is said, in the breeze? Where had gone the century and a half commitment to local control and the ardor of Connecticut's yeomen for their darling liberty?

An important part of the explanation lies in the fact of an economic revival that became apparent during 1787. The slowdown in business that hurt exporters and their agrarian suppliers was due principally to restrictions laid on their West Indian colonies by the French and English governments; the shortage of specie; and the inability of the state and national governments to pay their debts.[2] Tax reform in 1779 and in increments during the mid-1780s helped restore confidence in the state government on the part of the farming majority. The 50 percent reduction in 1784 of the specie tax to pay government officials was especially welcomed by hard-pressed yeomen. They were similarly cheered when cattle and swine under two years old were declared tax free, as were some sheep. Other tax-cutting acts and general tax forgive-ness were passed by the agrarian-dominated Assembly in 1784 and 1785.[3]

Additionally, state and Continental notes were made legal tender for state taxes and the state impost. The value this gave to various kinds of public IOU's made them a viable circulating medium.[4] Though the extreme eco-nomic democrats were unable to push through paper money programs, tax relief and fiscal policy were instrumental in keeping Shaysism confined to the two short-lived episodes in Preston and Sharon. Despite their brevity and lack of public support, the Shaysite incidents frightened many moder-ates into the nationalist camp, just as had Shays' Rebellion at the Philadel-phia convention. If Massachusetts, with all its resources, could not control its farmers without bloodshed, what state could feel safe without a stronger na-tional government?[5]

In a preview of the strategic line federalists were to take during the days leading up to ratification, Oliver Ellsworth and Roger Sherman downplayed the nationalist elements and exaggerated the similarities of the proposed Constitution to the old Articles. The new powers assigned to Congress, they claimed, "extend only to matters respecting the common interests of the Union and are specially defined, so that the particular states retain their *Sov-ereignty* in all other matters. . . . The Convention endeavored to provide for the energy of government on the one hand and suitable checks on the other hand to secure the rights of the particular states, and the liberties and prop-erties of the citizens." Sherman's strategy throughout the debate would be to minimize the changes to be wrought by the new system. It is quite possible that he believed his own rhetoric; he never seems to have grasped fully the nationalist implications of the Constitution.[6]

Two days after the Constitution was published in Connecticut, the high nationalist David Humphreys wrote optimistically to George Washington that "from what I hear . . . the opposition will be less than was apprehended." And Abraham Baldwin, a New Havener now transplanted to Georgia and one of that state's delegates to the constitutional convention, told James Madison that the Connecticut "opposition will be inconsiderable, that the Assembly, if it depended on them, would adopt the system almost unani-mously." Ezra Stiles believed that after the November election of delegates, known supporters of the Constitution outnumbered opponents 103 to 27. One correspondent reported that despite a majority of Litchfield County voters opposed to the Constitution, the county's delegates to the convention "are avowedly in favor of it"; but, he cautioned, with a minority view, "There will be powerful oppositions to it in Connecticut. . . . In short we are much divided; anarchy, I am afraid, is approaching."[7]

The situation in late 1787, then, was in flux and few observers were will-ing to predict an outcome. As Hugh Ledlie described it, writing from Hart-ford to W. S. Johnson in New York, "[I]t is very much as it was with our old Mr. Jennings who undertook digging a well at Norwich Landing in a very im-probable place for water. He told Captan Nathll. Backus that everybody said he would get water there but some says I shant." And it is true that not all the antifederalists had fled the field. Jeremiah Wadsworth reported "a strong party forming against the Convention, and much reason to fear the new gov-ernment will not go down."[8] But he was wrong. The General Assembly fol-lowed a path that could have been blazed by the most determined national-ists. The deputies approved a resolution calling for elections—open to all town meeting voters—to be held on November 12, followed by a ratifying convention to begin on January 3.[9] This timetable would not permit the anti-federalists to organize, scattered as they were across the countryside with no newspaper printer in their camp.

The tight-knit mercantile nationalists, centered principally in the state's five recently incorporated cities, the locus of eight of Connecticut's ten news-papers, were already organized.[10] They were a cohesive bunch, tied together by commercial connections, family relations, and to a large degree, college educations. Moreover, by the fall of 1787 they controlled the upper house of legislature, dominated the judiciary, and had turned their springtime bud-ding majority in the lower house into a full-blown one. As David Humphreys claimed, the nationalists included the "clergy, lawyers, physicians, and mer-chants . . . . [and] the officers of the late army." The nationalists, admitted an embittered adversary, claimed all the best speakers. Federalists, of course, agreed. "The leading Characters among our antifederalists," Roger Sher-man's son-in-law told a friend in New York, "are in general willful and Dog-matical—no speakers found among them—all their influence is by a low clandestine intrigue."[11]

The election of delegates to the ratifying convention by town meeting voters provided—with the exception of the mobocratic militia elections—for the most democratic procedure known to Connecticut government. Dep-uties, after all, were elected by the much smaller group of freemen. But the General Assembly merely called for the election of delegates—not for de-bate and instruction on the merits of the Constitution. Nevertheless, sub-stantive debate did take place in some towns, and eight towns instructed their delegates—four against and four for ratification. Of the seventy-nine towns whose records have survived, an additional five voted to approve the document and four voted not to. The rest merely elected delegates to a total of 174.[12] Those delegates included all three Connecticut members of the

Philadelphia convention, the governor, lieutenant governor, the five superior court judges, seven of the twelve-man council, and sixty-six deputies, numerous military officers, justices of the peace, and local officeholders.

David Humphreys noted in September that "the well affected have not been wanting in efforts to prepare the minds of the citizens for the favorable reception" of the Constitution. George Washington reminded his former aide a couple of weeks after the text of the Constitution arrived in Connecticut that because of the "sinister views of too many characters. . . . Much will depend . . . upon literary abilities, and the recommendation of it by good pens." And the pro-Constitution forces, that old plough-jogger, Hugh Ledlie, admitted disconsolately, "have got almost all the best writers . . . on their side."[13] Given the unusually high literacy rate of Connecticut voters, virtually every one of whom could read, it was especially important to control the press there. And indeed the federalists did their best. Essays by Roger Sherman and Oliver Ellsworth filled the newspapers.

Ellsworth, masquerading as a man of the soil, took upon himself the task of persuading Connecticut farmers that the commercial benefits of the proposed system would be theirs as much as the merchants'. Ellsworth's thirteen "Letters of A Landholder" were printed in Connecticut newspapers and widely reprinted across the country. "Your property and riches," he told the farmers, "depend on a ready demand and generous price for the produce you can annually spare." And this is to be found "where trade flourishes and when the merchant can freely export the produce of the country to such parts of the world as will bring the richest return. . . . Every foreign prohibition on American trade is aimed in the most deadly manner against the holders and tillers of the land, and they are the men made poor. Your only remedy is such a national government as will make the country respectable, such a supreme government as can boldly meet the supremacy of proud and self-interested nations. The regulation of trade ever was and ever must be a national matter."[14]

Economic and security matters could be approached on the level of reasoned debate. But the deepest fear of the provincial yeomen, accustomed to real self-government and over a century of traditional autonomy, was that they might lose those treasures—their darling liberty. As the Reverend Mr. Benjamin Trumbull summed it up, the basic objections to the Constitution in Connecticut were that "it is designed to take away our Liberties and will do us an injury as a nation or individuals." Indeed, "the only objections I have found in any public prints against it," he said, "are that no provision is made for jurors in civil Cases; That it contains no bill of rights; That it will annihilate our State assemblies, and deprive us of our Liberties."[15] This list reflects the fact that very few antifederal objections found their way into the "public prints" in Connecticut. We know that fear of an aristocratic takeover, emasculation of the militia, and insufficiently frequent election of representatives were all voiced in the state—but for the most part in private correspondence.

To combat these concerns, fundamental political values had to be addressed. Sherman and Ellsworth set out to do that. Their approach was to place the Constitution into the context of old-fashioned New England republicanism, and lay aside Madison's "new science of politics" that proclaimed mankind as vice-ridden and representative government a congeries of competing self-interested factions. The principal propagandist for the old republicanism was Oliver Ellsworth, who not only wrote the "Landholder Letters," but also led the pro-Constitution forces in Connecticut's ratifying convention.

Though a young man at the opening of the Revolution, twenty-four years Sherman's junior, Ellsworth's perception of republican society mirrored exactly that of the older man—which is to say, it reflected the Connecticut in which they practiced politics. They viewed republican government as organically connected to society; an elite chosen for their virtue—defined as selflessness—and wisdom to rule a hardy, hardworking, patient yeomanry and their families, whose principal virtue was their habit of electing their betters to office and deferring to them thereafter. In such a society, government is neither the servant nor the enemy of the people, but is rather the kindly father who always knows best. Representative assemblies consisted of the best of the yeomen and the most honest of the merchants who had been nurtured in the same soil as their constituents and from time to time returned to it to maintain their common perspective. There was no need for bills of rights or separations of powers. Liberty was best protected by practicing the virtues of labor, thrift, patience, regularity, and moderation, and electing one's most virtuous (and well-heeled) neighbors to run the government. No amount of Madisonian tinkering and governmental mechanisms like checks and balances and extended republics could protect ordered liberty, for "were it ever so perfect a scheme of freedom, when we become ignorant, vicious, idle, and regardless of the education of our children, our liberties will be lost—we shall be fitted for slavery, and it will be an easy business to reduce us to obey one or more tyrants."[16]

In light of his authorship of the Judiciary Act of 1789 and later evidence of high federalism, it is likely that Oliver Ellsworth was deliberately deceptive. On the other hand, it is probable that his colleague Roger Sherman was a victim of honest confusion or just did not understand or was unwilling to accept the theoretical underpinning on which Madison thought he had built the structure. Central to Madison's theory was the concept that government was the enemy of liberty and was only necessary to protect individuals as individuals, from themselves acting in groups. A form of graded and refined representation was the best system to channel the desires of the people in such a way that individual liberty would be protected; but such a government was also a hazard because it was prone to majoritarianism, which often led to tyranny over individuals and minorities. Thus the necessity for division and separation of powers. And in Madison's mind the Constitution was to be the product of the whole people, who had the sovereign power to delegate authority to as many different governments as they chose.

Roger Sherman reflected his long political experience in Connecticut, where there was no constitution or bill of rights unalterable by the General Assembly, no separation of powers, and where the government was the voice of the people—neither their servant nor their master. He never perceived a republican government as something to be regarded with suspicion and controlled; he misperceived separation of powers as arranged in the Constitution; and apparently he never fully understood the underlying theory of written constitutions. And in the context of the Constitution he construed the term "people" to mean the people of each of the states—radically different from Madison's "We the People of the United States."

On the basis of these misapprehensions Sherman was able to refute the arguments of the anti-Constitution forces, who so feared the threat to liberty and state sovereignty that the Constitution posed. Bills of rights, for instance, were not necessary because no such document ever bound the legislature unless the legislators themselves were committed to protecting the people's rights.[17] Ellsworth agreed. Bills of rights "are insignificant since government is considered as originating from the people." Connecticut's common-law system, which looked to frequent elections and judicial intervention, could be counted on to protect individual rights. "No alteration in the state governments," wrote Ellsworth, "is even now proposed, but they are to remain identically the same that they are now."[18] So much for Article I, Section 10.

Division of powers, one of Madison's central checks on government, was another modern complexity that Roger Sherman saw only through the simple-minded Montesquieuian plan that he had carried in his head to Philadelphia. "The General & particular jurisdiction ought in no case be concurrent," he insisted. "The immediate security of the civil and domestic rights of the people," he wrote on the eve of the state ratifying convention, "will be in the governments of the particular states. And as the different states have different local interests and customs which can be best regulated by their own laws, it would not be expedient to admit the federal government to interfere with them any further than may be necessary for the good of the whole."[19]

What "further powers may be necessary" seemed clear enough to Sherman in 1788, even if it took a generation longer for Congress and the Supreme Court to come to understand the terms so well—and so differently. "The powers vested in the federal government," he explained, "are particularly defined, so that each state still retains its sovereignty in what concerns its own internal government and a right to exercise every power of a sovereign state not particularly delegated to the government of the United States." He concluded, "[T]he objects of the federal government will be so obvious that there will be no great danger of any interference." So much for the "necessary and proper" clause. Indeed, if Sherman's description of the limits of national power had been widely shared, few antifederalists anywhere would have objected to the Constitution.[20]

Again reflecting the political system of Connecticut, where separation of powers did not exist, Sherman saw the mixing of legislative and executive functions in the presidential veto and appointive power shared with the Senate as positive attributes of the new Constitution. The executive should be "absolutely dependent" on the legislature, which "should have the power to remove [him] at pleasure." As we have seen, for Sherman, the idea that the executive and legislative powers "ought to be entirely distinct and unconnected," was a "gross *error* in politics."[21]

Thus Ellsworth and Sherman tried to cast the new Constitution into forms that Connecticut republicans could recognize and accept. It was also necessary for them to minimize the reach of the Union into citizens' daily lives. Sherman, recall, was the least nationalist of Connecticut's three delegates and the most effective defender of states' rights at the Philadelphia convention. He went there convinced that the central government had to be strengthened in only three respects: it must have an independent income; it must have exclusive authority over interstate and foreign commerce; and it must have an effective mechanism—civil and military—for national defense. He have would let stand the Articles with its single house, equal state representation, and legislative dominance; change would come through amendment.[22]

Now, after participating as a most influential states'-rights debater throughout the convention, after negotiating some of the crucial compromises, and after accepting a wholly new document, Sherman seems to have believed that the only changes made were those which he had been willing to accept in the first place. Thus as Connecticut antinationalists proclaimed their fear of a new dominating government that would circumscribe their individual freedoms and undermine the sovereignty of the state, Sherman insisted that almost nothing would be altered under the new government.

Sherman bent every clause of the document to minimize its impact on Connecticut yeoman. No feature was too petty to avoid his attention. The new government would be no more expensive than the old, Sherman claimed; Congress would not have to sit for more than "two or three months in a year"; the executive departments would be no larger than they were under the Articles (which was a total of twelve men). The security against standing armies would be strengthened by prohibiting Congress from appropriating money to support the military for more than two years. Direct taxes were unlikely because of the new national impost, but in any event would be small and proportionate to the population. The U.S. Supreme Court will deal only with great national issues, and it is probable that state courts will try federal cases so that no new lower courts will be established. And, he told his infamously litigious constituents in a state swarming with lawyers, "it is not probable that more than one citizen to a thousand will ever have a cause that can come before a federal court."[23] Sherman would live another five years and see every one of these predictions proved wrong.

Surely, then, Roger Sherman propounded a constitution his version of which, perhaps, was unique. It was the misperceived version of the new government that was sold to the Connecticut convention that ratified a document that would have been drummed out of the state if Hamilton's or Madison's or even Elbridge Gerry's or Luther Martin's version had been promoted there. Sherman and Ellsworth, one deluded and the other dishonest, presented to Connecticut voters a constitution far from what in fact the document brought about when put in place.

They might not have gotten away with their interpretations had an opposition voice been heard. But the pro-Constitution forces had firm and determined allies in all the state's printers. Though pages and pages of polemic in support of ratification were published, only a single article written by a Connecticut anti saw print, and it was not reprinted anywhere. The newspapers even suppressed the fact that several town meetings had rejected the Constitution.[24]

Vast amounts of pro-Constitution material reprinted from out of state newspapers appeared in Connecticut, but only five articles against the Constitution found their way into local newspapers. Efforts to distribute antifederal materials in Connecticut somehow came a cropper. Leading politicians like William Williams wrote secretly to friends in New York requesting copies of certain writings. But in general, antifederal pamphlets either never got sent or were somehow intercepted at the border. John Lamb in New York and others in Philadelphia intended to send materials and may have tried to. But antifederal publications widely available in neighboring states did not find their way into Connecticut except, perhaps, as single copies in the hands of individuals.[25]

Coupled with essays lauding the Constitution were others attacking the handful of anti-Constitution leaders in Connecticut. James Wadsworth of Durham, a longtime spokesman for the agrarian majority, took the brunt of the attack. Wadsworth was a seasoned politician who had served a term in Congress in 1784 as an outspoken opponent of the 5 percent impost. He was reported to have declared that "Rhode Island had saved the Liberties of the U.S. once & perhaps they might again." In 1788 he was a member of Connecticut's upper house and state comptroller. The little literary cabal known as the Connecticut Wits wrote in bitter jest that Wadsworth was "busied, daily, planning pop'lar schemes/ And nightly rapt in democratic dreams." Indeed, writes the leading authority on the Wits, "Their first campaign was to destroy the influence of General James Wadsworth."[26]

Hugh Ledlie, an old militia veteran, onetime farmer and Hartford shopkeeper, now gouty and retired, thought the Constitution "a gilded pill." He wrote an antifederal friend in New York that "General James Wadsworth is one of the many steeds that has behaved in character against the new Constitution and stood firm and intrepid not withstanding all the scoffs, flirts, browbeatings, flings, coughs, scuffles, threats, and menaces of the opposite faction." The new design, said Ledlie, "will work the ruin of the freedom and liberty of these thirteen dis-united states." Benjamin Gale, intrepid political gadfly of Killingworth neighboring Wadsworth's Durham, labeled the Constitution a *"dark, intricate, artful, crafty, and unintelligible composition."* He told the Killingworth town meeting that the Connecticut establishment had so "managed the matter that they have not left you a fortnight to weigh and consider of the most important affair that ever came before you."[27] Indeed, the town meetings of November 12 for the election of delegates to the state convention came only forty-seven days after the Constitution had been published in Connecticut papers.

The convention met at Hartford on January 3 at the State House, but adjourned to the First Church North Meeting House, where spectators could sit in the balcony. One hundred and seventy-four men had been elected, and 172 were present and 168 voted. They were "the very men that framed the new Constitution at Philadelphia," lamented Ledlie, "together with our present governor, lieutenant governor, judges of our superior and inferior courts, present delegates to Congress, judges of probates, lawyers, tagrag and bob-tail, with some reverend divines, and placemen, salarymen, sinecures, and expectants of every denomination whatsoever." Ezra Stiles thought it "the grandest Assemblage of sensible & worthy Characters that ever met together in this state." Indeed, the delegate from Norwich was Samuel Huntington, governor of Connecticut, and the first president of Congress under the Articles of Confederation.[28] The nationalist influence was everywhere.

Not only was the newspaper debate wholly dominated by the nationalists, but so was the debate at the ratifying convention. Hugh Ledlie was told that while opponents of the Constitution were speaking, galleries stacked by the nationalists, along with some delegates, were "shuffling and stamping [their] feet, coughing, talking, spitting, and whispering. . . . All these menaces and stratagems were used by a junto who tries to carry all before them in this state, as well by writing as every other diabolical and evil pretense. And as the presses in this state are open to them, but evidently shut against all those that would dare and presume to write on the other side . . . they have greatly the advantage."[29]

Another great advantage enjoyed by the pro-Constitution forces was the fact that conventions in three states had already ratified the Constitution with no dissenting votes. Only in Pennsylvania, where rioting and kidnapping marked the ratification process, had significant opposition been active.[30] At the convention the antinationalists never had a chance. A century and a half of deferential politics had fine-tuned the mechanisms of control. One old member of the establishment pointed out that the pro-Constitution forces included two governors, one lieutenant governor, six members of the upper house, a judge of the superior court, two ministers, eight generals, eighteen colonels, seven majors, thirteen captains, and sixty-seven others including many county judges and justices of the peace. On the other side were only one member of the upper house—the soon to be deposed James Wadsworth, two generals, four colonels, one major, three captains, a lieutenant, with only a sprinkling of county judges and justices of the peace.[31] It is significant that the titled antifederalists were almost all militia officers. As Ledlie pointed out, the constitutionalists overwhelmed the antis in power and prestige as well as information and rhetoric and, even he would have to admit, numbers. The balconies were packed with supporters of the establishment. They were in for a good show.

The pro-Constitution forces won much of the battle in their initial and uncontested thrust. To a harmless-sounding motion put forth by Lieutenant Governor Wolcott to permit the most free discussion, he deftly set the spring to the trap by adding the proviso that no vote be taken until the entire doc-

ument had been discussed. It would now be procedurally impossible for the
antis to chip away at the thing; it would be all or nothing at all.[32]

Ellsworth opened the debate and reiterated the points he had so fully
propounded in his essays. Again, now speaking to a mostly converted choir,
he emphasized the necessity and benignity of the coercive powers of the new
system. There must "be a parental hand over the whole, this and nothing
else, can restrain the unruly conduct of the members." Ellsworth did not
neglect the pocketbook issues, however. The Constitution, he said, in prohibiting states from levying import duties, would stop the flow of Connecticut money—which he estimated at £20,000 to £26,600 a year—into the New
York State treasury since an estimated seven-eighths of all goods imported
into Connecticut came through New York. Such sums would now be collected by the U.S. government for the benefit of all the states.[33] Though no
one pointed it out, it was also true that since Connecticut citizens were owed
proportionately much more of the national debt than citizens of any other
state, a good share of the national income would tend to flow its way.[34] To
make that point would raise a red flag before the numerous antiaristocratic
potential antifederalists since the holders of large amounts of U.S. securities
constituted only a small class.

Ellsworth gave full rein to his flamboyant and apocalyptic rhetoric. Union
is essential: Without a coercive power in the central government, "What is to
defend us from the ambition and rapacity of New York. . . . Do we not already see in her the seeds of an overbearing ambition? On our other side,
there is a large and powerful state. Have we not already begun to be tributaries? . . . A more energetic system is necessary . . . a power in the general
government to enforce the degrees of the Union is absolutely necessary."[35]
But, protested James Wadsworth in the only speech in opposition to ratification reported in the newspapers, the proposed system "gave the power of the
purse to the general legislature; another paragraph gave the powers of the
sword; and that authority which has the power of the sword and purse is
despotic."[36]

The newspaper report apparently included Wadsworth's remarks only to
set him up for a lengthy acerbic rebuttal by Ellsworth, who once again canvassed all the economic reasons for accepting the proposed constitution.
More speeches by Governor Huntington, Judge Richard Law, and Lieutenant Governor Wolcott were reported at great length. The central thrust
of their arguments was against the idea that the new government would
swallow up the states and annihilate the rights of the people. "So well
guarded is this Constitution," Wolcott declared, "that it seems impossible
that the rights either of the states or of the people should be destroyed."[37]

This defensiveness about the concern that the U.S. might swallow up the states, that greater centralized power was synonymous with antirepublicanism, and thus a threat to individual liberty, tells us that such concerns must have been voiced but unreported. The lone newspaper reporter was an ardent constitutionalist who neglected to report any but one speech in opposition. He declared that the Constitution "was canvassed critically and fully. Every objection was raised against it which the ingenuity and invention of its opposers could devise," none of which he chose to report perhaps because "all the objections to the Constitution vanished before the learning and eloquence of a Johnson, the genuine good sense and discernment of a Sherman, and the Demosthenian energy of an Ellsworth."[38]

A very different picture from the dispassionate and harmonious one drawn by Enoch Perkins, the newspaper reporter, comes from Hugh Ledlie, who wrote a friend that the business "was carried on . . . with a highhand against those that disapproved thereof," who "were browbeaten by many of those Ciceroes, as they think themselves, and others of superior rank, as they call themselves." As the disgruntled anti put it, "Theophistry, coloring, and smooth speeches of those great men which spoke last gave a turning cast to the whole and thereby gave the weaker brethren a different turn of mind from what they had when they came from home and or the instructions they received from the towns to which they belonged."[39]

As the convention closed, the nationalists brought out their biggest guns for the final salvoes. Governor Huntington declared to the delegates, "I am fully of the opinion that great council of the Union must have a controlling power with respect to matters of national concern. . . . The state governments, I think, will not be endangered by the powers vested by this Constitution in the general government." Indeed, said Chief Justice Richard Law, "we ought to consider that this general government rests upon the state governments for support. It is like a vast and magnificent bridge built upon thirteen strong and stately pillars. Now the rulers, those who occupy the bridge, cannot be so beside themselves to knock away the pillars which support the whole fabric." And concluding with an appeal to his Calvinist constituents, Law opined, "If it be the design of Providence to make us a great and happy people, I believe, that He who turns the hearts of the children of men, as the rivers of water are turned, will induce the people of the United States to accept of a Constitution which is so well calculated to promote their national welfare."[40]

After a few more comments, General Samuel Holden Parsons, a son of the Cincinnati and nephew of Matthew Griswold, recently governor and a delegate from Lyme, moved, "In the Name of the People of the State of

Connecticut . . . to assent to, ratify and adopt the Constitution."[41] A roll call
vote tallied 128 in favor; 40 against. Thus the great revolution was wrought,
and Connecticut without violence and with apparent equanimity surren-
dered the sovereignty that had been the darling of the people for a century
and a half.

To reiterate, however: Connecticut's voluntary—even enthusiastic—sub-
mission to the limitations of the Constitution comes as no surprise despite its
long history of autonomy and the provincialism of its people. To some, the
actual ratification may have looked like a coup by the commercial and professional class, but this had been the leadership group for generations. And
in this case they had the support of the overwhelming majority of representatives of the remote agrarian hinterlands. It was no coup; it was a consensus.

But why, then, did forty thoroughly representative Connecticut leaders
stand outside the consensus and refuse to accept the promise that the new
system would bring? It is conventional to look for some ideological, or at least
rhetorical, differences between antifederalists and federalists. In the Connecticut context this is not possible. Not a single delegate who voted against
ratification left a statement of his position. The fullest statements we have
were made by men who were not delegates to the convention. One is the
draft of a speech by Benjamin Gale presumably prepared for delivery at the
Killingworth meeting to elect delegates; the other is a long letter from Hugh
Ledlie to the New York antifederalist John Lamb.[42]

From Gale and Ledlie and bits and pieces, hints and implications found
scattered among the literary remains of the era, we can reconstruct something of the antifederalist side of the dialogue, if such a one-sided conversa-
tion can be called that. Ledlie, for instance, characterized the federalists as
self-proclaimed "Ciceroes . . . of superior rank" and "upstart sons of Apollo."
Gale thought that members of Congress "will be of the higher class of people
who will know but little of the poverty, straits, and difficulties of the middling
and lower class of men." The Constitution, said Ledlie, "will work the ruin
of freedom and liberty of these thirteen disunited states," and in ratifying it
the people "by one stroke . . . have lost all the liberty and privileges, both
civil and sacred, as well as all their property, money, etc." For Gale, in "this
newfangled Congress" the framers "have taken care that . . . we resign into
the hands of Congress the *impost, excise, duties,* and a power to tax for as
much as they want and to make all necessary laws to regulate . . . matters, to
appoint their supreme and inferior courts, to eat up ours, and we take our
militia out of the hands of our governors, reducing our governors into the
quality of drill sargeants, [and] convert our militia into a standing army." But,

of course, neither of these men were chosen by their townsfolk to represent them at the convention. Among the antifederal delegates, we know only that James Wadsworth, the principal antifederalist at the convention, objected that the Constitution gave the power of both the purse and the sword to Congress.[43]

There is nothing in this antifederal lament that rises to the level of an ideology. However, two elements of protest are clear: fear of an aristocratic takeover and fear of the loss of local autonomy and individual liberty. But the statements are inchoate, unfocused, and disorganized, or as Ledlie admitted, presented in an "unconnected scrawl" full of "inaccuracies and incoherence."[44] The rambling and inarticulate presentation of the Connecticut antifederalists, along with the absence of literary remains, leaves us with guesses as to the intellectual content of their opposition.

Perhaps there was no intellectual content; perhaps it was visceral. In Connecticut state sovereignty had always been more a practical and emotional commitment than an ideological one. For the delegates to accept what only a few months earlier would have been considered treason goes a long way toward disclosing their frame of mind in January 1788.

Noah Webster called it jealousy: "The federal men suppose the antifederal to be knaves, designing artful demagogues. The anti-federal suppose the federal to be ambitious tyrannical men, who are aiming at power and office at large." Webster left no doubt about which side he stood on, for "people in general are too ignorant to manage affairs which require great reading and an extensive knowledge of foreign nations." Webster's skepticism had driven him, by 1786, to "prefer a limited monarchy" to a republic. With federalists taking this sort of a stand, others can hardly be blamed for perceiving the proposed new executive to be "an *Elective King*," part of a "*dark, intricate, artful, crafty and unintelligible*" system. The finished document seemed to fulfill Abraham Granger's darkest forebodings that it would "produce a royal government in this country."[45]

As antifederalists had little faith in the governing class, federalists had little faith in the people. Suspicion ran deep on both sides The antifederalists, Oliver Ellsworth explained somewhat ambiguously, were "men of much self-importance and supposed skill in politics, who are not of sufficient consequence to obtain public employment, but can spread jealousies in the little districts of the country where they are placed; these are always jealous of men in place and of public measures, and aim at making themselves consequential by distrusting every one in the higher offices of society." Ellsworth, of course, was one of those delegates who would be perceived as "delicately bred" (although he wasn't) and living in "affluent circumstances" (which he was) whose domination of the convention some men had anticipated with such trepidation.[46]

Just weeks after he cast his vote against changing the national system, James Wadsworth was characterized as what has become the stereotypical antifederalist. Wadsworth was, wrote an intemperate federalist, "as remarkable for his stubbornness, as for his contracted politics and local prejudices, who has gained some consequence by an uniform opposition to every measure which was unpleasing to the knavish and licentious."[47] The antifederalists, the stereotype ran, constituted a class of unscrupulous demagogues, like those so unmercifully satirized by the Wits in *The Anarchiad.*

Provincials' suspicions of an aristocratic and centralizing conspiracy of the educated rich were salved by the honest assurances of Sherman, the dissemblings of Ellsworth, and the apparent good sense of men like Samuel and Jedediah Huntington, whom they trusted. The antifederalists in Connecticut, like those across the country, were unable to put forward a comprehensive, consistent, and focused argument against the new system. Also, as elsewhere, Connecticut antifederalists were not cohesive. Delegates from the northern towns did not join in a coordinated movement. Nor did they attempt juncture with Wadsworth's coterie in New Haven. Each group—indeed each individual—had its own reasons for opposing the Constitution. But in Connecticut deference still made a difference, and there were more worthies than libertines. For every man of little faith in established leaders, there were many who trusted them. The federalist steamroller had crushed the antinational leadership.

The lopsided majority of 128 to 40 was a result of scores of individual decisions made on the basis of individual concerns and local conditions. At bottom, the explanation of the antifederal vote at Connecticut's ratifying convention demonstrates the adage that in America "all politics is local." Though general theories and broad generalizations open up insights and guide intuitions, they cannot tell us why particular people did the things they did. Only a study of particular people can do that. There was no "antifederalist" ideology in Connecticut, not even a cohesive set of articulated social attitudes to hold those forty stubborn antifederalists together. Local, factional cohesiveness there was, but its core lay in something much more tangible than ideas and attitudes. We shall investigate that core in Chapter 6.

6

Constitutional Crosswinds

A correspondent writing from out of state was amazed that Connecticut's yeomen, famed all over for their independent ways, would succumb to such an overarching national system. Was it not a state, he incredulously asked, where men "are so jealous of their representatives and fond of elections that they cannot be trusted but six months, and all the legislative and executive officers but one year." How could "a state whose privileges are so guarded . . . so greedily destroy itself" by adopting the Constitution?[1]

That was a reasonable question to ask at the time, based as it was on Connecticut's long heritage and accurate reputation as an insular, provincial, jealously autonomous little republic. But the war and its aftermath had changed things. The end of the empire had set the states afloat without the protection of the British fleet. The wartime breakdown of law and order had created the potential for internal assaults on the establishment. And the annihilation of imperial mercantile restrictions had opened the nation and the world to commerce if only it could be channeled and regulated. Security concerns and commercial opportunity overbore concern for local autonomy and stimulated the urge for commercial expansion. Connecticut was part of a new nation with the world just outside its gates. The reasons in favor of joining the new union were overwhelming. The real question, so obvious to many in the winter of 1788 and to most only months after ratification, was why would any rational Connecticut man oppose subscribing to the new Constitution?

The analysis that follows shows that the traditional division into agrarian antifederalists and commercial federalists needs major qualifications. True, most delegates with mercantile interests or from commercially oriented towns voted to ratify—indeed all ten from the five incorporated cities did;

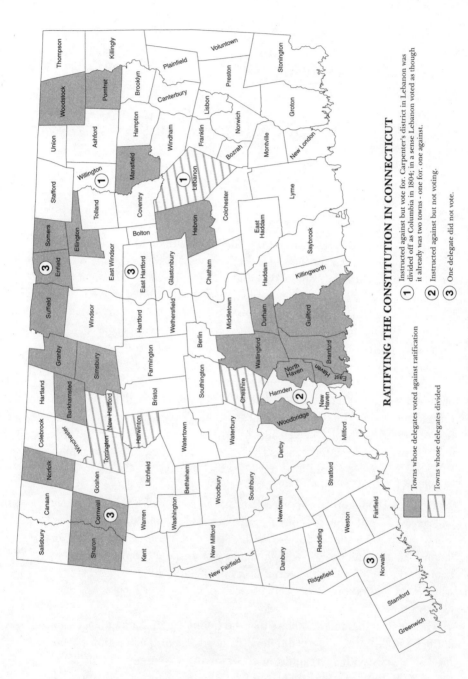

RATIFYING THE CONSTITUTION IN CONNECTICUT

① Instructed against but vote for. Carpenter's district in Lebanon was divided off as Columbia in 1804; in a sense Lebanon voted as though it already was two towns - one for. one against.

② Instructed against but not voting.

③ One delegate did not vote.

▨ Towns whose delegates voted against ratification

▨ Towns whose delegates divided

2. Ratifying the Constitution in Connecticut.

and most of the delegates who voted against ratifying the Constitution came from predominantly agricultural communities. However, most farmer delegates and about two-thirds of the delegates from remote, underdeveloped towns voted to ratify, contrary to what the conventional wisdom would have us believe.

The Federalists

As we have seen, the convention's ratification of the Constitution is not so surprising despite Connecticut's long tradition of provincial autonomy. Ratification certainly was not due to the election of an unrepresentative body, as some antifederalists claimed.[2] Delegates voting for the Constitution came from all over the state. They were sent by commercial towns and farm towns; cities and small towns; port towns and inland towns; old towns and new towns. They included political nonentities from remote country villages as well as governors and congressmen; Continental privates and generals, and militia privates and generals; public debtors and creditors, private debtors and creditors; merchants and farmers, artisans and professionals; young men and old. In short, the pro-Constitution forces constituted a highly representative selection not, of course, of Connecticut's late eighteenth-century body of yeoman voters, but of its traditional leadership cadre.

The federalist political spectrum ranged from nationalists like Samuel Holden Parsons, who thought that "all authority in the States should be derived from the Supreme sovereignty of the Country,"[3] to last-minute switch-overs like localist leader Joseph Hopkins, who spoke against the Constitution and then voted for it. Indeed, many delegates—perhaps two or three dozen—who had gone to Hartford inclined—even instructed—against ratification, voted for the Constitution in the end.

In other states, the core of antifederalists' fear of the new form of government lay in their perception that it would undermine or overpower local control, and raise up an expensive aristocracy of former Continental military officers and national officeholders. This perception prevailed among Connecticut antis, as well. But in the absence of the documentary remains of Connecticut-generated polemic, it must be seen as more of a gut feeling than an articulated ideology.[4] Inchoate and largely unarticulated, the fear of centralized aristocratic government could be quelled by rhetoric and appeals to common sense and shared values. The federalists were supported also by the visible presence of power and prestige, and the characteristic deference of many in the face of a virtually unanimous standing order. Perhaps the most

significant reason for ratifying the Constitution was the objective reality of
the economic and security benefits of a strengthened central government
and a national free-trade region.

The effects of Shays' Rebellion were also significant in bringing moder-
ates—especially in northern Litchfield County—into the nationalist column.[5]
As one might expect, in the Land of Steady Habits the reaction against,
rather than the reflection of, Shays' Rebellion dominated. Moderate localist
and antiaristocratic delegates like Charles Burrall of Canaan, Daniel Miles of
Goshen, near neighbors of Shaysite Sharon; or such delegates as East Haddam's Dyar Throop and Jabez Chapman, all of whom voted against granting
Congress authority to levy a national impost, were no doubt shaken by the
Sharon episode.[6] They all ultimately voted to ratify the new Constitution.

After the Constitution was published in Connecticut, propagandists reported a movement for a "kingly government" in reaction to Shays' Rebellion, and set up the proposed federal system as the golden mean. "Many of
our people feel the Influence of the Disease . . . [which] catches across the
state line," one correspondent wrote privately. A polemicist warned of "the
precarious state of property, . . . every hour subject to the prey of a Shays, or
some like miscreant."[7] Federalists pointed to the paper money supporters
and their sympathizers in high places like William Williams as soft on Shaysism. Another anxious newspaper correspondent wrote accusingly that "'tis
by no means to be wondered at that such an infection should take effect
in this state, when . . . some of our rulers and leading men . . . afford their
council and personal assistance to have this most horrid distemper become
universal."[8]

But secretly some federalists saw the rebellion as helping their cause. Jeremiah Wadsworth wrote Henry Knox that "if the Massachusetts rebellion
had continued" it would have helped the cause of ratification.[9] It is clear that
the Shays activity on the Connecticut border in the late winter of 1786 and
early the next year put a damper on the enthusiasms of the democratically inclined deputies at the Assembly session in May 1787, when the decision was
made to send delegates to Philadelphia. It is very likely that it helped move
some previously reliable antinationalists into the nationalist camp as well.

The Antifederalists

Like the federalists, the antifederal delegates constituted a highly representative selection of Connecticut's late eighteenth-century leadership. They
ranged the political spectrum from die-hard James Wadsworth, who, after

ratification, refused to take an oath to uphold the Constitution, to Constant Southworth, who admitted that he "was restrained from voting for it only by his instructions" from the Mansfield town meeting.[10] Like the federalists, too, the antifederalists represented coastal towns and inland towns; old towns and new towns; commercial towns and farm towns; large towns and small towns; debtors and creditors; young and old. The antis, however, numbered no representatives of the five incorporated cities—the centers of the state's commercial life.[11] Among the federal voters were thirteen merchants (10 percent); among the antis, two (5 percent). Indeed, with significant exceptions to be discussed below, one side of the conventional wisdom that equates federalists with commercial orientation holds up.[12] The other side does not; most delegates representing small, remote agricultural communities—some only a decade or two away from wilderness—voted to ratify.

In fact, the distinguishing characteristics did not distinguish federalists from antifederalists so much as they distinguished leaders from the hoi polloi. As individuals, the men who voted to ratify the Constitution are remarkably similar to those who voted not to. Indeed, three of the four principal antinational leaders finally voted for the new government. As individuals, the nay voters look much like the ayes. They were local leaders, usually of above-average wealth, often from old-line families. They were militia officers, justices of the peace, and selectmen. It is usually impossible on the basis of economic or geographic data to predict how a man would vote.[13] Though a biographical picture does not always yield a reliable basis of prediction, such biographies are always illuminating and often explanatory.

Federalists and antifederalists shared many characteristics. The median age of both groups was fifty-one.[14] Of those whose church affiliation has been discovered, among antifederalists 95 percent were Congregationalists; among federalists at least 92 percent were. Of those a third of the antifederalists and a quarter of the federalists were deacons. Eight Episcopalians voted for the Constitution, two voted against—6.2 percent of former group, 5 percent of the latter.[15] Among the antifederalists 7.5 percent were physicians; among the federalists, 7 percent were. There were nine (6 percent) federalist and five (12.5 percent) antifederalist taverners.[16]

But when each is viewed collectively the two groups reveal some telling differences. Four of the forty antifederalists were college graduates; forty-two (33 percent) of the federalists were.[17] Only one anti held high state office, but sixteen federalists were or had been governors, lieutenant governors, members of the Council or Congress. Among the federalists only 8 percent had never served as deputies in the lower house; 12.5 percent of the antifederalists had never been deputies. Of the twenty men who served

Connecticut as congressmen between 1774 and 1788, sixteen were delegates to the convention. (Of the remaining four, one was dead, one was dying, one was in exile in England, and the fourth was a suspected antifederalist.) Fifteen voted to ratify.[18] As we have seen, there were thirteen men known to be merchants among the federalists; two among the antifederalists. Both minister delegates voted aye. To cap off the dominance of the establishment among the federalists, thirty-six (28 percent) of them were lawyers; only two of the bar voted nay.

And although service in the Continental army was not helpful in getting elected to go to the convention, only one antifederalist held a military commission from Congress, but thirty-four federalist delegates had served as officers in Continental regiments or the Connecticut Line when attached to Continental units.[19] Cincinnati membership could hurt. Jonathan Trumbull, Jr., reported to George Washington that he was not elected a delegate because of "being in my particular circle, under the cloud of commutation and Cincinnati." Indeed, of 270 men who joined the Connecticut branch of the Society of the Cincinnati, only twelve were sent to the convention. They all voted aye.[20]

On the other hand, association with the intellectual—as opposed to the military—elite did no harm, and may have added some attractive cachet. The Connecticut Society of Arts and Sciences, founded in 1786, numbered among its forty-five members twenty-one who would go to the convention.[21] Every one of these voted for the Constitution.

Generally speaking, those whose primary occupation was other than farming were much more likely to favor the Constitution. In a society in which about 80 percent of the adult men were farmers, at least seventy-two federalists (56 percent) but only eighteen antifederalists (45 percent) were not principally farmers.[22] Indeed, that I was able to discover the primary occupations of 73 percent of the federalists, but only 57 percent of the antifederalists, tells something about the relative prominence of the men constituting the two groups.

Thus a collective portrait shows a kind of a class division. The college educated, merchants and professionals, high state civil officers and Continental military and civil officers clustered in the federalist camp.

The ability to find commonalities that distinguish federalists from antifederalists does not, however, provide the wherewithal to predict how any of the 174 delegates at the ratifying convention would vote. Many of those who voted aye on January 9 had been opposed to ratification on January 2. Not all the delegates from commercial centers voted to ratify, but most delegates from remote undeveloped agricultural towns did. The most interesting question that remains, it seems to me, is why did anyone—especially those from commercial suburbs of New Haven—vote against the Constitution?

Among the forty delegates who voted against the Constitution in 1788, there were several who as deputies in the General Assembly during the 1780s voted against supporting or increasing the powers of Congress. They are Nathaniel Atwood, Andrew Ward, Elihu Marvin, Street Hall, and Daniel Hall. In addition, certain other delegates emerged as local "democratic" leaders between 1784 and 1786 because of their support of legal tender or paper money bills or opposition to congressional requisitions and antidemocratic alterations in the state government. They were James Wadsworth, Joseph Hopkins, William Williams, Constant Southworth, Charles Burrell, Abel Pease, and Erastus Wolcott. On the basis of their previous voting record or their earlier published polemics, we would expect all these men to vote against ratifying the Constitution. Charles Burrell did not, however, nor did the three principal antifederal leaders, Williams, Wolcott, and Hopkins.[23] The defection of these three men from the antinationalist camp—which no doubt influenced a number of followers—was a lethal bloodletting of the wounded antifederalists.

The Antinational Apostates

A short biographical side trip will demonstrate the social similarity of the federal and antifederal leaders and may at the same time reveal some clues as to why at the crucial moment some men voted to ratify and others voted against.

Joseph Hopkins was born in 1730, the son of Waterbury's most prominent political and economic figure, a descendant of an original settler. Hopkins was the largest landowner in town, a watchmaker and silversmith, and Waterbury's second-wealthiest taxpayer, and a deacon of the First Congregational Church. Hopkins had been prominent in Waterbury government since 1758, and between 1764 and 1796 he served forty-four semiannual terms in the Assembly. He was a judge of probate for thirty years. He did his nominal militia duty as a young man, but never served under arms in either the French and Indian War or the Revolution. He was, however, on Waterbury's earliest Committee of Inspection in 1774. He was related by marriage to Waterbury's other delegate at the ratifying convention, John Welton, who also voted to ratify, and connected by marriage—though somewhat remotely—to the leading antifederalist, James Wadsworth. However, he was more closely related to high federalists, among them his first cousin, Lemual

Hopkins, one of the acerbic Wits who pilloried him unmercifully for his anti-nationalist stand.[24]

Hopkins owned at least 447 acres of land in Waterbury, and in May 1787 he introduced a bill to prohibit the forced sale of land to meet tax payments. As an artisan in business, however, he opposed legal tender laws and paper money. He was a friend and confidant of William Williams and, like Williams, the butt of federalist ridicule from their relations. He did not oppose sending delegates to the Philadelphia convention, but said on the Assembly floor in 1787 that "he had very little to expect" from it.[25] Hopkins' anti-Constitution inclinations were well known, and a federalist writer in the *New Haven Gazette* attacked his character as one of "hideous deformity," and the man as "tired and jaded" and possessed of "a rotten and unprincipled heart." He was an anti-Constitution leader at the state ratifying convention, where among other things he decried the absence of a bill of rights. In the end, however, he was persuaded to vote in favor. His erstwhile antifederal colleagues then turned on him, calling him "Weathercock," and declaring he had turned from "light to darkness."[26]

Though not a farmer, Hopkins was a popular leader—even populist. His hundreds of acres would have been farmed by tenants or hired labor, but his income came largely from his public service—he had long since given up silversmithing. It is not unlikely that Hopkins' change of heart resulted both from his desire to join the winning side and his recognition that the new federation would do him no economic harm, and might well help his business. And, of course, federalist relations were leaning on him. Soothing comment by Roger Sherman that a national bill of rights was unnecessary may have calmed fears on that account. And, finally, Sherman no doubt convinced him that the new government would not threaten his local offices, from which—especially the probate judgeship—he derived a significant income.[27] Pro-Constitution leaders, of course, made it clear almost to the point of extortion that he would lose these appointive positions if he voted against ratification. Family pressure, rational analysis, and fear of losing these lucrative jobs no doubt determined Hopkins' vote in the end.

William Williams, who served as the clerk of the town of Lebanon, moderated three stormy meetings at which the proposed new Constitution was debated. He was easily elected a delegate to the ratifying convention.[28] With less unity, Ephraim Carpenter was elected to join him. Carpenter was a militia captain, county surveyor, and frequent local officeholder who lived in "the Crank," Lebanon's second society in the remote northwest section of town. He was a blacksmith and innkeeper and a large real estate dealer and land speculator. He had been a leading anticommutation figure. Carpenter, following instructions, voted nay. Like so many oppositionists, he left Connecticut, moving to Vermont in 1790 when he was fifty-two.[29]

After the choice of delegates, the Lebanon meeting decided to instruct them. An up or down vote on the Constitution on a rainy November 12 gave a tally of thirteen for, forty-nine against. The matter was called up again at the annual town meeting three weeks later, and with fuller attendance the negative vote was confirmed eighty-one to forty-one. Instructions—the text of which has not been discovered—were written and Williams and Carpenter went off to Hartford bound to oppose the new government.[30] But while Carpenter, a leader of the antifederalist forces on the eve of the convention, fulfilled his townly obligations, Williams turned apostate. Why?

William Williams, fifty-eight years old in January 1788, was typical of the old Connecticut leadership. His father was minister of the First Church of Lebanon, Williams' lifelong dwelling spot. He graduated from his father's alma mater, Harvard College, in 1751 and became a local merchant. He climbed the militia ladder customary for well-connected local officials after getting a head start as an ensign at the age of twenty. In 1775, in due course, he was promoted to colonel, a position he resigned in December 1776 at the age of forty-five. He never served under arms, and was distinctly not a military man. Civil public office was his main interest and he was elected town clerk and treasurer at the age of twenty-one, and served in those offices for forty-four years. He also served twenty-seven consecutive annual terms as selectman and was almost continuously a deputy from 1757 to 1776, when he was elevated to the Council. He was a deacon of his church for most of his adult life. Aside from his time at Harvard, about eighty miles from Lebanon, he left the state of Connecticut twice: once in 1761 to go to Crown Point on Lake Champlain on a commercial venture, and once to visit Philadelphia to sit in the Continental Congress, where he signed the Declaration of Independence. He was a Calvinist parochial. At age forty-one he married a daughter of his neighbor, Governor Jonathan Trumbull.[31]

In the 1780s Williams broke with his nationalist Trumbull in-laws over congressional policy, most pointedly over the commutation issue. The rivalry split the town, but Williams led the anticommutation majority. In the course of the statewide political struggle he lost his place on the Council, but was elected to the lower house, where he was chosen clerk and then speaker. He was a major antinational leader from 1783 to 1787. Williams sympathized with the farmers and, as a county court judge, refused, during the Shaysite disturbance in Massachusetts, to hold court when so many debtors were being sued.[32] In 1787 he received the third-highest number of votes for a seat on the Council, to which he had been reelected in 1784. In 1787 he was set up—unsuccessfully—by the localist agrarian faction as a competitor to Oliver Wolcott for the lieutenant governorship.[33]

In 1786 Williams wrote an attack on the Cincinnati, linking its members to commutation and a scheme by which the nationalist faction would control the sale of Connecticut's Western Reserve. A copy, sent confidentially to Joseph Hopkins, was intercepted and Williams' identity revealed. Williams blamed Samuel Holden Parsons for the indiscretion and a public squabble between the two men raged. A cartoon broadside circulated in the winter of 1787–88 shows Williams and Parsons in poses that make them appear as though they are defecating at each other.[34] Because of his leadership—or perhaps patronizing—of the agrarian faction among the statewide electorate, Williams had long been the butt of the commercial nationalists' ridicule. When he was at Congress, John Trumbull, the Wit—not Williams' brother-in-law of the same name, but that man's second cousin—had written,

> A man of Congress asked thus
> "How comes it, *Poet Timbel!*
> "Your State doth send a Fool to us
> "Whose Name is William Wimble?"
> The poet did this speech relate —
> "From honest views we sent him;
> "The fools are many in our State,
> "He goes to represent 'em."

Such intellectual scorn, however, did not necessarily damage Williams' political career. One young federalist partisan wrote a friend that "the course of politics seems rather against the wits & Poets . . . It would be odd, if instead of writing W.W. Esqr. into political annihilation, they should write him into the second seat in the State."[35]

At the ratifying convention in Hartford, Williams objected to the omission of a religious test for federal officeholders; he wanted at least "to require an explicit acknowledgment of the being of a God," he explained later. The only account of his participation in the debate that we have is from the hostile Perkins, who said "Williams rose and talked a great while, partly on one side and partly on the other, and finally observed with striking propriety that *his arguments concluded nothing.*" His brother-in-law, Jonathan Trumbull, Jr., explained that "among objections, the consolidating idea has catched his noddle. He is afraid of being swallowed up at one gulp."[36]

About a month after Williams' surrender and affirmative vote at Connecticut's ratifying convention, he wrote of the "calm, dispassionate and ra-

3. **"The Looking Glass for 1787." See Appendix E, pages 157–59 for a descriptive analysis of this cartoon.** Reproduced with permission of the Connecticut Historical Society, Hartford, Connecticut.

tional discussion" there and characterized its conclusion as "so happy an issue."[37] This was a far cry from his sentiments in the first week of January. What had happened? Williams, like Hopkins, was more politician and public servant than anything else. In 1788 he was not only a delegate to the ratifying convention, but also town clerk, county court judge, probate court judge, and a member of the Council of Assistants. He would lose both judgeships if he voted contrary to the establishment's wishes. Perhaps more to the point, for twenty-seven years he *had* been a town selectman until removed in an unusual local revolution in 1786.[38] Trumbull's doggerel about Williams' representative character is telling. Williams always had a wet finger to the wind. He knew which side blew cold. At the convention he was no doubt under very heavy pressure from his family and some old political friends and contemporaries like Roger Sherman and Samuel Huntington.

Furthermore, it is not impossible that rational argument played a part in persuading him to abandon his instructions. Eighteenth-century minds expected mankind to follow rational self-interest. It should come as no surprise that some of them did. After all, it was pretty clear just two years after ratification that those who voted aye had exercised the better judgment. Connecticut's political stability and economic strength both gained immeasurably as one of the new united states. And it appears that Williams' constituency soon came to see it that way, too. Where Carpenter—who obeyed town meeting orders—had his political career nipped in the bud, Williams was returned to office at the next election and for many more after that.[39]

If William Williams was well connected to the top echelons of government, Erastus Wolcott was hip deep in high-placed kin. Wolcott's younger college-educated brother, Oliver, was lieutenant governor for ten years beginning in 1786. His father was governor from 1750 to 1754, when Erastus was just entering his thirties and of an age to benefit politically and economically from the relationship, which he did. Erastus was also the brother-in-law of Matthew Griswold, who was governor from 1784 to 1786. Unlike all these close relatives, Wolcott was not a college graduate, but he learned enough mathematics to practice surveying and in his first public appointment was made, at the age of twenty, Hartford County Surveyor, a particularly fruity plum. This appointment would put him in an excellent position to speculate in lands to add to the very large family holdings in which he would ultimately share. In 1788 he was landlord to tenants on many hundreds of acres held in several towns.[40]

Wolcott was a leading figure in bringing about the division of East Windsor from Windsor in 1768, served as moderator of the new town's meetings and was a frequent selectman there. He began his legislative career as deputy from Windsor in 1758, when his father sat on the Council. He served fifty-eight semiannual terms in the lower house and rose to the Council in 1785, where his brother, about to become lieutenant governor, also sat. He was a justice of the peace, a probate judge, and he sat on the county court all through this period.[41]

Wolcott's militia career followed the trajectory typical of bright, ambitious and, especially well-connected young men. He was appointed lieutenant in 1759—the year after election to the General Assembly—at the age of thirty-seven. In June 1776 he was a colonel. He became a brigadier general later that year (on the same day that his brother Oliver was also appointed to this rank), a rank he held until his resignation in 1781. (He was succeeded in that position by his sister's husband, Roger Newberry.) Wolcott served as a colonel of one of three Connecticut regiments sent to aid Washington outside Boston in 1776. He commanded the guard at New London in that and the next year. He also took three regiments to Peekskill in 1777, but his military service was limited to militia duty.[42]

Wolcott's lack of Continental service might have been partly a function of age—he was fifty-four in 1776. But it may also have been a function of his lack of enthusiasm for the revolutionary cause. After an intense analysis of Connecticut's participation in the Revolutionary War, Richard Buel concludes that Wolcott and Anglican-neutralist William Samuel Johnson were "the two most influential advocates of moderation in the legislature." Wolcott and Johnson arranged to be appointed emissaries to General Gage in Boston in 1775, an ill-fated mission that could have cost a less well established man his political career.[43] One close scholar has identified Wolcott as the principal opponent of the new loyalty oath required of all adult men after independence in 1776, an opposition that brought a quick repeal of the act.[44] There is no evidence that Wolcott's reputation was in any way besmirched, but frequent charges in the mid-1780s that the antinationalists included many former loyalists or lukewarm patriots no doubt reflected the behavior of this agrarian leader during the opening years of the war. In 1787 he was elected a delegate to the old Congress, but declined to go, as was the case when he refused to attend the Philadelphia convention in that same year.[45] He was, it seems, a dyed-in-the-wool, stay-at-home conservative. Other than his military expeditions to West Point, Boston, Long Island, and Providence—all within about seventy-five miles of his home—he apparently never left Connecticut.[46]

Wolcott was of the rentier class, owning many hundreds of acres of land both for farming and speculation, but he was also a businessman. He owned the busy ferry across the Connecticut River and in 1787 he bought a tavern at the ferry slip.[47] Most of all, however, Erastus Wolcott, like Hopkins and Williams, was principally a local and state public servant, in close touch with his constituents and ambitious to win and hold office. His constituency was heavily agrarian,[48] and he became the intellectual leader of the localist-agrarian faction in 1782, when he began publishing essays urging tax reform that would equalize the burden by shifting some of it to the commercial and professional class. His reforms would halve the poll tax on men under twenty-one, reduce land taxes, and exempt young livestock. He would increase the faculty tax levied on professionals and tradesmen, and also raise taxes on certain personal property and luxury items.[49] Within a year after these essays were published, Wolcott's faction included a majority in the lower house.

Additionally, Erastus Wolcott sought to protect state creditors' interests. He favored a state impost over a national one and would accept all kinds of state securities for tax payments. Since employers of apprentices and artisanal and farm labor paid poll taxes for their employees, artisans and large-scale farmers would benefit. Merchant-artisans would also benefit from the duties on imports. Thus Wolcott spoke not only for the agrarian majority, but also for the incipient and still locally oriented manufacturing class. In the General Assembly he voted consistently against expanding congressional authority, opposed the national impost under all circumstances, and was a major anticommutation leader.[50]

When a statute of 1784 outlawed concurrent membership on both the Council and the Superior Court, four assistants resigned their places on the Council. Wolcott, who had been waiting patiently since 1772, when he first appeared on the upper house nomination lists, finally obtained one of the seats in 1785. His brother was lieutenant governor; his brother-in-law, governor. It was heady times for the family; it is unlikely that Erastus would want to spoil the party. Certainly, had he continued his allegiance to the localist faction he would have faced heavy familial pressure. It is also likely that Roger Sherman, an old friend and contemporary, and Oliver Ellsworth had persuaded him that state notes—of which he possessed at least $1,825 worth[51]—would be funded by the new national government under the proposed document. It is clear, too, that he was not of the democratic antiestablishment wing of the agrarian faction.

Wolcott no doubt represented the localist-agrarian view when appointed to Connecticut's delegation to the Philadelphia convention. His refusal to serve fit the pattern established previously when he declined to attend Congress. Given his antinational record, it is quite likely that in this case where he protested fear of catching smallpox in the distant city, he did not support the idea of a stronger union.[52]

By November 1787, however, Wolcott seems to have changed his mind. The town meeting called to elect delegates to the state ratifying convention, moderated by Erastus' first cousin William, voted to "accept and approve the Constitution." Wolcott was far and away the most influential man in East Windsor. It seems highly unlikely that this motion would have been put forward had he not wanted it so. The town meetings were under no obligation—legal, political, or moral—to vote one way or the other on the Constitution. Perhaps Wolcott wanted this vote as cover for the defection from his antinational allies he knew he was going to make in January at the ratifying convention.[53]

A significant factor underlying Wolcott's abandonment of the localist position was the elimination from his constituency in 1787 of Ellington parish, which was incorporated as a separate town, taking nearly 30 percent of East Windsor's population and roughly 40 percent of the territory, the most thoroughly agrarian section of that town.[54] Ellington's lone delegate would vote against the Constitution. At any event, Wolcott's position at the ratifying convention must have brought a significant number of potential antifederal votes over to the nationalist side.

While it is interesting to ruminate upon the motives of these three agrarian and antinationalist leaders for abandoning their well-established principles and disappointing the expectations of their constituents, it is perhaps more to the point to wonder why they parted from the governing party line in the first place. All three came from secondary commercial towns. They were all exceedingly successful politicians, very well connected to governors and councilors, and they all derived a significant income from public office. They were cut from the same cloth as were those of the ruling circle. Indeed, Williams and Wolcott, certainly, were part of that circle. For a few years, however—1784 to 1787—agrarian voters made up a majority of the freemen.[55] As professional politicians, it may have been the prevailing winds of the early 1780s that blew them into the agrarian fields, and their change of direction in 1788 merely reflected gales from a different quarter.

It is more likely, however, that popular opinion was not clear in January, and, in fact, that all three politicos gave way to the federalist juggernaut of 1788 captained by friends and family to keep their friends, quiet their families, and hang on to their state appointments. One old plough-jogging farmer told a friend in New York that those in office who went to Hartford determined to oppose ratification "were told plainly that if they did not turn and vote for it, they must not expect any places either of trust or profit under the new Constitution."[56] Given those political family pressures along with the clear economic benefits Connecticut would gain, one can understand their change of mind. Our focus, indeed, must be on the other side of the coin: Why would anyone in Connecticut oppose ratification, and who were the men who did it?

7

Those Who Voted No

It should be clear by now that the interests of Connecticut's farmers, artisans, tradesmen, and all the professionals who served them would be best protected by accepting the government under the new Constitution. The liberty enjoyed under a century and a half of autonomous government was threatened by foreign foes, neighboring states, and internal mobs. The new system would provide protection. The promise of commercial riches could only be realized as a member of the new United States. Oliver Wolcott, Sr., wrote to Oliver Wolcott, Jr., both future governors, "So farr as the pecuniary Part of the Plan can affect this State, I mean relative to commerce and its consequences, it is altogether in our favor."[1]

The advantages of the government under the Constitution would fall to all the people: farmers great and small, self-sustaining and commercial; merchants of the backcountry and busy ports; artisans, lawyers, ministers, and printers—all dependent for their incomes on the prosperity of the economy in general. As one Hartford County diarist put it, "[T]here can no weighty arguments be advanced against it—when, on the other hand, reason, experience, justice, safety, and the present as well as the future well being and safety of this country depend on its taking place."[2]

One of the dualities of Connecticut's localism was the provincial perspective its delegates brought to national affairs—an approach, no doubt, taken by most of the delegates from all the states. The second element of the dual localism is the effect that town and parish affairs had on deputies and delegates sent to the statewide assemblies and conventions. A very close examination of these little communities and the political players they sent to Connecticut's ratifying convention reveals clearly the force of local and personal connections and conditions. A collective portrait has not helped us identify the forces or motives behind the vote of any individual delegate. Indeed, the collective characteristics would lead us astray more often that they would provide an explanation; look, for instance, at the hundred or so dirt farmers who voted to ratify. Thus the class analysis sketched in chapter 6 above is wholly inferential. It does not explain the behavior of a single nay voter at the state ratifying convention.

By the time of the vote on January 9, the browbeating, political intimidation, one-sided polemical assault, reasoned argument, and personal pressure had done their job. Three of the four leading antinationalists had capitulated and so had their potential followers. But one long-standing, high-ranking member of the establishment held out, and he was able to bring in his antifederal train a number of upper-level officeholders and powerful local leaders. Other delegates, impelled by local circumstances and personal connections, joined them to make forty votes against ratifying the Constitution.

This brings us to the second tier of the dual localism that drove Connecticut's response to national developments: The dynamics of village politics and personal relations determined the stance of many delegates to the state ratifying convention. Our attention now turns to those men who voted no in the face of the heavy weight of both rational security and economic arguments and personal political and economic threat.

Conventional efforts to account for antifederal votes point to economic and geographic factors, ideology, and social-cultural attitudes. Old "Progressive" historians saw a division of voters at state ratifying conventions between those from interior agrarian regions and those representing coastal and riverine commercial areas. Another economic dichotomy pitted public creditors against private debtors, i.e., holders of state and national securities against the farmers who would be taxed to pay them. A variation of this analysis juxtaposes holders of state paper of all sorts against holders of U.S. securities.

More recent efforts to characterize antifederalists focus on ideological factors such as states'-rights opposition to centralization and the promotion of commerce over agriculture. Other historians have seen the differences between federalists and antifederalists as a cultural divide of the worthy against the licentious, and the antiaristocratic localists against a perceived nationalist elite. A much-bruited argument developed among historians as to whether the struggle over the Constitution was a reflection of a division between those who promoted an old-fashioned republicanism of civic virtue against those who promoted a modern liberal individualism.

The old Progressives—including their mid-twentieth-century followers—

reasoned from more or less concrete factors of geography and economics to locate their antifederalists in interior, agrarian regions known to have been inhabited by disproportionate numbers of debtors. This conclusion, however, does not fit the Connecticut distribution of antifederal delegates. The other interpretations rest on analyses of written works: essays published in newspapers and as pamphlets principally, but also private correspondence. Thus one leading scholar has said, "Planter aristocrats, middling politicians, and backcountry farmers were bound together by a tenuous connection provided by the world of print." "Print," he says "provided the glue that held the Anti-Federalist coalition together."[3]

If this were true, there would be no basis for discovering unifying elements among Connecticut antifederalists. There is virtually no body of Connecticut-originated antifederalist writing; nothing in print and only the two manuscripts of Gale and Ledlie discussed above, neither of which was publicly disseminated. But the statement is not true when speaking of Connecticut.

There is little evidence that Connecticut antifederalists, before their vote on January 9, communicated with opponents of the Constitution elsewhere; and there is evidence that antifederal materials were kept out of the state and suppressed by newspaper editors. Thus "print" did not connect them to other antis in other states. Nor is there evidence of any organization throughout the state. Indeed, one close observer wrote a friend that the Connecticut antifederalists' objections were not only "very trifling," but also "very different . . . many will condemn the same articles [of the Constitution] which others with zeal recommend. None of them agree in their objections."[4] Blocs of delegates from neighboring towns sometimes did vote together, however; and why they did is the focus of the analysis that follows.

The traditional dichotomy of agrarian versus commercial towns provides only a very incomplete picture. True, all five cities—the major commercial centers—sent delegates who supported the Constitution. But delegates from four secondary commercial towns voted against ratification, and those from another split. Even more subversive of the old analysis is the fact that most agrarian towns—including some of the most undeveloped and remote ones—sent delegates who voted to ratify. Of forty inland towns, the delegates from twenty-three voted to ratify; four more delegations split. Thus the delegates from overwhelmingly agrarian Litchfield County with no primary commercial town—and only three secondary ones out of twenty-two—voted 75 percent federalist, while those from heavily commercial New Haven County voted only 41 percent federalist, against an average for the state of 77 percent.

Perhaps a more helpful analysis is that which pits democrats and/or localists against antidemocratic nationalists. It is here where a close look at those delegates who have voting records in the General Assembly might be most helpful. But such an examination does not yield an identifiable pattern. Certainly unique regional economic interests are not reflected in any regional voting blocs. In order to discover why individual delegates voted the way they did, it is necessary to study them individually. Though this analysis does not "prove" anything, it is, it seems to me, highly suggestive. It should at least lead us away from broad generalizations based on an aerial view of the forest.

New Haven County

We can start with New Haven County, locus of the state's major port and seven secondary commercial centers out of its thirteen towns—Connecticut's most commercial county. There is no reason why delegates, for instance, from Milford and Guilford on Long Island Sound should have voted on opposite sides. Yet thirteen of New Haven County's twenty-two delegates (59 percent) voted to reject the new Constitution. Why?

New Haven County was the apparent cockpit of antifederal activity. The delegates from eight of its thirteen towns voted against ratification. Four of these towns were those recently separated from New Haven in the city incorporation movement, and one, Cheshire, had just been set off from Wallingford. The others, Durham, Guilford, Branford, and Wallingford, were all old, first-generation towns. All of them were agricultural, with appropriate levels of artisanal activity. But Branford and Guilford were port towns with significant coastal and West Indian trade, secondary commercial centers; and East Haven, liberated from New Haven in 1785, was potentially such. The populations of the eight antifederal towns in 1790 ranged from East Haven's 1,025 to Guilford's 3,460, a range that would include eighty-four of Connecticut's ninety-nine towns. They were not in any distinctive way different from any other collection of eight towns in Connecticut aside from the five cities at one edge of the economic spectrum and the remote agrarian towns in the northwest corner at the other edge.

The fulcrum of New Haven County antifederalism was James Wadsworth of Durham. His recalcitrance was anticipated. Just days after the Durham town meeting, which he moderated, had voted forty-seven to four to oppose ratification, Oliver Wolcott, Sr., wrote his son that Wadsworth "certainly will not be employed in his office of comptroller nor in any other that has any resemblance to it later than next May."[5] But friends and followers continued to support Wadsworth. Until January 1788, when his political career crashed on the rocks of ratification, James Wadsworth's life exemplified almost perfectly the career trajectory of Connecticut men born to the ruling circle.

One of four college men among the forty antifederalists, Wadsworth graduated from Yale at age eighteen in 1748. His grandfather, a founder of Durham, was a deputy and councilor in the General Assembly from 1710 to 1751. In 1738 Wadsworth's father became a deputy. Both father and grand-father served as justices of the peace, sometimes simultaneously, thus monopolizing justice in Durham. At other times James and his father were the only j.p.s in town. They also served as judges of various courts. Wadsworth's grandfather was the town clerk from 1707 to 1756, when the young man took over the job that he then held for thirty years. Thus the two family members held the position for seventy-nine consecutive years—not an extraordinary feat in eighteenth-century Connecticut. For two sessions, in 1759 and 1769, both father and son represented Durham in the lower house. James was appointed to the Council along with Erastus Wolcott in 1785, when four councilors resigned in order to keep their seats on the superior court. Wadsworth was continued in that office by vote of the freemen the next year. He was elected to Congress each year, 1783 to 1786, and actually served in 1784. Of the twenty men to go to Congress from Connecticut, sixteen of whom served in the convention, he was the only one to vote against the Constitution.[6]

A man who knew Wadsworth well described him about ten years after the General's political Waterloo as "very dignified but very courteous." He could be seen on his Narragansett pacer, "with his large, erect military figure, with his broad brimmed hat, with his Olympian locks" returning with dignity the bows of the boys in the school yard. The town library was kept in his house, and he encouraged the schoolchildren to read certain of books there.[7] Wadsworth's wife bore him two daughters, both of whom died in infancy. The fact that he had no heir and thus no political legacy to protect and pass on might help explain Wadsworth's politically destructive behavior in 1787 and 1788 in a society where family connection were central to political promotion.

Wadsworth's militia service was the frame on which he built his political career. His grandfather was a militia colonel, and Wadsworth's first militia appointment as an ensign came in 1752, when he was only twenty-two years old, family connection as helpful in the militia as in civil politics. After service as a captain during the French and Indian War, Wadsworth was appointed major in 1772 and colonel in October 1774. In December 1776 he was made a brigadier general, and six months later he became the junior major general—next to the top position. He resigned in May 1779 and Oliver

Wolcott was appointed to his place.[8] He commanded a tour at New York in 1776, where his brigade took part in the general retreat at Kip's Bay. He was then stationed at Harlem Heights, but otherwise does not appear to have served outside the state during the war. The retreat from Kip's Bay was general, but Wadsworth was accused in Connecticut newspapers of having contributed to the defeat there because of an alleged delay in carrying out Washington's orders. A similar charge of delinquency and cowardice was made against Wadsworth at the time of the British raid on Danbury, where he "spar'd the foes' lives, and gladly screen'd his own." Later, he suffered insults from Continental officers, and, in 1780 was embroiled in a public shouting match with officers who had bivouacked troops and foraged horses on the Durham town green opposite his house.[9] These unpleasant relations with Continental units might explain Wadsworth's hard-line antinational stance. Indeed, as we shall see, officers whose service was limited to militia duty constitute a core antifederalist cadre.

Wadsworth owned a small farm of about twenty-five acres that he had inherited and managed as a gentleman farmer. But he, like the other local leaders, was much involved in public business and derived the bulk of his income from state and local officeholding and public administration assignments that were compensated on a per diem basis. He lived in a modest family home built by his grandfather that still stands on the Durham green near the Congregational church. In 1791 he ranked forty-ninth out of 230 taxpayers. But he had £420 out at interest—which was not taxed—over ten times as much as the next nearest.[10] The man was an old-line protocapitalist, distinctly not an agrarian reformer.

In 1785 James Wadsworth was very close to the pinnacle of the political mountain. He had been second-in-command of the state militia and now was a justice of the peace, and county court judge; recently speaker of the lower house, he had just been elected to the Council. He was among the three or four principal leaders of the antinationalist faction. In 1785 the Assembly, briefly dominated by localists, appointed him to the new position of comptroller. The position had been established as a result of the fiscal chaos left by the treasurer, John Lawrence, who had not reported to the Assembly in years and who now, mired in fraud and forgetfulness, fled a financial fiasco with a timely resignation. The comptrollership was a job of great responsibility and very considerable drudgery; it paid £150 per annum.[11]

Wadsworth was a power in the state and could expect, if he lived another ten or fifteen years (which he did), to have a good chance at the gubernatorial seat. Instead, he threw away his political career and much of his income along with it by staying true to his convictions and constituents, or perhaps imprisoned by some self-destructive psychological imperative.

With rare exceptions Wadsworth was elected a deputy from Durham beginning in 1759 at the unusually young age of twenty-nine, explained of course by family connection, when his colleague was his father. He was elected Speaker in 1785, but then succeeded to the Council. After twenty-five years of service in the House, Wadsworth bade farewell in a short statement he read to his fellow deputies. It is a bundle of the usual bromides, but fateful events would show that for Wadsworth the phrases were not mere boilerplate. He considered his elevation to the Council "a call of Providence" to "exert myself to the utmost of my abilities to promote and protect the liberties and privileges of the state." This was a pledge he would keep even unto his political death. In the meantime, he begged the Deputies to exercise wisdom and patriotism to "secure the rights, perpetuate the liberties, and promote and increase the true interest, real happiness, peace and prosperity of the people of Connecticut." The members of the House complimented him on his "assiduity, probity, and ability . . . [and] rigid impartality."[12]

Wadsworth owed his elevation to the Council to his support among the agrarian and antifederal freemen. Wadsworth's antinationalism was well known. His elevation to the Council was fought by a majority of the councilors, but insisted upon by the brief localist majority in the House. Alone among the antinational leaders, he maintained his loyalty to that faction until his political ruin. His position in the Council was always tenuous, however, never rising above twelfth, last among the elected Assistants. He held that spot only from May 1786 to May 1788, the first elections after the ratifying convention.[13] Wadsworth's antinationalism and especially his opposition to the 5 percent impost made him a lightning rod for the nationalists, in particular the Continental officers. Four of those—all of whom were eligible to receive the commuted pensions—pilloried him in their collectively written *Anarchiad*. The authors have Wadsworth, whom they call Wronghead, praying to the Devil for assistance, in his "pop'lar schemes," "democratic dreams."

> Fair discord as a godess I revere . . .
> *Cant pretense* of *liberty* . . . gained me all the posts I hold,
> With numerous salaries heap'd my chest with gold
> And fed my hopes that fed'ral ties no more
> Shall bind the nations of the western shore;
> That local schemes shall lift their narrow scale,
> And our own statesmen through the land prevail; . . .

It was Wadsworth's aim, his literary tormenters claimed,

> From federal ties to guard the rights of man;
> At power's deep root to lay the patriot ax,
> Oppose the impost and prevent the tax;
> Bid depreciation pay the public debt,
> And teach the noblest art, the art to cheat; . . .[14]

There was more of this attack published in the winter of 1787, before the call for the Philadelphia convention. Wadsworth's antifederalism was well known.

Wadsworth's antinationalism was, perhaps, stimulated by his resentment against Continental officers. His leadership at Kip's Bay had been less than glorious at best, and cowardly at worst. Continental officers were not his friends. He chaired the committee that wrote the Durham resolutions against the commutation—a bitter document accusing the Congress of acting dishonestly, unconstitutionally, and under cover of secrecy.[15]

In the face of the closing ranks of the federalist commanders, Wadsworth led the opposition to the Constitution in the convention, voted against it, and kept his followers in his camp. It was, indeed, his following that constituted the principal antifederal bloc. This following is identifiable because it was geographically based and cohesive. It consisted of the delegates from eight towns in New Haven County, mostly eastern satellites of the port city.

Though militia relationships were not necessarily determinative of political connections, there can be no doubt that neighborly and family alliances were strengthened when supported by companionable military service. When, in December 1776, James Wadsworth was appointed general of the 2nd Brigade, which encompassed New Haven County, two of his four colonels were Andrew Ward and Street Hall of neighboring Guilford and Wallingford, both delegates to the ratifying convention.[16] Both these men supported Wadsworth in voting against the Constitution.

Andrew Ward, a descendant of one of Connecticut's founding families, represented Guilford, a secondary commercial town on Long Island Sound. He owned a spinning mill, two hundred acres of farmland, some silver plate, $400 in Continental notes, and other money out at loan. He lived a life that, if not exactly baronial, was high gentry. Ward held may local offices and represented his town in the General Assembly about thirty times, the most prominent figure in local politics for many years. He served with Wadsworth as fellow captains at Crown Point in 1759 and trailed along in Wadsworth's militia wake, finally rising to his mentor's brigadiership when Wadsworth was appointed major general in 1777. He converted to Anglicanism in 1770.[17]

Here is a federalist profile if there ever was one; but he voted against the Constitution.

Another of Wadsworth's antifederal colonels was Street Hall of Wallingford. Hall descended on both paternal and maternal sides from original settlers of Wallingford and thus had an easy climb up the local civil and militia ladder. He owned a farm of 120 acres and ranked in the top 8 percent of taxpayers. Hall served as an officer in the French and Indian War and made his way through the militia officer ranks to become, as we have seen, a regimental colonel serving under Wadsworth in New York. When his regiment was placed under Continental command in 1776 and he was reduced to lieutenant colonel, he resigned. His wife was first cousin to Andrew Ward.[18]

Another Seventh Regiment colonel to join the antifederal forces was John Eliot, son of the famed minister and agronomist, Jared Eliot. John Eliot, Ward's Guilford colleague, owned an inherited farm and was fourth on a tax list of 432. He served in many local offices and often as a deputy in the Assembly. Eliot resigned his lieutenant colonelcy in 1775 along with his commanding officer, his brother Aaron. Aaron was replaced by Andrew Ward; Eliot by his brother-in-law, William Worthington. The Eliots were conservative, Old Light, cool revolutionaries. Their sister was married to the leading antifederal polemicist, Benjamin Gale. John Eliot was also related by marriage to Andrew Ward and Street Hall.[19]

Neighboring Guilford to the west is Branford, which sent Timothy Hoadley and William Gould to the convention. Hoadley served as an ensign in Wadsworth's regiment, but did not rise farther. He was a surveyor and well-to-do farmer addressed as squire. He was first cousin of Street Hall and of Andrew Ward's wife. He was also Ward's brother-in-law. Hoadley's Guilford colleague, William Gould, was a physician and a frequent deputy with service extending from 1762 to 1799. He made his way up the militia ladder in the Second Regiment of James Wadsworth's brigade, appointed lieutenant colonel in 1773, but resigning in 1775 at the age of forty-eight. Gould and Hoadley were cousins.[21]

Adjoining Branford is North Haven, a suburb cut off of New Haven in 1784. Its lone delegate was Daniel Basset. He ranked sixty-first out of 226 taxpayers in this small town "showing the marks of poverty." Basset was a leader in the movement to separate from New Haven and a deputy to the General Assembly. He served as an ensign in the Second Regiment under Gould. He was first cousin to Street Hall.[22]

Another newly separated suburb of New Haven, East Haven, sent Samuel Davenport, a high officeholder in town since its establishment in 1785. East

Haven lay on New Haven harbor, with commercial potential, but its very small area slowed the development it hoped to see. Two years after its separate incorporation it was in the bottom 10 percent of towns on the tax list. Davenport was cousin to Street Hall and connected to Hall by marriage as well.[23]

Cheshire presents an interesting test of the thesis that New Haven County delegates who voted against ratifying the Constitution were influenced by the family-militia web. David Brooks was an eccentric. A Yale graduate who briefly served as a minister in various pulpits, he settled down as a farmer and prominent citizen. He served as a private in the Second Regiment when it went to Peekskill under James Wadsworth in 1777. He voted no.[24]

Brooks' colleague was Samuel Beach, also a Yale graduate. He did not serve in the military during the Revolution but may have served during the French and Indian War. He had been married to a Wallingford Hall, but she died in 1769, thus severing his relationship with the antifederal family. He remarried that same year. His uncle was the enthusiastic Loyalist Anglican minister John Beach; a first cousin was married to William Samuel Johnson. Beach, a lawyer, was closely related to the aye-voting Holbrooks of Derby. He was the only delegate from this bloc of towns not connected to the no voters; and the only one who was connected to the aye voters west of New Haven, and the only one to vote to ratify.[25]

To summarize: The antifederalist delegates from the towns of eastern New Haven County were all related by either blood or marriage. Thus Andrew Ward was a first cousin of Street Hall's wife, and connected by marriage to his fellow Guilford delegate John Eliot, to William Gould of Branford, and probably Daniel Hall of Durham. Samuel Davenport of East Haven was married to a Street, a cousin of Street Hall. Timothy Hoadley of Branford was a first cousin of both Andrew Ward and Street Hall; Hall and Daniel Basset were first cousins. The lone federalist was the only delegate not part of this family web.

Thus at least eight of James Wadsworth's New Haven County followers were tangled in a web of family and militia connections. As these family relationships helped members climb the militia ladder, so they also tied them together in a knot of mutual support in this unpopular political cause.

Conversely, many of the turncoat localists who finally voted in favor of the Constitution constituted their own family network. Joseph Hopkins, a leading localist who nevertheless voted to ratify, was connected to the federalist Holbrook cousins of Derby, his fellow Waterbury delegate John Welton, and Samuel Beach of Cheshire, all of whom joined him in approving the Constitution. Hopkins and his relations do not appear to be connected to members of the antifederal Ward-Hall network. As we have seen, William Williams and Erastus Wolcott, similarly, were restrained securely at the crucial moment by their own family webs.

Militia Connections

As must be clear by now, family relationships often determined political success in eighteenth-century Connecticut. Such connections apparently also helped one's militia career, as well. Commissions in the militia depended on the ability to recruit enlisted men. An obvious pool would be family members, and, indeed, multiple family names are commonly found in company rolls. Thus fathers, uncles, brothers, and cousins were in positions to push their relations up the militia ladder. The close association is no coincidence. The militia was very political; indeed it may have more often acted as a political organization than as a military one.[26] Many of the antifederalists had served in close peer and hierarchical relationships in the militia dating back to the French and Indian War.

Forty men voted against ratification: Thirteen had no reported military service, though some of them must have served their requisite time in the peacetime militia; eight served in the French and Indian War or other pre-1775 actions; sixteen served in the Revolution; three served in the Connecticut Line while operating in association with Continental units. Six or seven never became officers, mostly men who served as privates or non-commissioned officers in the French and Indian War and were overage by 1775. No one who would have been eligible for commuted payments voted against ratification. With a single exception, all the Continental officers and soldiers at the convention voted to ratify, including every delegate eligible to receive commuted payments. Beyond this, among the federalists there is no pattern: Ratifyers included many militia officers and soldiers and many men who never served under arms in any war.[27]

Indeed it appears that the family connections were further cemented by service in James Wadsworth's New Haven County militia: the Seventh Regiment of the Second Brigade, a brigade that consisted of the five regiments roughly encompassing New Haven County and Middletown. From the establishment of the Seventh Brigade in 1776 to at least the end of the eighteenth century, the general officers always came from the three contiguous towns east and north of New Haven—Middletown, Durham, and Guilford. Most surprising is the fact that during the period under study no regimental or brigade commander came from the most populous town, New Haven,

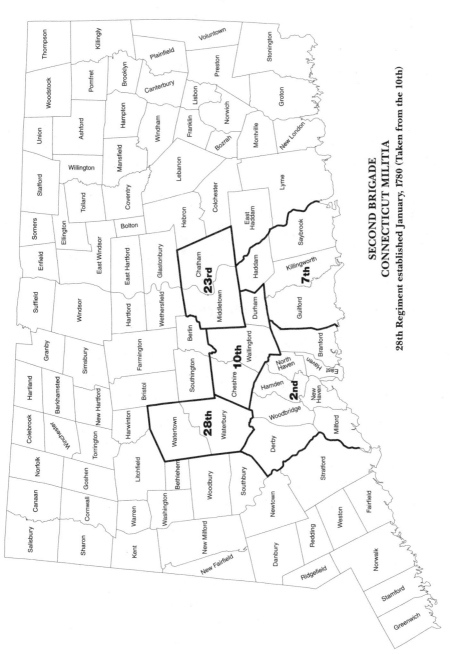

SECOND BRIGADE
CONNECTICUT MILITIA

28th Regiment established January, 1780 (Taken from the 10th)

4. Second Brigade Connecticut Militia.

even though the county's major political figures of the day lived there. Apparently, there was a militia-based political ladder that paralleled that of civil office.

Career militia officers, led by James Wadsworth, formed the antifederal core in the ratifying convention. Street Hall, John Eliot, and Andrew Ward all rose to the ranks of colonel or general in the Seventh Regiment of James Wadsworth's brigade; Wadsworth himself made his career for the most part in the neighboring Tenth Regiment. And though many prominent New Haven County politicians—both federal and antifederal—served as officers in the Second Regiment—also in Wadsworth's brigade—which included the city of New Haven and its environs, none of them rose above the rank of captain after 1775.

Wadsworth's militia connections could reach well beyond New Haven County, too. To take another case in point, there is no apparent reason why Hebron, a centrally located town about sixteen miles east of Hartford, should send two antifederal delegates to the convention, but it did. One of them was Elihu Marvin, a physician and one of four Yale graduates to vote against the Constitution. He was Hartford County Surveyor, and a frequent justice of the peace and deputy. Marvin had large business interests in Norwich, but in 1786 he was bankrupt and appealed to the General Assembly for protection from his creditors, a deal that would have to be approved by the Comptroller, James Wadsworth.

Marvin had begun a promising militia career as a twenty-five-year-old lieutenant, but resigned in a huff in 1777, when he was "superseded or neglected after serving through the winter at Valley Forge." In 1779 Marvin went as a volunteer aide to James Wadsworth during the New London alarm. Later, Wadsworth petitioned the Assembly for his own compensation for that tour and wrung an increase for Marvin, too. Marvin voted with Wadsworth's New Haven County antis at the convention. Marvin's antifederal colleague was Daniel Ingham, a militia captain and frequent local officeholder, many times a deputy through the years 1773–92. He was a substantial farmer of little formal education, but reputed to be a good public speaker. Hebron was one of those towns that elected deputies from its parishes; Ingham represented Gilead parish. His mother was a Guilford Stone, and he had many cousins in that town. Perhaps more significantly, he was married to a Phelps.[28]

When militia connections were linked to family connections they could have a very long reach indeed. Such certainly was the case of Noah Phelps of Simsbury. Phelps was a militia captain in the Ticonderoga expedition, and in 1776, at the age of thirty-six, was appointed captain to serve under the Branford antifederalist Andrew Ward in a regiment raised for the Continental service. Phelps was a career militia officer who ended his service as a major general in 1796. He was a prominent figure in Simsbury, many times a deputy, a probate judge, and a frequent moderator at town meetings. Indeed, he moderated the meeting at which anticommutation resolutions were passed. He was a member of the localist bloc in the General Assembly.[29]

More to the point, Phelps' sister was married to Daniel Humphrey. Daniel Humphrey, a lawyer and often a deputy, was a frequent officeholder in Simsbury, referred to as squire. Humphrey served as a lieutenant in Phelps' company, and as a captain when Phelps was made colonel. He voted with the localist bloc in the Assembly, and in December 1787 Hugh Ledlie reported Humphrey had declared "that if the new Constitution take place, he would not value all his estate worth three coppers in clover."[30] Phelps and Humphrey made two of the six antifederal votes among Hartford County's twenty-six delegates. There is no generalized economic, regional, or ideological reason why Phelps and Humphrey should join the antifederalists. Militia connections might provide an explanation, however. The militia reach can then be extended through close family connections. The Humphrey family carries that connection into Norfolk.

Norfolk, on the Massachusetts border in Shays country, might be expected to send antifederal delegates to the convention. And it did. But not because of its location; neighboring towns voted to ratify, as did, indeed, New Marlborough just over the Massachusetts line. And so did Canaan just to the west. Canaan and Norfolk were very similar. They shared the same institutional and geographic history. Why did their delegates vote on opposite sides of the issue?

Norfolk's two delegates were Daniel Humphrey's brothers, Asabel and Hosea, ten and twenty years younger than Daniel. Hosea, only thirty-one in 1788, had been a saddlemaker early in life and now was a physician. He was in the General Assembly in May 1787, where he spoke against sending delegates to the Philadelphia convention. He had lived in Providence for a time and he applauded Rhode Island's negative response to the call for delegates. That he could be elected a deputy at the age of twenty-nine or thirty attests to the dominance of his family in this town of about 1,300 people. He left Norfolk soon after 1788.[31] He was otherwise undistinguished, and one can only surmise that he and his brother, Asabel, were actually surrogates for Daniel. Asabel was a deputy from Norfolk in the late 1770s and again in 1786 through May 1788, but not again until 1792 though frequently after that. He, like Daniel, was a lawyer, and a localist in the Assembly. Like Hosea, he was no doubt fully influenced by his older brother. The Norfolk meeting that elected them decided not to instruct.[32]

Indeed, the clue to Norfolk politics in this period is that the town was dominated by immigrants from Simsbury, which was, as we have seen, a militantly antifederal town. A half-dozen leaders could shape town politics, and there were that many Humphreys there alone, along with many other Simsbury immigrants. The influence of Daniel Humphrey of Simsbury, a day's journey to the east, explains Norfolk's delegates' votes.

The Massachusetts Border Towns

If family and militia connections provide the cement of antifederal cohesiveness in New Haven County, local history and politics, rather than either ideology or economic interest, best explain the votes of the delegates from the towns along the Massachusetts border. Though in a number of instances the reach of Wadsworth's long militia arm grasped antifederal votes in this remote region, local political factors seem to have been most influential. This is an area where, using the traditional commercial/agrarian measures, we would expect an overwhelming antifederal sentiment. But half the towns in this Shays-like countryside sent federal delegates to whom our attention will turn later. Let's look first at the thirteen towns on the Massachusetts border. One did not send a delegate. Among the six antifederal towns on the border were five that had changed jurisdictions, joining Connecticut in 1749 after a decades-long bitter controversy. They were consistent and unanimous in their antinational stance. Four were part of the Springfield orbit and no doubt shared some of the antigovernment attitudes of the Shaysites. Somers, Enfield, Suffield, and part of Granby were constituted from lands disputed by Connecticut and Massachusetts. A bit farther east, Woodstock shared the same history.

All these towns had been settled largely by Massachusetts people. In the 1740s the towns petitioned to be attached to Connecticut and, in 1749, after considerable acrimonious backing and filling, were so joined. Jurisdiction in Woodstock remained controversial till the opening of the Revolution, with sections along the border not resolved till 1793 when Massachusetts reclaimed three thousand Woodstock acres. A small area lapping the boundary in Suffield and Enfield in Connecticut and Southwick in Massachusetts continued in dispute into the nineteenth century. These towns' representatives to the General Assembly through the 1780s were consistently localist.[34] That this localist tendency is related to these towns' history of intercolonial controversy is evinced by the fact that every delegate from every neighboring and intervening town that did not share that history voted to ratify.

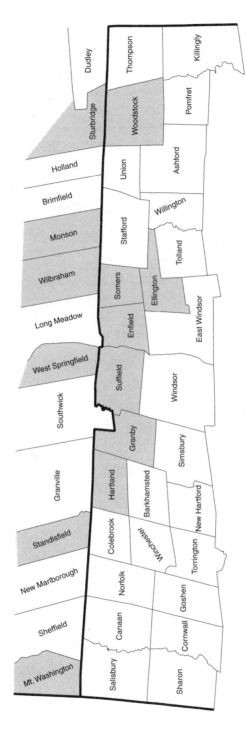

5. The vote on ratification in the towns on the Massachusetts-Connecticut border (antifederal towns on the border are shaded).

Perhaps the long effort to attach themselves to Connecticut had brought into being a network or coalition of families and leaders that had long been accustomed to coordinating political efforts. In Woodstock, at least, there were many men still active who could remember the days of 1749. Perhaps they feared that Massachusetts would take advantage of the new Supreme Court's authority to hear controversies between the states or that there might be some retroactivity implied in Article IV, Section 3′ prohibition of state partitions.

Two other border towns joined the five former Massachusetts towns. Both were small, remote outposts of larger towns, divided off in 1786. Each was limited to a single delegate. Ellington voters no doubt still harbored resentments against their former mother. The citizens' perspective was marked by extreme localism: They once characterized the East Windsor town fathers five to eight miles away as "Strangers to Our Circumstances." Similarly, Granby citizens complained in 1786 that traveling six or seven miles to Simsbury for town meetings "deprived many . . . from having a voice in Electing their Town Officers or the Civil Rulers of the State." Both delegates voted as the conventional wisdom would predict—against ratification. Ebenezer Marsh, Ellington's lone delegate, was rewarded with election to selectman three months later.[35]

The five former Massachusetts towns, Somers, Suffield, Enfield, Granby, and Woodstock, and the recently liberated Ellington supplied ten of the forty votes against the Constitution.

Litchfield County: The Antifederalists

Litchfield County, twenty-two towns in the northwest region of the state—rural, agrarian, remote from waterside commercial centers—was in Daniel Shays' backyard. Windham County, where Woodstock was, together with Litchfield County had 28 percent of the state's population but saw more land seizures for taxes than all the rest of Connecticut.[36] On the basis of conventional ideological or economic analysis, Litchfield County towns would be expected to elect antifederal delegates. But of the county's twenty-two towns only five went against the Constitution; of thirty-six delegates, twenty-six voted in favor. Colebrook, a presumed antifederal town, chose to send no delegate at all. There is no discernable voting pattern in Litchfield County explicable in geographic, economic, or debtor/creditor terms. Nor is there any information that hints at a division on antiaristocratic or localist/nationalist grounds.

Sharon, a paper money town with a wisp of Shaysism, and Barkhamsted, the most primitive town in Connecticut, both sent known antifederalists to the convention. They voted no, fulfilling the old economics-based thesis.

Cornwall, in the northwest corner of Connecticut near New York and Massachusetts, is a town that exhibits the agrarian remoteness that is supposed to breed antifederalism. The town sent two delegates to the ratifying convention. Both attended; one voted nay, one failed to vote. Why did they act as they did? Local politics tells us. Indeed, Cornwall exemplifies so well the impact of local politics that a detailed picture of the scene there will be illuminating.

A mixture of militia and church politics seems to have influenced the vote on ratification in Cornwall. The town bordered antifederalist Sharon in Shays country and was sharply divided over local issues and contending local leaders. Matthew Patterson, forty-three in 1788, was a prominent local officeholder who had moved with his parents to Cornwall from Stratford in 1762. He was a strong localist deputy in the General Assembly, where he served ten sessions between 1781 and 1787, but not again after the convention. He is the only antifederalist voter who served in the Continental forces; but he is the exception that proves the rule. He saw only brief duty as a lieutenant at Ticonderoga and in Canada, where he was taken prisoner in 1776, and quickly paroled, ending his military career. He would not have been eligible for the commuted payments. Patterson served so briefly that he did not internalize the "continental" perspective that was otherwise universal among Continental officers at the ratifying convention. Significantly, at Crown Point and other engagements during the French and Indian War, Patterson was a fellow company commander of James Wadsworth in the Second Regiment. Patterson's earlier militia career overweighed his very brief Continental service.[37]

Patterson's colleague was Edward Rogers, who at age twenty-five in 1760, moved with his parents to Cornwall with a large contingent from Branford— part of Wadsworth's antifederal bailiwick. Rogers was a farmer, but he also owned a potash mill and became a merchant of considerable wealth and local standing. He was a longtime antinationalist and was sent by the Cornwall town meeting to the Middletown convention in 1783. While still a resident of Branford, Rogers served in the French and Indian War as an ensign under James Wadsworth at Crown Point, Lake George, and other engagements. Later he served as lieutenant under Patterson. Rogers was a member of the Cornwall Committee of Correspondence and served as a captain under Wadsworth at the Battle of Long Island and after the retreat from Westchester County did no more military service. He was then forty-one.[38] Militia service, especially the connection to James Wadsworth, might have tied Patterson and Rogers together in the antifederal camp. But, in fact, militia politics helped drive them apart. And there is much more in the way of local politics that helps explain their split.

Cornwall exhibited during the 1780s a local history that culminated in one of the most bizarre political episodes of the decade. In the mid-1770s one of two rival political leaders, John Sedgwick, was promoted to captain in the militia ahead of Edward Rogers, who ranked him. Rogers blamed Sedgwick's brother-in-law, the minister Hezekiah Gold, for pushing Sedgwick's advancement: By 1783 Sedgwick was a lieutenant colonel; Rogers never got past captain. This personal animosity lay behind a long-term opposition to the minister that culminated in 1780 with Rogers leading a majority of the townsfolk—but not a majority of the church members—to establish a second Congregational church. Rogers' new church was based ostensibly on the strict principles of the revivalists of the 1740s, but according to both nineteenth-century historians of the event, the basis of the schism was "really . . . personal."[39] The embroilment determined the course of local politics through the 1780s, including the unique election of the town's two ministers to the General Assembly in September 1787.[40]

In November 1787 the town meeting rejected Sedgwick's federalist leadership and chose antifederalists Matthew Patterson and Edward Rogers to go to the ratifying convention.[41] Patterson voted against. But Rogers had a problem. As a wealthy merchant his economic interest lay on the side of ratification. But his local political support lay with the antifederalists, opposed to Sedgwick, the local federal leader. Rogers was reported absent for the vote. Perhaps in the end he couldn't bring himself to vote against a constitution that would support the stability that as a merchant he would so desire. But neither could he, a localist leader and enemy of the Sedgwicks and a member of the old Wadsworth militia network, vote in favor.

Divided delegations offer clear examples of the influence of local and family connections on the way men voted at the ratifying convention. We have already described the situation in William Williams' Lebanon and as well in Cheshire in New Haven County. A trio of undeveloped, interior, agrarian towns allow some fairly concrete analysis. In addition to Cornwall, three other Litchfield County towns sent two-man delegations that split.

Is it a coincidence that the three towns are neighbors? Was there an agreement among them to neutralize their votes as a matter of politics or individual political cover? There is no way to know; but it is an odd coincidence, since only two other delegations from Connecticut's ninety-nine towns divided.

Torrington was a town of a little over a thousand people and a grand list seventy-fourth out of the eighty-five towns that reported their lists in 1788. It was settled late, but was growing fast. Located in the northwestern part of the state, its center was about fifteen miles from the Massachusetts line. In 1783 the town meeting had been the spearhead of the statewide anticommutation movement. Perhaps more important, in the mid-1780s the town was in an uproar over a split in the church that was caused partly by traditional differences over who should be baptized, but even more by disagreement about the new minister—a mulatto named Lemuel Haynes.[42]

One delegate was Epaphras Sheldon. Sheldon had come to Torrington from Windsor in 1769 at the age of forty-three. He took up a prosperous farm, established a tannery, a distillery, and opened a tavern, "the head quarters for most doings of the town." He quickly became a leading figure, serving often as a justice of the peace and a deputy to the General Assembly. His military career was launched as a lieutenant and then major under high nationalist Oliver Wolcott when the latter was appointed colonel of the Seventeenth Regiment in 1774 and made his former neighbor an aide. Three years later, Sheldon succeeded Wolcott as colonel and in 1784 Sheldon, a career militia officer, followed Wolcott as brigadier general of the Sixth Brigade.[43]

In 1788 Sheldon was in debt, sharing the hard times of his agrarian constituents. "Money is hard to be Got & our Grain Much Damaged by ye Buggs," he wrote his principal creditor. His militia career, debtor status, agrarian constituency, and interior residency should, according to the old interest-based orthodoxy, make him a committed antinationalist. He helped write Torrington's anticommutation resolutions and went as a delegate to the Middletown convention. At the very moment of the ratifying convention he was begging for a stay from his principal creditor. Significantly, his militia mentor was the nationalist Oliver Wolcott, now sitting as a delegate from neighboring Litchfield; and his principal creditor was high nationalist Jeremiah Wadsworth (not James), sitting as a delegate from Hartford. Their eyes were on him.[44]

The other delegate was Eliphalet Enos, a farmer "of considerable reputation." Enos was elected to the General Assembly in alternate sessions—that is, once a year—for ten years beginning in 1782. He was otherwise undistinguished but ultimately became a Baptist and a leading Litchfield County Jeffersonian. He never served in a major local office or as a militia officer; indeed, he appears never to have served in the military at all. Enos' wife was the niece of Samuel Whiting, the Wallingford antifederalist, and Enos was a brother-in-law of Mercy Gillet, the sister of the Sharon antifederalist. Enos' father-in-law was the deacon of Cornwall's First Church and leader of the strict pro-Haynes faction.[45]

Enos' colleague, Epaphras Sheldon, was also a member of the riven First Church, apparently of the minority faction opposing the strict tenets of Enos' father-in-law and the ordination of Lemuel Haynes. Sheldon and Enos split also on an effort, led by Enos' father-in-law, to move the meetinghouse away from the southwest corner of town, the early center of population and the location of Sheldon's tavern. The conflict over the meetinghouse location, its nineteenth-century chronicler tells us, was "a mighty struggle of moral elements, not quite as thoroughly modified by grace as could have been desired." When the new location, next to a rival tavern on the green, won out, Sheldon lost the patronage of militia training days, Sabbath diners, and even his town clerkship of sixteen years past. Lemuel Haynes gave his first sermon in the rival tavern.[46] Thus Sheldon's military career gave him a personal tie to a man who became a high nationalist; he was a pressed debtor of another high nationalist; and he was a rival tavern owner and church schismatic of the leading localist. Perhaps he would have voted for the Constitution if none of these personal and local matters had existed; but he had plenty of personal and local reasons to vote as he did.

Like its neighbor Torrington, Harwinton also split. This was a poor town of about 1,200 inhabitants, in the bottom fourteen on the state's grand list, and unable to pay its taxes in full. One delegate was Mark Prindle, an Episcopalian and Loyalist early in the war who never served under arms. He was often a selectman and after the war served many times as a deputy and as a justice well into the 1790s. This Loyalist Episcopalian voted to ratify the Constitution.[47]

The antifederal delegate from Harwinton was Abner Wilson, who was present as a lieutenant at James Wadsworth's disastrous flight at Kip's Bay. After the war he rose to lieutenant colonel in a different regiment, but resigned in 1788, militia advancement presumably foreclosed by his vote against the Constitution. Wilson was, like Prindle, a frequent deputy, selectman, and justice of the peace. He was deacon in the Congregational society in a town with no settled minister just when Prindle was organizing the Episcopal church and depriving the Congregationalists of much of their tax base.[48] Local religious divisions with heavy political overtones relating to wartime loyalism no doubt played a significant part in splitting the town's vote.

The third of the three contiguous Litchfield County towns to split its vote was New Hartford. The federalist delegate was Aaron Austin. Austin was a local officeholder, twenty-seven times a deputy in the General Assembly, and a lieutenant colonel in the militia, serving under Charles Burrall, Canaan's federalist delegate. His father, also a high militia officer, was a longtime officeholder in neighboring Torrington. Austin was a conservative who would ultimately rise to the upper house and live long enough to serve in the state constitutional convention of 1818. In 1788 he was forty-three years old. The antifederalist delegate was an obscure merchant named Thomas Goodman. The only statewide position he ever held was as a civilian commissary to the army in 1780. He is one of only two nay voters I have been able to identify as merchants.[49]

Most of the other Litchfield County towns voted solidly federal. Canaan, Goshen, Hartland, Kent, Salisbury, Warren, and Winchester were remote, agrarian towns. The list includes the three poorest towns in Connecticut. Yet all their delegates voted to ratify. Why? The most compelling reasons, no doubt, resulted from their rational analysis of the benefits the new Constitution would bring. But there are also matters of individual biography that help explain their federalism. One was the son of former governor James Fitch; two were Yale graduates; another was related to federalist delegate Wait Goodrich of Glastonbury; four or five served as militia officers under Charles Burrell, federalist delegate from Canaan; and four were jointly associated in the development of the iron mines in Salisbury.

This discussion of Litchfield County seems necessary because of the predominance of the economic interpretation of the division over ratification in Connecticut. Even if three secondary commercial towns—Litchfield, Woodbury, and New Milford—are cast into the economically determined federalist camp, only nine of thirty delegates from poor, remote, agricultural towns voted against ratification. As noted elsewhere, 75 percent of this agrarian county's delegates supported the new nationalist system. In other words, any way you count it, the exceptions greatly outnumber those conforming to the conventional wisdom. The agrarian-commercial class and geographic thesis set forth first by Owen Libby in 1894 and perpetuated by the old and neo-Progessive historians just doesn't hold—at least not for Litchfield County, which constituted about 20 percent of the state's territory and nearly a quarter of its towns. Too many delegates from archetypically antifederalist constituencies voted for the Constitution.

The point should be clear enough by now that the sinews of antifederalism in Connecticut were built on personal relations and local conditions, not interest or ideology. And there are many similar tales to be told; readers will find some of them in Appendix C.

Conclusions

My effort in this monograph has been twofold: first, to convince readers that a full understanding of the political dynamic of the constitutional convention of 1787 must include attention to the social and economic structures, political context, and attitudes, habits, and needs of each of the states represented at Philadelphia; and second, to suggest that in the context of ratification the grassroots political actor was motivated predominantly by local and personal concerns; only the behavior of a small intellectual elite is driven by ideas and ideologies. Not all politics is personal and local, but much of it is—and was; and that which was personal was always the most potent.

Historians accept the fact that there were many "original intentions" among the fifty-five men sitting in Independence Hall and the 1,750 who voted in state ratifying conventions. Phrases, terminology, even whole provisions were shaped by the perspectives and needs of certain states as propounded and pursued by their delegates. Latter-day interpreters of the Constitution have looked for theoretical, philosophical, and ideological meanings in words that found their way into the Constitution without reference to any of those concerns. To insist that historians and jurists include these state perspectives in their analyses of the document vastly complicates their work; but to omit those perspectives misses the dominating motive of many of the delegates all of the time and all of them some of the time. Thus the social and economic context and the politics of each state must be studied separately. A close analysis will show that the objectives and the context from which they sprung were different in each state.

With the possible exceptions of the supernationalist ideologues James Madison, Alexander Hamilton, and James Wilson, the delegates from each state reflected the geographic, economic, and political conditions back home. Every one of them had provincial interests to protect and foster. A most authoritative scholar writes that "the disaffection of Virginia's two nonsigning members can be traced beyond dispute to state and regional considerations."[1] Georgia's vast forests of Indian inhabitants were untenable without a national army; South Carolina's hegemonic planter aristocracy could not maintain its culture if the institution of slavery was not protected; Massachusetts wanted its maritime interests—in commerce and fisheries—secured by a navy greater than a single state could provide and treaties with foreign nations that must involve all the states; New Jersey and Delaware insisted on guarantees for their territorial and political integrity.[2]

Topography and climate were important. Did a state's bounds encompass natural deep-sea harbors, inland waterways, coastal plains, and broad river valleys? Was the rainfall ample and the growing season lengthy? These factors largely determined the economy and demography of each state. And each state's economy and demography—aside from individual personal biography—largely determined the position each state's delegates would take on each of the elements of structure, allocation of authority, and specific powers addressed at the convention.

A vast coastal plain and scattered alluvial deltas combined with heavy rains and a long growing season fostered the tobacco, rice, and sugar economies of some states; and the cultivation of those crops gave rise to the demographics of place and race in the South. Well-positioned and contoured natural harbors gave New York, Boston, and Philadelphia in particular, but also Baltimore, Norfolk, and Charleston, a class of commercial families that, along with the large plantation owners, gave rise in some states to an aristocracy of wealth.[3] Other states became economic tributaries to their commercial neighbors. Some state bounds included vast unsettled tracts of forest promising future wealth, but calling at the moment for large military expenditures to quell Indian residents there. Other states had defined limits with no access to the west; some of these had reached their demographic limits, others soon would. The inhabitants of these demographically and/or spatially confined states feared not only commercial, but political domination as well. "Maryland's leading men possessed a well-developed corporate consciousness by 1776," and "they fought and died and gave generously of their resources to preserve their own form of government, their own sovereignty as an independent state."[4] North Carolina's leaders "evidenced extreme concern over the need to protect the rights of the states and the individuals within them," some "seemed almost paranoid about these issues."[5] And so it went; every state had its own axes to grind at Philadelphia.

Thus every delegate to the Philadelphia convention, regardless of his degree of nationalist aspiration, had to attend *as a threshold concern* to his state's needs and desires. What one close analyst has said about Virginia holds true for all the states: "*all* Virginia politicians were particularists in the sense that their perspectives, hopes, and fears were shaped by calculations and concerns arising from their regional position and the state's historical relationship with other members of the Union." As Gouverneur Morris pointed out at Philadelphia, "The States . . . had many Representatives on the floor. Few . . . were to be deemed Representatives of America."[6]

These statements by eighteenth-century contemporaries and modern scholars provide more than hints that state concerns drove much of the debate at Philadelphia and mandated certain clauses and provisions of the Constitution. The failure to fulfill states' particular requirements would have doomed the adoption of the new system quicker and more completely than a lack of certain principled inclusions like an independent judiciary, reelectability of the executive, or short terms for representatives. The states' delegates at Philadelphia were looking over their shoulders at their constituents' shadows hovering over their deliberations every minute of every day. Gouverneur Morris had to plead with them to "extend their views beyond the present moment of time; beyond the narrow limits of place from which they derive their political origin."[7]

True, there were a few high nationalists like the doctrinaire Madison, who urged his colleagues to cease trying to second guess their constituents and consider only what was "right & necessary in itself for the attainment of a proper government."[8] But the great majority over and over again rejected specific proposals because they believed that their constituents would not adopt the document if local needs were threatened or neglected. Thus C. C. Pinckney "declared it to be his firm opinion that if himself & all his colleagues were to sign the Constitution & use their personal influence, it would be of no avail towards obtaining the assent of their Constituents" if the slave trade was not protected. Elbridge Gerry knew that among his people "great opposition to the plan would spring" if standing armies were not prohibited. On the core issue of representation in the legislature, William Paterson declared that the delegates should hold to the rule of suffrage as practiced under the Articles of Confederation or "we should be charged by our constituents with usurpation. . . . We must follow the people; the people will not follow us." Pierce Butler summed up the constituent-focused sentiment: "We must follow the example of Solon who gave the Athenians not the best Govt. he could devise; but the best they would receive."[9]

For the most part, each delegate heeded his constituents' desires and fulfilled his state's essential needs. New York was the loser, if there was one. That state had to give up fiscal control of not only its own trade, but that of neighboring states as well. Only the political and polemical exertions of Alexander Hamilton—with James Madison's assistance—pulled off ratification there. In all the other states—with the possible exception of North Carolina—the delegates brought home the bacon. But in every state there were some who didn't like the way it was cooked. Objections to the structure of the new government, with is potential for political dominance and its lack of a bill of rights, were heard everywhere.

The first tier of "dual localism," then, sees the delegates to the constitutional convention as advocates for their states' interests, interests that usually overrode their personal hopes for a stronger national government. At the second tier of this "dual localism"—ratification in the states—motivations were even more parochial. Local politics, social and family connections, just downright orneriness, and other individual peculiarities played a part in determining a delegate's vote on ratification. Underlying statements of some rational abstraction like a violation of state sovereignty—often mere rationalizations— lay nonrational impulses that resulted in opposition to the Constitution. In New York "[p]ersonalities rather than principles dominated the political alliances . . . in the 1780's," and the constituents of each faction—federal and antifederal— were too disparate for their closest analyst to categorize.[10] In Pennsylvania, ethnic and religious connections and an ongoing dispute over the structure of the state government underlay the division of federalists and antifederalists. Ratification there was put over by a minority, and in its wake political discourse degenerated into "personal attacks and narrowly partisan polemics."[11] On the surface, ratification in Virginia was brought about by an adherence to republican ideology. But it is not "possible to fully comprehend this theoretical dispute without consideration of the 'local interests' that concerned both sides." Even a universal state perspective among Virginians at their ratifying convention "produced no uniform conclusions. . . . Individuals who *should* have thought alike or *should* have split into opposing camps— made various decisions."[12] The objections to the Constitution by Maryland's antifederalists were "discordant," and "no two objecting individuals . . . concur in making the same exceptions."[13]

These are hints again that underneath the rhetorical and polemical verbalizations of antifederal objections to the Constitution—even more compelling than class or individual economic interests—lay very local, political, family, and personal motivation for individuals' opposition to ratification of the Constitution.

Connecticut was not unique in its relationship to the creation and adoption of the Constitution. But it did have a particular combination of requirements that was different from those of any other state; and the part played by its delegates to the Philadelphia convention in the intersection of the demands of nationalization and the special needs of Connecticut stands as an example of the necessary behavior of almost all the other delegates.

Connecticut's interests could be promoted and protected by enhancing the powers of the central government in certain areas: nationalizing the impost to distribute its benefits among all the states and deprive New York of its control over Connecticut's transatlantic commerce; protecting the state's claim to the Western Reserve; providing for security against neighboring states and foreign nations and from uprisings in neighboring states that might spill over the borders; stabilizing currency, and making interstate and national fiscal arrangements; and establishing a thirteen-state free-trade zone. And the new government had to be strong enough to do all these things, while at the same time prevented from intruding on traditional individual rights and the state's civil and jurisprudential systems.

The Connecticut delegates believed they had accomplished all these things, and so did a great majority of the political, social, and commercial leadership in the state. By January 1788 this traditional oligarchy was able through persuasion and intimidation to rally most Connecticut voters behind the new Constitution. Nevertheless, forty delegates to the state ratifying convention, many of them members of the oligarchy, chose to reject the Constitution. They did so, my research shows, because of individual circumstances having to do with local and personal concerns. There is no evidence of ideological articulation or cohesion among these forty antifederalists. For a hundred and fifty years after the Constitution began its long and illustrious career, historians swept these antifederalists into the dustbin of history. In the case of Connecticut, at least, perhaps they were right to do so.

That the Constitution as drafted in 1787 still stands as a framework for our evolving political system is testimony enough to the genius of its framers. It is the nationalizing elements, of course, that give it its greatness. The manifestations of parochial interest do not glorify the charter. To mention the insistence by states of the Deep South that the slave trade be protected and the expansion of slavery be allowed to continue is enough to demonstrate that. But some of the elements that arose out of local interests helped to make the system work. Maintaining a degree of prerogative in the state governments was important just for practical administrative purposes, for instance. Other elements, like an equality in the Senate and the electoral college, may seem atavistic in the twenty-first century, but no doubt they help demographically small states cohere in a nation where without it they would feel overwhelmed and ultimately alienated.

The supernationalism of Madison would not have worked in 1787. His core requirements—proportional representation in both houses and a national veto of state legislation—would have doomed ratification. The states'-rights members of the convention may have been shortsighted and parochial, but the fruits of their work didn't seem so to most Americans then, or indeed for several generations after. In the meantime, the nation had seventy years to try varied applications of the system before two of them met in a struggle that left the nationalist version victorious.

Appendixes

APPENDIX A

Town Locator

84. Ashford	62. Middletown
29. Barkhamsted	37. Milford
46. Berlin	74. Montville
15. Bethlehem	11. New Fairfield
59. Bolton	31. New Hartford
75. Bozra	38. New Haven
42. Branford	73. New London
47. Bristol	12. New Milford
92. Brooklyn	9. Newtown
24. Canaan	40. North Haven
93. Canterbury	25. Norfolk
63. Chatham	3. Norwalk
44. Cheshire	76. Norwich
15. Colchester	94. Plainfield
26. Colebrook	89. Pomfret
21. Cornwall	96. Preston
81. Coventry	8. Redding
10. Danbury	7. Ridgefield
35. Derby	23. Salisbury
68. Durham	71. Saybrook
66. East Haddam	20. Sharon
58. East Hartford	49. Simsbury
41. East Haven	53. Somers
55. East Windsor	13. Southbury
56. Ellington	45. Southington
52. Enfield	85. Stafford
4. Fairfield	2. Stamford
48. Farmington	6. Stratford
77. Franklin	98. Stonington
61. Glastonbury	51. Suffield

22. Goshen
50. Granby
 1. Greenwich
99. Groton
69. Guilford
67. Haddam
39. Hamden
91. Hampton
57. Hartford
27. Hartland
32. Harwinton
64. Hebron
18. Kent
90. Killingly
70. Killingworth
78. Lebanon
95. Lisbon
19. Litchfield
72. Lyme
80. Mansfield

88. Thompson
82. Tolland
30. Torrington
86. Union
97. Voluntown
43. Wallingford
17. Warren
16. Washington
34. Waterbury
33. Watertown
 5. Weston
60. Wethersfield
83. Willington
28. Winchester
79. Windham
54. Windsor
36. Woodbridge
14. Woodbury
87. Woodstock

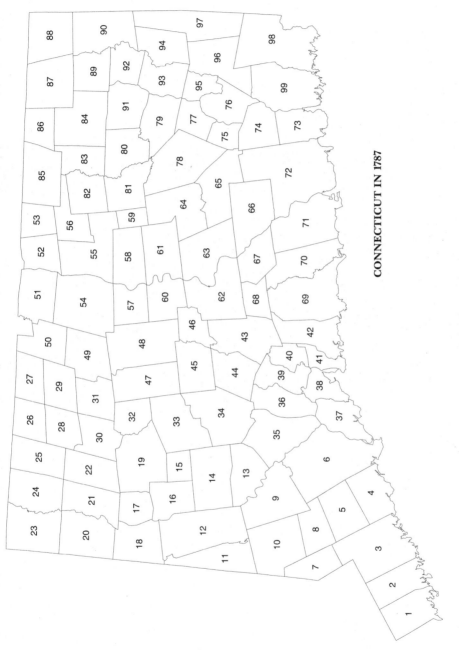

CONNECTICUT IN 1787

6. Connecticut town locator.

APPENDIX B

New England Turnpike Routes
and Mill Villages

A glance at maps of turnpikes as they existed in the early nineteenth century graphically illustrates the difference between Connecticut's economic and demographic dispersion as contrasted with Massachusetts and Rhode Island. In the latter two states, the great majority of turnpikes converge on the states' single major port city. In Connecticut, no such convergence occurs; rather, the roads meander from town to town quite equitably. Similarly, a map of mill villages during the era of waterpower shows this economic and demographic dispersion. At the mouth of the Connecticut River, New England's greatest waterway, where one would expect a busy seaport, there is only vast marshland and a small village. The turnpike maps are on pages 331 (Connecticut), 57 (Massachusetts), and 287 (Rhode Island) of Frederic J. Wood, *The Turnpikes of New England*. The map of towns, villages, and mills is from the endpapers of Ellsworth Grant, *Yankee Dreamers and Doers* and is reproduced here with the author's generous permission.

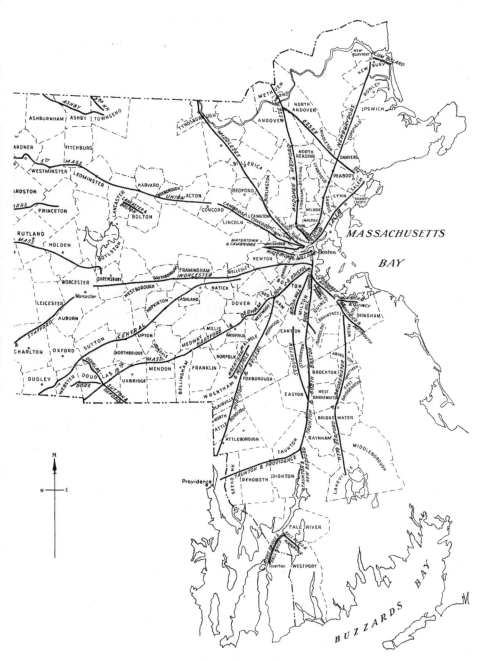

7. **Turnpikes of Massachusetts.**

145

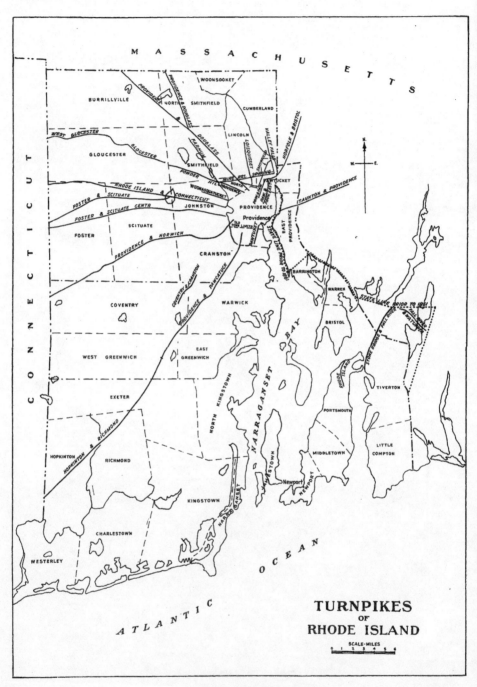

8. Turnpikes of Rhode Island.

146

9. Turnpikes of Connecticut.

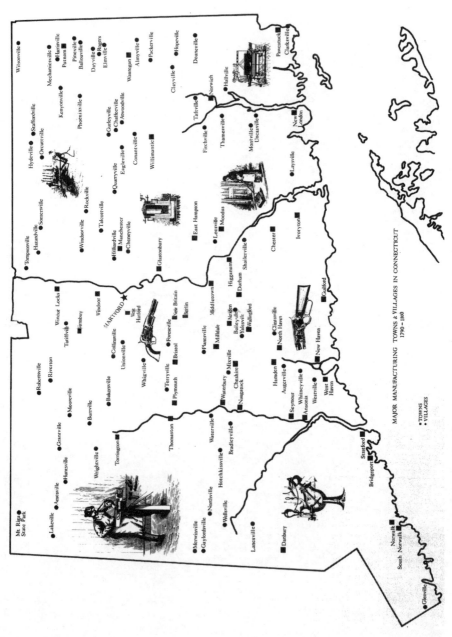

Map showing towns and villages with labels including:

Wilsonville, Mechanicsville, Harrisville, Putnam, Pineville, Ballouville, Daysville, Rogers, Elmville, Alumville, Packerville, Clarksville, Staffordville, Orcuttville, Kenyotville, Phoenixville, Clayville, Doaneville, Hazardville, Somersville, Windsorville, Talcottville, Rockville, Hydeville, Gurleyville, Chaffeeville, Atwoodville, Quarryville, Eagleville, Conantville, Willimantic, Taftville, Norwich, Fitchville, Thamesville, Uncasville, Montville, New London, Hallville, Leesville, Moodus, East Hampton, Hillardville, Manchester, Cheneyville, Glastonbury, Leesville, Chester, Ivoryton, Tompsonville, Winsor Locks, Windsor, HARTFORD, West Hartford, New Britain, Berlin, Higganum, Shailerville, Durham, Middletown, Guilford, Robertsville, Riverton, Tariffville, Simsbury, Unionville, Collinsville, Whigville, Forestville, Bristol, Plainville, Milldale, Meriden, Baileyville, Yalesville, Wallingford, Clintonville, North Haven, New Haven, West Haven, Mooreville, Granville, Bakersville, Terryville, Plymouth, Cheshire, Mixville, Waterbury, Naugatuck, Hamden, Augerville, Whitneyville, Ansonia, Westville, Burrville, Wrightville, Torrington, Thomaston, Waterville, Seymour, Amesville, Huntsville, Lakeville, Merwinsville, Gaylordsville, Northville, Wellsville, Hotchkissville, Bradleyville, Lanesville, Danbury, Stamford, Bridgeport, Norwalk, South Norwalk, Glenville, Mt. Riga State Park

MAJOR MANUFACTURING TOWNS & VILLAGES IN CONNECTICUT
1790 – 1860

■ TOWNS
● VILLAGES

10. Major manufacturing towns and villages in Connecticut, 1790–1860.

148

Some Additional Local Contexts

The material included in this Appendix further strengthens my thesis that many of those who voted against the ratification of the Constitution did so for personal or local reasons. It was withdrawn from the body of the text so as to streamline the analysis there.

Barkhamsted was the most primitive town in Connecticut in the 1780s. Set out in 1732, where fifty years later only seventy-eight adult males resided, "generally very poor & low, & many of them have neither Land nor Stock of their own, but live entirely upon hire both as to land and Cattle." They taxed themselves for ministerial support, but begged the Assembly to permit them to tax the many absentee landowners as well. As in equally primitive Colebrook, at its northwest corner, they were not self-supporting and had to import grain. But unlike Colebrook, despite the fact that they sent no deputy to the General Assembly until 1796, Barkhamsted sent one delegate (they could have sent two) to the ratifying convention; he voted no. He was Joseph Wilder, sixty-three in 1788, in a town where "most of the men were in ye younger part of Life & have numerous Families of small Children." Wilder, like everyone else in town a farmer, was probably the only solvent householder in Barkhamsted. He was the sole justice of the peace in town for most of the 1780s, "a man of extended power and influence," and clearly the only man of parts in the frontier settlement.[1]

At the time of the convention, Barkhamsted was under great financial pressure because two areas had been set off to neighboring parishes at a moment when the few scattered inhabitants were trying to finance their own church and ministry. The local collector attempted to tax the absentee holders of undivided lands—since tenants paid on their leased lands—but was rebuffed by the General Assembly when the absentees objected. The leader of the absentee landlords was Erastus Wolcott, agrarian spokesman, but himself of the rentier class. Joseph Wilder, Barkhamsted's antifederalist delegate, was in 1788 at loggerheads with this turncoat localist. In addition, Wilder's nearest neighbors were two families of the Simsbury Humphreys—leading antifederalists.[2]

Hartland, bordering Massachusetts in the Springfield orbit, and in the bottom 15 percent of towns on the tax list, sent two delegates who voted aye, Isaac Burnham and John Wilder, Joseph's brother. In 1783 the Hartland town meeting resolved that the pensions proposed for Continental officers were "unjust Making an unreasble [sic] Distinction Betweene the officers & the Soldier Laying a foundation for Innumerable Evils." Wilder and Burnham were two of three men sent as delegates to the Middletown convention protesting the pensions. Burnham was often a selectman and served as a deputy at least six times in the 1780s, including 1788, after he had cast his affirmative vote.

Hartland's other pro-Constitution delegate was John Wilder. His father, an original settler of Hartland, gave him fifty acres in 1762, when he was twenty-one or twenty-two years old, and the next year John was twenty-seventh on a list of fifty-one taxpayers in town. Over the years he bought a good many more acres. Wilder was selectman in 1782 and 1787 and a deputy in 1788—but that's the total of his known political service. He apparently did not serve in the militia during either the French and Indian War or the Revolution, though he was in his mid-thirties in 1776. However, he did serve on local committees in support of the war effort in the 1770s. He was an original member of the Second Society when, for reasons of distance, it split from the First in 1780. In 1794 he would become a deacon of that church. Hartland was one of those towns that permitted each of its two parishes to nominate a deputy to the General Assembly to be rubber-stamped at freemen's meetings, and apparently this routine prevailed in electing delegates to the ratifying convention.[3]

As noted above, John's brother Joseph, a delegate from Barkhamsted, voted against ratification. Joseph had a close connection to Hartland. His father was an original settler there; Joseph served as Hartland's deputy to the General Assembly in 1776, when he was living in Barkhamsted;[4] he lived close enough to the population center there that he was an organizer and original member of the West Hartland Society and at one time lived in a school district that straddled the line between the two towns. Indeed, he had been an original member of the First Society way over in East Hartland. He was ten to fifteen years older than John.[5] That brothers with identical backgrounds, both farmers living as near neighbors in virtually identical towns divided on the issue of ratifying the Constitution while countering the much more common fact of family coherence, points up the fact that decisions were individual and personal.

In Tolland County, the contrasting behavior of the delegations from Mansfield and Willington, both instructed to vote against the Constitution, is telling. Constant Southworth is the all-time champion officeholder of Mansfield; a selectman and justice of the peace in 1775, he served as town clerk continuously from 1756 to 1806, and as deputy to the General Assembly nearly continuously from 1769 to 1801. Southworth, a cripple, was a deacon of his church, taught school locally, and made a living as a surveyor, ultimately becoming Windham County surveyor. He owned agricultural acres, did well financially, and left a substantial estate. Southworth was a prewar reformer, and he usually voted localist in the General Assembly, though he would have allowed the national impost.[6]

Southworth's public activities brought him into frequent contact with William Williams of neighboring Lebanon, and when Williams was attacked for closing down the Windham County Courts in the winter of 1787–88, Southworth defended him in letters to newspapers. Mansfield freemen were highly agrarian and localist in sentiment and even after the nationalist rout at the convention, continued to give their votes for statewide office to James Wadsworth and other localists.[7] Southworth reflected that constituency. How else could he count on reelection as clerk, selectman, and deputy over and over for decades?

Southworth's colleague was Nathaniel Atwood, also a very frequent officeholder and deputy. He owned a large farm on the main road that ran from Norwich and Windham on the south to Willington and the Massachusetts line to the north. Atwood is not recorded as having done any military service ever. Like Southworth, he had a mildly agrarian voting record in the Assembly. He was over fifty in 1788.[8]

Willington, adjoining Mansfield, sent to the convention Caleb Holt and Seth Crocker. They represented the two families that had dominated town government for decades. Both were almost certainly farmers. Holt never served as a deputy, but he was a very frequent town officer, serving as a selectman whose prominence continued after 1788. He was referred to as Sergeant Holt in the early 1770s, probably—though not certainly—a rank earned in the French and Indian War. He did not serve under arms during the Revolution. He was fifty-seven years old in 1788.[9] Holt's colleague, Seth Crocker, was also a frequent local officer; unlike Holt, Crocker went very often to the General Assembly, was reelected once after his vote at the convention, but that was the last of his fourteen terms. He was appointed a militia captain in 1780.[10]

Willington and Mansfield, virtually identical towns, demonstrate the idio-syncratic nature of delegates' behavior at the convention. At an adjourned town meeting in Mansfield on December 17, "the question was put whether said inhabitants do approve of the new proposed Constitution." Southworth as clerk then wrote, "Resolved in the negative." In Willington, a town meet-ing of December 3 "[v]oted to reject the new-proposed Constitution" and further "voted that the delegates to [the] Convention be instructed to act agreeable to the vote of the town," instructions the town reaffirmed a month later.

Southworth, a major Windham County leader, secure in his elective of-fices, but hazarding his appointed judicial offices, followed his instructions to vote no even though he was personally willing to vote in favor, and his close association with the flexible William Williams might inspire him to do so. At-wood followed Southworth. But Caleb Holt and Seth Crocker of neighbor-ing Willington disobeyed their very unambiguous instructions.[11] There is nothing in the record that explains these different actions; nor is there any element of the economic or political context of the towns the men repre-sented that might explain what they did at Hartford. The explanation must lie in the unreported relations of the men with their constituencies, or in the unfathomable personal characters of each of them.

These examples together with those described in the text do not exhaust the evidence that the delegates' votes in the ratifying convention reflected local political and social relationships and individual decisions. I have stud-ied the locales and biographies of all forty antifederalists and many of the federalists. In no case do I find an ideological basis for their stand for or against the Constitution. I certainly find no ideologically cohering web among either group. On the other hand, there are clear and demonstrable family connections among like-voting delegates—especially among the federalists. Often these connections are strengthened—but sometimes broken—by local political factors. Family, friends, and local factional squabbles played the strongest part in determining who would vote against—and often who would vote for—the ratification of the U.S. Constitution in Connecticut.

Occupations of Convention Delegates

The information on which these lists is based is drawn from scores of local histories, genealogies, and some additional miscellaneous sources such as town tax and other records. These sources are listed in the bibliography to this work only if they carry information used in the text. The totals in my lists do not always agree with the figures I give in the text because there I deal only with a man's primary occupation, while here some men appear in more than one category.

Most of the men listed here were involved to some degree in farming. I know for sure that eighteen federalists and ten antifederalists were primarily or exclusively farmers; it is safe to assume that all the men for whom no other occupation had been found were primarily farmers. Another category I might list is "officeholders." Quite a few men on both sides of the debate on the Constitution spent most of their time and earned much, if not most, of their income as public servants in elective and appointive office. Insufficient information is available to draw up such a list with any accuracy. Too many judgment calls would be necessary, so I have not attempted to make such a list.

My list might be compared to that of J. T. Main in *The Antifederalists*, pp. 289–90:

Antifederalists

Lawyers
A. Humphreys
D. Humphreys

Physicians
H. Humphreys
King
Marvin

Merchants
Goodman
Marvin

Taverners
Carpenter
Cotton
Enos
N. Phelps
Hez. Holcomb

Surveyors   **Other**
Southworth   Carpenter (blacksmith)
Hoadley   Nash (tanner)
Coleman   Todd (owned an iron foundry)
Teamsters   Ward (owned a spinning mill)
Nash   **Non-Practicing Minister**
Enos   Brooks
Landlords   **College Graduates**
Wadsworth   Brooks   Yale '65
Carpenter   King   Yale '59
Ward   Marvin   Yale '73
Newton   Wadsworth   Yale '48

Not Voting
Goodyear—taverner
Kingsbury—farmer
Pitkin—mill owner, merchant
Rogers—mill owner, merchant
Silliman—taverner/merchant
Utley ?

Federalists

Lawyers   Judd
S. Beach   Law
Brinsmaide   A. Learned
Buckingham   Miller
Chandler   Minor
Cleaveland   Mitchell
James Davenport°   Newberry
John Davenport   Parsons
B. Dow   E. Root
H. Dow   J. Root
Dyer   R. Sherman
Edwards   D. Smith
Elderkin   Strong
Ellsworth   Sturges
Everitt   Throop
Fenn   Treadwell°
Griswold   E. Whittlesey
Hale   **Sea Captains**
Halsey   H. Goodrich
S. Huntington   W. Goodrich
Johnson   Halsey

°Non-practicing

Surveyors
Heron
Shipman
J. White
Mill Owners
Elderkin
Dyer
J. Phelps
E. Pitkin
Porter
Ministers
H. Dow°
A. Learned°
White°
Chandler°
A. Lee
Robbins
Landlords
Barns
Burr
Canfield
S. Chapman
John Davenport
Hall
J. Holbrook
Mitchell
C. Phelps
Watson
E. Wolcott
Other
Hopkins (silversmith)
Miles (carpenter)
Sheldon (tanner)
E. Wolcott (ferry owner)
Physicians
Brainard
Chandler
Mead
Orton
C. Phelps
Porter
Warner
West
O. Wolcott

Taverners
Barns
S. Beach
Canfield
B. Dow
Danielson
Mosley
Porter
Sheldon
E. Wolcott
Ship Builders
Halsey
Shipman
Merchants
Bradley
Chapman
Coit
Edwards
H. Goodrich
W. Goodrich
Halsey
S. Hart
Hopkins
Howe
J. Huntington
D. Learned
Miles
Mills
Morgan
E. Pitkin
Raymond
Ripley
R. Sherman
Jery Wadsworth
E. Wolcott
Woodbridge

College Graduates (41)

S. Beach	Yale '57
Bradley	Yale '38
Brinsmade	Yale '72
Buckingham	Yale '65
Burr	Princeton '58
Chandler	Yale '59
Chester	Yale '66

Cleaveland	Yale '77	Noyes	Yale '65
James Davenport	Yale '77	E. Pitkin	Yale '53
John Davenport	Yale '70	Porter	Yale '54
H. Dow	Yale '84	Robbins	Yale '60
Dyer	Yale '40	E. Root	Yale '82
Edwards	Princeton '68	J. Root	Princeton '56
Ellsworth	Princeton '66	Strong	Yale '61
Hale	Yale '69 A.	Sturges	Yale '59
Heron (Dublin?)	Trinity	Throop	Yale '59
J. Huntington	Harvard '63	Treadwell	Yale '67
Johnson	Yale '44	Watson	Yale '64
Judd	Yale '63	West	Yale '74
Law	Yale '51	J. White	Yale '60
A. Learned	Yale '72	E. Whittlesey	Yale '79
Lee	Yale '66	Williams	Harvard '51
Miller	Yale '78	O. Wolcott	Yale '47
Mitchell	Yale '66	Woodbridge	Yale '71

APPENDIX E

"The Looking Glass for 1787"

This political cartoon, the earliest example of the genre listed by Frank Weitenkampf in *Political Caricature in the United States,* was printed in the *Connecticut Courant* on March 26, 1787. [*DocHist*, Microfiche, 7A.] In 1988 there were only two known copies of this cartoon, each a different varient. One was offered at auction by Sotheby's in 1988; the other, which is reproduced here with permission, is at the CHS. [Sotheby's, *Fine Printed and Manuscript Americana,* New York: April 16, 1988. unpaged; Weitenkampf, *Political Caricature.* p. 11.] The engraver was almost certainly Amos Doolittle of New Haven. A character in the lower left corner sits in "Tweedles Studdy," a reference to the fictional poet whom the Connecticut Wits conjured up as the author of *The Anarchiad.* [Riggs, ed., *Anarchiad,* p.35.] Indeed, it was probably the Wits who inspired the cartoon and contributed to its substance. The phrase, "As I sit plodding by my taper," is an allusion to a bit of doggerel written by one of the Wits signing himself "Trustless Fox." [Howard, *Connecticut Wits,* pp. 182–87.]

"The Looking Glass for 1787" centers on a wagon labeled "CONNECTI-CUT." The wagon carries "currency" and is mired in a mud hole. A military figure sits in the wagon brandishing a sword—perhaps a reference to the Society of the Cincinnati. He is exclaiming, "Gentlemen, this Machine is deep in the mire and you are divided as to its release." He is probably speaking to the "Council of Twelve"—that is, the Assembly's upper house—five tugging in one direction, six the opposite way. (We shall discover the twelfth anon.)

The nationalists on the left certainly include Governor Samuel Huntington, probably the fellow saying, "Comply with Congress"; and Lieutenant Governor Oliver Wolcott, Sr. My best guess at the identities of the others are: Benjamin Huntington of Norwich, not sent to the ratifying convention because Governor Samuel and General Jedediah—both Huntingtons—took

157

precedence; Johnathan Sturges of Fairfield, a lawyer, frequent officeholder, and establishment figure; and John Treadwell of Farmington, a solid pillar of the establishment, governor, 1809–11. [Dexter, *Biographies,* II:614–15, III: 247–50; Jordan, "Connecticut Politics," pp. 256–57.] They are intoning, "Pay Commutation," "Drive them to it," and "I abhor the anti federal faction."

James Wadsworth, of course, finds a place at the other end of the wagon, perhaps saying, "Confusion to the Federal Government." The man closest to the wagon on the antifederal side, saying "Tax Luxury," is Erastus Wolcott. William Hillhouse was a known localist; Joseph Platt Cook was reputed to have opposed sending delegates to Philadelphia; and Stephen Mix Mitchell was known to have. [Gossbart, "Revolutionary Transition," p. 268; *DocHist,* pp. 485, 501.] They add two more to the antifederal contingent; that makes five. Andrew Adams, the sixth, joined the antinational faction as an outgrowth of a bitter personal dispute with Oliver Wolcott, Sr. [Jordan, "Connecticut Politics," pp. 213–14; Loucks, "Reformation and Revolution," pp. 985–87]. They exclaim, "the People are oprest," "Success to Shays," and "Curse Independence," the last an allusion to the belief that among the antifederalists there were many closet Loyalists.

The twelfth councilor is William Williams, identified as "Agricola," his newspaper pseudonym. He holds one end of the antinationalists' chain and moans, "I fear & dred the Ides of May," election day for the upper house. His frock coat is awry. At Williams' feet is a skunk shooting accurately at Parsons. Parsons, in military attire complete with spurs, also with coat awry, fires a cannon at Williams, hits him, and exclaims, "A good Shot." He holds a quill in his right hand.

The Sotheby's copy of the cartoon is much embellished in respect to Williams and Parsons. Both men have been redrawn. Parsons is identified by initials SHP, and the quill is removed from his hand. There is no cannon; Instead Parsons defecates, hitting Williams in the rear-end. He wears a scabbard with a tag that says "—?——?—of the Cincinnati." Williams defecates, too, but misses, hitting well short of his target. The trousers of both men are down around their knees. The only other alteration I find is that, in the Sotheby's version, the swamp in which the wagon is mired leaks muddy water down to the feet of Williams and Hopkins. The Sotheby's version, obviously, is the more scathingly and anti-antinationalist. Which of the versions is the original is not evident, but the less ribald of the two is the one published in the *Courant.*

To the left of Williams is a farmer standing at his plow, holding in one hand a rake and in the other what I take to be a duck. He complains of the disproportionate burden placed on farmers: "Takes all to pay Taxes."

To the left of the farmer is the antinationalist, Joseph Hopkins, a watchmaker of Waterbury, a metalsmith who had just shut down his copper penny mint. He dangles one of the coins bearing the motto, AUCTORI CONNEC, next to the letter J and says to CATO, "Curs Commutation." CATO, a pseudonymous newspaper polemicist, responds, "I dispise your coppers."

At the left margin of the picture is Mt. Parnasus—the home of the ancient Greek gods Apollo and Dionysus, and the Muses. At its summit stand three of the four authors of "American Antiquities," *The Anarchiad:* David Humphreys, Joel Barlow, and Lemuel Hopkins. The fourth, John Trumbull, sits in "Tweedles Studdy" at the foot of the mountain.

While the sun shines on the nationalists, storm clouds threaten in the upper right corner and lightning ignites a fire, which the antinationalists will encounter if they are able to release the wagon from the mire and pull it their way. More lightning hits at New York at bottom right, the destination of profits and duties "From Connecticut to New York paying £40,000 per annum impost." Below the cartoon, commenting on its message, are the words, "A house divided against itself cannot stand. Mat[thew] Chap. 12 verse 26."

Notes

Abbreviations

AHA   American Historical Association

CHS   Connecticut Historical Society

CR   *Public Records of the Colony of Connecticut*

CSL   Connecticut State Library

DAR   Daughters of the American Revolution

MHS   Massachusetts Historical Society

NHCHS   New Haven Colony Historical Society

SR   *Public Records of the State of Connecticut*

DocHist   *Documentary History of the Ratification of the Constitution.* Merrill Jensen, ed. Volume III. *Ratification of the Constitution by the States: Delaware, New Jersey, Georgia, Connecticut.* Madison, Wisc.: State Historical Society of Wisconsin, 1978.

Introduction

1. Lubell, Samuel, anecdote told at a talk at the University of Connecticut, spring 1976.

2. Wiebe, *Search for Order,* p. xiii. Some historians have distinguished local face-to-face politics from national politics that were "abstracted from society." One says explicitly that antifederalists' failure to make this distinction was one cause of their ultimate frustration. See Bender, *Community and Social Change,* passim, but especially pp. 84–85, 137 for a summary of some of these historians' claims.

3. Fischer, *Revolution of Conservatism,* p. 220.

4. Zeichner, *Years of Controversy,* p. 228.

5. O'Neil, *Man of the House,* explains his introduction to the phrase. pp. 25–26; Tocqueville, II: 95, 274; McDonald, ed., *Plunkitt.* See especially "To Hold Your District," p. 62; Joseph Jones to James Madison, May 31, 1783, quoted in Roeber, *Faithful Magistrates,* p. 199.

6. The collapse of Congress is described in Burnett, *Continental Congress,* Chs.

XXXIII and XXXIV. William Grayson quoted in Ibid., p. 689. [Faux Latin: The head is perishing of bitter cynicism.]

7. Biographical analyses of convention delegates can be found in many works, perhaps handiest Rossiter, *Grand Convention;* Morris, *Forging the Union;* and my own *Decision in Philadelphia.*

8. Farrand, *Records,* I:8, 10n.

9. Henry is quoted in Morris, *Forging the Union,* p. 269. For Wolcott's refusal to attend, see Connecticut State Library (Hereafter CSL), *Arch.* Ser. I, I:56ab and p. 175, n. 56.

10. Madison on New York: Smith, ed. Letters. 24:111 (February 21, 1787). There are a number of monographic discussions of ratification in single states. They are listed in separate bibliographies that accompany the essays in Conley and Kaminski, *The Constitution and the States.* In the same volume, a bibliographic tour de force, "Posterity Views the Founding," by Patrick T. Conley, surveys the scholarly treatments of the creation of the Constitution as of 1987. Another state-by-state collection of scholarly essays is Gillespie and Lienesch, *Ratifying the Constitution.* Eight of the contributors are political scientists rather than historians, a fact which gives their essays a more theoretical than narrative emphasis. The shortcomings of this approach are illustrated in the extreme by Lutz's essay on Connecticut.

11. Banning, "Sectionalism and the General Good," p. 268; Farrand, *Records,* III:101; Kaminski, "Homogenized History," p. 34; McDonald in Gillespie and Lienesch, eds., *Ratifying the Constitution,* p. ix.

12. Every scholarly study of the debate over ratifying the Constitution includes an historiographic discussion that gets around to the question, who were the antifederalists. The most pointed of these is that by John Kaminski in a 1989 review of Herbert Storing's *The Complete Anti-Federalist.* Storing tried longer, more laboriously, and at greater length than anyone to show a unified set of attitudes, even something that could be called a common ideology. Kaminski convincingly undermines that contention. Another useful summary of the historiography of antifederalism is Saul Cornell's "Changing Fortunes" (1989), which is updated in the "Introduction" to his *The Other Founders* (1999). In a masterly one-page paragraph, Jack Rackov limns the interpretations of the late twentieth century. *Original Meanings,* p. 133.

13. After an exhaustive study of the determinants of voting patterns in the Confederation era, *Political Parties Before the Constitution,* Jackson Turner Main concludes that regional residence is the most consistent predictor. Men who lived along lines of communication—coastal and riverine cities, for the most part—were more inclined toward nationalism and commercialism; those who lived in hinterlands were focused more on local concerns. Main equates these regional similarities to economic factors—small farmers as distinguished from merchants and plantation capitalists.

14. This is the approach taken by Cornell in *The Other Founders.* His research into literary sources is the most thorough done to date and it is unlikely that it will be surpassed. Cornell focuses on written materials; his is a study of rhetoric, largely. He, like me, finds virtually no antifederal rhetoric emanating from Connecticut. This leaves him with no basis from which to infer reasons why forty delegates voted against the Constitution.

15. Cornell, *Other Founders.*

1. Geography, Politics, and Society

1. Madison, *Papers*, X:205.

2. Rush, *Autobiography*, pp. 145–46.

3. Thomas Ruggles, *The Usefulness and Expedience of Soldiers* (1737), quoted in Marcus, "The Militia of Colonial Connecticut," p. 258.

4. On Connecticut and royal disallowance see Andrews, "Intestacy Law." passim. A rare, perhaps unique, exception to Connecticut's freedom from disallowance is the King's veto of the General Assembly's anti-Quaker law in 1705 and 1706. *Public Records of the Colony of Connecticut* (Hereafter *CR*). IV:546, 546n. In a similar two-year period fifteen of forty-five Massachusetts laws were disallowed. Bushman, *King and People*, p. 107. Rhode Island shared Connecticut's autonomy. (Perhaps they were "binique.") An antagonistic Massachusetts agent "reported to the Privy Council that in 'Rhode Island government they deem his Majesty's royal authority to be entirely given up by their charter.'" Lovejoy, *Rhode Island Politics*, p. 75.

5. Connecticut Historical Society (Hereafter CHS) *Collections*. III:90; Fane, *Reports*. p. 2; Bushman, *King and People*, p. 156.

6. "Our ancestors, who emigrated from England to America, were possessed of knowledge of the laws and jurisprudence of that country; but were free from any obligations of subjection to them." Root, *Reports*, I:iii. See also Swift, *System*, p.57 and Nutting, "Charter and Crown," especially Section II, where Nutting describes how through obfuscation, delay, court challenge, and downright disobedience, Connecticut officials effectively implemented their own concept of the colony's relationship to the crown and Parliament.

7. Abraham Granger in Jensen, ed., *Documentary History of Ratification* (Hereafter *DocHist*). Microfiche 8-B, p. 50.

8. Franklin quoted in Weaver, "Review," p. 105. Main, *Society and Economy*, passim. Main concludes in an earlier work, "The major element in Connecticut's society was the middling sort, respectable, independent, enjoying a decent standard of living. At any one time, half of the population belonged to it, half of those below would move into it, and a third of those above had come from it." In Connecticut, he writes, "Liberty, challenges to authority, an adherence to republican ideas, and allegiance to middle-class ethics started with the founding, were favored by the environment, found expression in the Glorious Revolution, emerged strengthened from the Great Awakening, and finally helped to create the United States." Main, *Connecticut Society*, pp. 70, 71.

9. Webster, "An Examination," in Ford, ed., *Pamphlets*, p. 44n. There is a considerable literature on the suffrage in colonial Connecticut. The consensus of the best of it is that statutory requirements for voting at town meetings were often disregarded and when challenges to "illegal" voters arose, the General Assembly acting as a court usually upheld the de facto voters' right to vote. Historians estimate variously that 65 percent to 80 percent of adult males could qualify for freeman status on the eve of the Revolution. Most of those not qualified were young men who some day would qualify. Main, *Society and Economy*, pp. 321–22. See also Daniels, *Connecticut Town*, pp. 128–31, 192–93; Grant, *Democracy in the Frontier Town of Kent*, pp. 107–14; Williamson, *Connecticut Property Test*, pp. 101–04; Grossbart, "Revolutionary Transition," pp. 154–57.

10. Daniels, *Dissent and Conformity*, pf. 49; Lovejoy, *Rhode Island Politics*, pp. 15–18. In the eleven years from 1779 through 1789, twenty-eight new towns were created in Connecticut, adding thirty-five new deputies to a house of 146. All the new deputies came from agrarian regions. Twenty-eight new towns resulted in thirty-five deputies because eighteen were granted only one deputy, and ten received two. But in three cases the mother town, e.g., Kent, gave up a deputy to the new town, so the *net* gain in number of deputies was only thirty-five.

11. Lovejoy, *Rhode Island Politics*, p. 65 and passim; Boyd, *Politics of Opposition*, p. 25.

12. In the 1780s the requirements for town meeting voting were a 50 shilling ($7) freehold (real) estate or £40 ($134) personal estate. To become a freeman eligible to vote for statewide officers, the freehold estate required was only 40 shillings, but the personal estate was £40 not counting the poll, which was £18. Free blacks were not legally barred from voting until 1814. I have not found any who did, though one account implies such a vote. Waldstreicher and Grossbart, "Abraham Bishop's Vocation," 649 n44.

13. Sheehan and McDowell, *Friends of the Constitution*, p. 384n. If no one received a majority of the freemen's votes, the General Assembly chose the governor by a majority of each house—a frequent occurrence.

14. See Main, *Society and Economy*, pp. 322–23; Main, *Connecticut Society*, pp. 48–49; Daniels, *Connecticut Town*, p. 131–32; Selesky, "Patterns of Officeholding," pp. 166–72; Stark, "Upper House," pp. 137–47. This turnover was not usually the result of local politics. Rather, it was most often due to the practice of rotating deputies through different parishes in those towns that had more than two of them and serving alternately in the semiannual legislative sessions. Another factor influencing turnover was an apparent unrecorded but widely practiced tradition of voluntary retirement at age seventy. Some men, of course, became incapacitated or dead before that age.

15. Olson, "Economic Aspects," pp. 12–14, 19, 27; Bushman, *Puritan to Yankee*. See especially Part II. Bushman's thesis is very explicitly and concisely anticipated by Olson. See, e.g., Olson, pp. 24–25. See also, Daniels, "Large Town Power Structures," pf. 63.

16. Daggett, *Oration*, p. 6. After surveying the ratification process in all thirteen states, two scholars note that all states had "distinctive social structures, with their own relationships of authority and deference." Connecticut's Standing Order "was . . . an extreme case." Gillespie and Lienesch, *Ratifying the Constitution*, p. 19. The pervasiveness of family webs in Connecticut may have been extreme, but it was not unique. Every state exhibited a fair degree of family oligarchy. This fact has been fully demonstrated by James Kirby Martin in *Men in Rebellion*. See especially Ch. 4.

17. See generally *CR* and the *Public Records of the State of Connecticut* (Hereafter *SR*) for relevant years. On the Pitkins' role in Hartford politics see Daniels, *Connecticut's First Family*. In Ch. I, Daniels' case for family dominance is compelling. Between 1701 and 1785 Pitkins held elective office in Hartford 227 times, 35 percent of the highest local offices including deputy to the General Assembly. Scores more must have been held by close relations who did not share the same last name.

18. Caulkins, *Norwich*, p. 415, 625, 701 and passim.

19. Ibid.

20. Ibid.

21. Gerlach, *Samuel Huntington*, pp. 8–9.

22. Davenport, *Davenport Genealogy*, pp. 53, 55–56, 87, 90, 91.

23. On Sherman and Ellsworth see above Chapter 2. Adams' statement is Adams, *Works* VI:530. Jefferson's is in Cappon, ed., *Adams-Jefferson Letters*, p. 389. See also "The Family Compact of Connecticut" reprinted in Beard, *Economic Interpretation*, p. 364 from *The Aurora*, September 13, 1800. See also Bates, ed., "Sketch of Roger Wolcott," CHS, *Collections*, XVI:xxv. Bates speaks of a "small aristocracy . . . made up of descendants of families of the earliest settlers." Charles Loucks challenges Adams' characterization. "Connecticut drew its leadership not from a few dominant families but rather from scores of important clans scattered throughout the colony." Loucks, "Reformation and Revolution," p. 63. The difference is a matter of degree. Adams says families; I say family networks; Loucks says clans. Not only was local politics dominated by family networks, but so was local business enterprise in this same era. See, e.g., Robert K. Lamb, "Entrepreneur and Community."

24. For at least a half century following the 1950s historians have debated the meaning of the term "deference" and its practical effect on internal colonial politics. I do not mean to enter that debate here. A quick way to get up to speed on the matter is to read the "Special Issue" of the *Journal of American History* 85 (June 1998) devoted to the subject. For a full discussion of deference in America in its colonial context see Kirby, "Early American Politics"; in its Connecticut context see Daniels, *Connecticut Town*, Ch. 3. Deference was, of course, more than a habitual attitude. It had deep roots in England and the colonies in economic relationships such as landlord and tenant, artisan and customer, etc. It was, certainly, the breakdown in deference during the 1760s and 1770s that supported the revolutionary movement, as it was the Revolution itself that hurried on that breakdown. See e.g., Wood, *Radicalism*, pp. 63–64; and "Interest and Disinterest" in Beeman, et al., eds., *Beyond Confederation*, pf. 73; Martin, *Men in Rebellion*, Ch. 7. Nevertheless, Connecticut voters of the "middling sort" still in the 1780s and after hesitated to cross their "betters" in overt ways. See, e.g., Purcell, *Connecticut in Transition*, pp. 125, 139, 156, where he discusses the "stand-up" law of 1801. As it happens, the best published test case of whether voters deferred to those of high social rank examines Connecticut officeholders in prerevolutionary eighteenth-century Connecticut. The authors conclude that voters did *not* defer to men of high socioeconomic status; repeated reelection to colonywide office resulted from a record of long-term successful public service. I see this almost automatic reelection as deference—deference to men of *earned* superior rank. That their way up the political ladder was aided by family connection is admitted by the Gilsdorfs in at least 25 percent of the cases. I think they vastly understate the effect of family connections and I try to make that case in this essay. Gilsdorf and Gilsdorf, "Elites and Electorates."

25. Gale, "Brief, Decent but Free Remarks," p. 31; Stark, "Upper House," pp. 140–42. Legislation of 1784 outlawed concurrent congressional and Council officeholding.

26. Code of 1650 in *CR*, I:548. See also Jones, *History of Taxation*, p. 25n1; Loucks, "American Revolution," p. 133–34.

27. Loucks, "American Revolution," pp. 168, 170; *CR*, XV:204. When, for instance, in 1785 Elijah Lothrop of Norwich applied for permission to establish a snuff

manufactory, he discovered to his dismay that the General Assembly had just granted Pitkin an exclusive monopoly for its manufacture. Grossbart, "Revolutionary Transition," p. 292; *SR*, V:400.

28.*Warren-Adams Letters*, I:75.

29. Warfel, ed., Webster's *Letters*, p. 64. One scholar believes that town meetings reflected the people, while the General Assembly reflected a less popular opinion. Grossbart, "Revolutionary Transition," passim. Grossbart's conclusions, however, are based on a small number of towns, all in eastern Connecticut and mostly from Norwich, an unusual protoindustrial town.

30. I have surveyed all the pre-1820 petitions from outlying parishes asking to be incorporated as towns. Virtually all of them cite the distance to town meeting as the principal basis justifying their claim for separate town status.

31. There are thorough descriptions of militia elections in Connecticut in the two dissertations so often cited below: Marcus, "Militia of Connecticut," pp. 241–50; Gates, "Disorder," Ch. II. Legally, local election was merely nomination. As a constitutional matter, the General Assembly appointed all militia officers. This system, according to James Duane in 1775, was practiced only in Connecticut and Rhode Island. In all other colonies military commissions came from the governor. Butterfield, ed., *Adams Papers*, II:203.

32. Marcus, "Militia of Connecticut," p. 242; Gates, "Disorder," p. 72.

33. Selesky, "Military Leadership," p. 418.

34. Selesky, *War and Society*, p. 196. In the seventeenth century, Connecticut officers received their first commissions as captains at a median age of over fifty. Main, *Society and Economy*, p. 320.

35. Marcus, "Militia of Connecticut," pp. 338, 364–65. In 1739, 50 percent and in 1763, 44 percent of the deputies were captains or higher militia officers. After 1725 deputies who held ranks below captain were no longer identified by their military titles, so many more than the figures show actually held militia office. Ibid., p. 240. In 1772, 64 of 139 deputies (46 percent) held military titles of captain, major, or colonel. *CR*, IX:1–3. It was not customary, apparently, to use noncommission titles—corporal and sergeant—in political office. After the reorganization of the militia in 1739, members of the Council did not customarily use their military titles when acting in a civil capacity. Marcus, "Militia," p. 240. In 1783, 77 of 153 deputies (50 percent) used military titles, five of whom were generals. *SR*, V:430–32.

36. Selesky, "Military Leadership," p. 381. Selesky's figures for new militia commissions are:

	1745–55	1755–64	1765–74	1775–81
field (major, colonel)	31	34	104	236
company (lieutenant, captain)	1338	1588	2324	3305

37. Marcus, "Militia of Connecticut," p. 349; Gates, "Disorder," pp. 96–98, 100; *CR*, XIII:580.

38. Marcus, "Militia of Connecticut," pp. 243–45. In 1691 Wallingford militiamen

attempted to replace Thomas Yale as ensign, but the General Assembly in which Yale represented Wallingford refused to accept his replacement and finally, because of "great difficulty and disturbance in the spirits of the good people of Wallingford," promoted Yale to captain. Ibid., p. 243.

39. Turner, ed., *Journal of Williams,* pp. 25, 26, 28; Marcus, "Militia of Connecticut," p. 245–47. Thomas Rose of Preston was a deputy when he was elected lieutenant of the trainband in Preston. But he was unruly, guilty of "insulting candor and carriage to the Governor," and the Assembly negatived his commission. It was said that Rose had a "considerable number of relations" in his militia unit who with "other inconsiderate persons" under the influence of "flattery and insinuations" elected him to office. It is interesting to note that in the Rose imbroglio, of the two men appointed by the Assembly in lieu of those locally elected, one, Mark Williams, refused the promotion while the other, Daniel Woodward, accepted. Williams, a few years later, was elected captain of the trainband and deputy to the General Assembly; Woodward disappears from both civil and military lists. *CR,* VII:227, 465, VIII:3, 53. Gates, "Disorder" also tells the Rose story, pp. 107–08. The more usual circumstance is illustrated by a failed attempt of Captain Elisha Sheldon, a long-term deputy soon to be a councilor, to insert himself as colonel over the more senior lieutenant colonel Ebenezer Marsh. Turner, *Williams Journal,* p. 43; *CR,* XI:16 (1757).

40. Those between fifty-five and sixty were excused in 1708, and those between forty-five and fifty in 1772. But by that time it was customary to excuse all over forty. Marcus, "Militia of Connecticut," pp. 234, 349; *CR,* V:83–84, VIII:36. On the other hand, large numbers of boys down to the age of ten voluntarily trained with the local companies. Stiles, *Literary Diary,* I:288–89. Those excused because of their office or occupation were: assistants, justices of the peace, church officers, the president, secretary, teachers and students at Yale, lawyers, millers, "constant herdsmen," full-time sailors, sheriffs, constables, ferrymen, and the certified disabled. *Acts and Laws . . . of 1769,* p. 157.

41. Harold Selesky believes that the militia officers came from outside the political leadership ranks. His impression is that service as a militia officer did not help promote political careers—at least in the colonial era. *"War and Society,"* pp. 204, 212. However there is a very great coincidence of numbers of deputies and selectmen who are officers. If military office did not help one's political advancement (and I will make the case later that it did), it is certainly true that political advancement helped one's military career. For a case of a sitting deputy trying to push himself forward for appointment to officer rank, see, e.g., Samuel Mott's deposition of February 10, 1778. CSL, *Arch,* "Militia," 2nd ser. XIII:253a. See also Turner, *Williams Journal,* e.g., pp. 25, 26, 28.

42. *Connecticut Journal* (March 26, 1779) quoted in Loucks, "American Revolution," p. 148.

43. See, for instance, *CR,* XV:226.

44. Marcus, "Militia of Connecticut," p. 364.

45. CHS *Collections,* II, "Correspondence of Silas Deane," p. 141 (April 13, 1774). Leffingwell was a lieutenant at the time. *CR,* XIII:92.

46. *CR,* VIII:277–79; Marcus, "Militia of Connecticut," pp. 231–32. Field grade officers were nominated by a caucus of the representatives from the towns included

in the regimental bounds. Very rarely were those nominations rejected. Gates, "Disorder," p. 34; Deposition of Samuel Mott, February 10, 1778. CSL, *Arch,* "Militia," 2nd series, XIII:253a–c.

47. Perhaps Lawrence Gipson goes too far when he claims that "popular officers . . . at times . . . exercised . . . a degree of authority in political affairs which brushed aside any and all opposition." But as John Brooke has shown for Massachusetts, political careers could be built on militia elections, just as military careers could be enhanced by civil service. Gipson, *Jared Ingersoll,* p. 31. He repeats these words in his much later work, *British Isles,* III:89; Brooke, *Heart of the Commonwealth,* pf. 114.

48. Selesky, "Military Leadership," p. 419; Washington quoted in Kohn, *Eagle and Sword,* pp. 9–10 (December 20, 1776). It is not possible on any social or economic basis to distinguish men who chose Continental service from those who chose or acquiesced in militia service. A possible difference is the level of commitment to the revolutionary cause. To enlist in the Continental army as a private soldier was a long-term commitment to an arduous, dangerous life with a high probability of becoming a casualty. Militia service was short-term, often close to home, usually much safer, and frequently coerced. See Royster, *Revolutionary People,* pp. 373–78; Shy, *People Numerous and Armed,* passim, especially Chapter IX.

49. CSL, "Farmington Revolutionary War Records," May 6, 1783; David Humphreys to Thomas Jefferson (November 29, 1788) in Humphreys, *Humphreys,* p. 436.

50. The best general discussion of the Cincinnati in Connecticut politics is in Wachtell, "Localism and Nationalism," pp. 174–80.

51. Burnett, *Continental Congress,* pp. 315–16. A new act was passed in 1781. Ford, ed., *Journals of the Continental Congress,* IX:502, XVIII:958–59.

52. Burnett, *Continental Congress,* pp. 557–58, 568. For the Connecticut implications of these acts see Buel, *Dear Liberty,* pp. 297–303. The act commuting the pensions to a lump sum is Ford, ed., *Journals of the Continental Congress,* XXIV:207–10. Even friends of commutation in Connecticut admitted it would cost the state over $400,000 to pay. Wachtell, "Localism and Nationalism," p. 148.

53. Kohn, *Eagle and Sword,* p. 21. The reality of the conspiracy is thoroughly documented by Richard Kohn in "Newburgh Conspiracy" and *Eagle and Sword,* pp. 19–39. For a discussion of the pension controversy from the perspective of the Continental officer corps see Royster, *Revolutionary People,* pp. 345–51. The best discussion of the commutation controversy in Connecticut in its national context in print is in Main, *Antifederalists,* pp. 107–09. Main says that of all the states it was in Connecticut that "[t]he most extensive and interesting controversy occurred." Ibid., p. 107. The best description of the Connecticut delegates' part in the matter is Gerlach, "Connecticut and Commutation," in CHS, *Bulletin,* published unfortunately without citations. The fullest discussion is in Grossbart, "Revolutionary Transition," pp. 218–40. There is also a good discussion in Buel, *Dear Liberty,* pp. 297–310. See also Jordan, "Connecticut Politics," pp. 135–156; and Wachtell, "Localism and Nationalism." Ch. III; Gerlach, "Connecticut Delegates," pp. 103–14; *DocHist,* pp. 319–21.

54. Dyer's anguished vote in favor of commutation cost him his seat on the Council at the next elections and, he said, ruined a twenty-five-year career in Connecticut politics. Wachtell, "Localism and Nationalism," pp. 75, 108. See also, Willingham, *Eliphalet Dyer,* pp. 38–41.

55. Selesky, "Military Leadership," estimates that about 30,000 Connecticut men

served in some military capacity during the Revolution, of which about 10,000 served in Continental units. p. 423. This was out of a 1774 population of 198,000.

56. Burnett, *Letters of Members,* VI:407, V:429.

57. Quoted in Main, *Antifederalists,* pp. 108–09. At least sixteen towns passed resolutions condemning commutation. They are listed in Jordan, "Connecticut Politics," pp. 147–48, 147n84; and Grossbart, "Revolutionary Transition," p. 223n63. Noah Webster claimed that the lower house was so incensed at the Council's refusal to endorse the protest that the deputies as a matter of spite voted to have the General Assembly meet sequentially at each of the six county seats instead of alternately at Hartford and New Haven. Nothing came of this proposal, but Webster cites it as an example of the occasional irresponsibility of popularly elected legislatures. Webster, "An Examination," in Ford, ed., *Pamphlets,* p. 33.

58. Conventions are more threatening in states without constitutions because in effect the legislature is a convention—not limited by constitutional restrictions or even legitimated by a constitution. A convention really parallels the traditional legislature and could be seen as overwhelming it at some point. Indeed, that is exactly what did happen with Committees of Correspondence during the Revolution. On conventions as a threat to established republican government, see Noah Webster, *Collection of Essays and Fugitive Writings.*

59. *Connecticut Journal,* March 31, 1784; *American Mercury,* November 22, 1784, and October 11, 1783. Five years later, sixteen of the sixty-four Middletown "conventioneers" were sent as delegates to the U.S. Constitution ratifying convention. Eight of them voted against (20 percent of the antis); seven voted for (5 percent of the federalists); one absented himself on voting day. There is a slight correlation of Middletown participation with antifederalism.

60. Richard Buel guesses that most of the promoters of the Middletown Convention were prewar leaders who had besmirched their reputations by inept military leadership or lukewarm support of the war. He implies that several of them had Tory leanings. He surmises that they were using the commutation issue to "regild" their reputations. These are not improbable guesses—but still they are guesses. Buel, *Dear Liberty,* pp. 311–12. It seems to me, however, that Buel exercises his intuitions too strenuously when he characterizes the antifederalists as "men in ruthless pursuit of political rehabilitation [who] would not stop to consider" that their opposition to an impost that would establish the national credit "might tempt Britain to reopen hostilities." p. 312.

61. *DocHist,* p. 320. Buel, *Dear Liberty,* pp. 304–14. See also Wachtell, "Localism and Nationalism," pp. 108–14. Buel, *Dear Liberty,* says 56 percent of the deputies in the session of October 1783 had not been there in May. Turnover rates between May and October sessions had been 48 percent in 1781 and 58 percent in 1782. A "normal" turnover rate between spring and fall sessions in this era ranged from 48 percent to 61 percent. Ibid., p. 208. See above note 14.

62. *Susquehannah Papers,* XI:359. The Susquehannah Company episode has been extensively and intensively studied. The basic source is the eleven-volume edition of the *Papers.* Its place in Connecticut politics is discussed in Collier's *Roger Sherman* and three unpublished dissertations by Richard T. Warfle, Paul Moyer, and James Edward Brady. Other relevant items are discussed in Collier, *Literature of Connecticut History,* pp. 84–86.

63. Taylor, "Trial at Trenton."

64. The course of the Connecticut cession is best studied through relevant volumes of Smith's *Letters of Delegates* and the "Introduction" to volumes VIII and IX of the *Susquehannah Papers* and the documents referred to there. Especially useful are Onuf's *Origins*, Ch. 3; and Gerlach, "Firmness and Prudence." See also, McCaughey, *Samuel Johnson*, pp. 199–205.

65. These internal factional differences are thoroughly described in Moyer, "Wild Yankees," esp. Ch. 4. On Allen's intervention, see Bellesiles, *Ethan Allen*, pf. 248; and Onuf, *Origins*, pp. 69–70.

66. Smith, *Letters*, 23:227.

67. Ibid., 23:266–67.

68. Ibid., 23:318.

69. Ibid., 23:318, 314–15, 318.

70. Farrand, *Records*, I:316–17.

71. *Susquehannah Papers*, IX: 21–22. The rights to soil were to have been tried at Annapolis in June 1784, but the Wyoming leaders were in refuge in the woods outside Wilkes-Barre at the moment and could not attend. Brady, "Wyoming," p. 189.

72. Ibid., IX:119, 141–42. It would have been more appropriate for the House to direct its resolution to Connecticut's congressmen—of which Johnson was one—but none were in attendance at Congress at the moment.

73. Ibid., IX:509. The disposal of the Western Reserve had become the focus of a bitter conflict played out in 1786 and the spring of 1787, even before Congress had accepted Connecticut's proposal to abandon its settlers in Pennsylvania and disavow its claims west of the Reserve in exchange for the Reserve. One faction would sell the land at fifty cents an acre in thousand- acre lots payable in Continental notes as well as specie and certain Connecticut notes. Its liberal payment plan and large minimum lots would favor grand speculators, many from outside the state. It would also reward Continental officers who held the hated commutation notes. The plan that won approval in the General Assembly provided for an orderly tier-by-tier sale at about the same price (three shillings), payable in State notes, with no minimum-sized lot, but not less than 20 percent down. Lieutenant Governor Oliver Wolcott and Cincinnati leader Samuel Holden Parsons led the proponents of the former plan; William Williams was the leader of the latter—successful—plan. The hot political imbroglio is described in detail in Jordan, "Connecticut Politics," pp. 252–69, and Wachtell, "Localism and Nationalism," pp. 233–39.

2. The Economic and Political Context

1. The economy of colonial Connecticut is described in summary form in Daniels, "Economic Developments," and more fully in Main, *Society and Economy*. The most detailed analysis is Saladino, "Economic Revolution." The New England context is described in McCusker and Menard, *British America*. A contemporaneous description of the export trade is Gale, *Brief, Decent but Free Remarks*. For a discussion and listing of relevant works published before 1982, see Collier, *Literature*, pp. 59–63.

2. *CR*, III:297. These large vessels had to transfer their cargoes to barges and little sloops to get their cargoes ashore.

3. This and the next two paragraphs are taken largely from Saladino, "Economic Revolution," Chs. 1, 3, 5.

4. Daniels, *Dissent and Conformity,* p. 113; Lovejoy, *Rhode Island Politics,* pf. 19.

5. Blocs of deputies tended to vote alike on various combinations of issues that came to the floor of the General Assembly. A full analysis of all known recorded votes for the period 1782 to 1795 has been reported by Stephen Grossbart in "Revolutionary Transition," pp. 359–66. Historians have variously characterized these groups as localists and nationalists; localists and cosmopolitans; provincials and expansionists; agrarians and merchants; federalists and democrats, etc., depending on the kinds of issues they are describing. In Connecticut, they were very fluid, constantly changing membership.

6. *CR,* VIII:133. See also Walradt, *Financial History,* pp. 22–23.

7. Saladino, "Economic Revolution," p. 174.

8. Ibid. In 1787 Noah Webster asserted that Connecticut's state debt—that is, taxes owed to the State by local taxpayers and by the State to the Congress—was the heaviest in proportion to its population of all the states and that Connecticut "cannot discharge its debt, on any principles of taxation ever yet practiced." Webster, "An Examination," in Ford, ed., *Pamphlets,* p. 62. For a general discussion of tax policy, controversy, and reform in Connecticut in the revolutionary era, see Becker, *Politics of Taxation,* pp. 145–53.

9. See chapter 6, pp. 106–9.

10. Stiles, *Windsor,* I:414, 614–15, 766, II:811. Wolcott was appointed to lieutenant in 1759 and moved through the ranks to brigadier general in 1776. *CR,* XI:338, 579, XII:88, XV:422; *SR,* I:134, III:326.

11. McDonald, *We the People,* p. 144. McDonald says Wolcott held $1,825 in state notes and $103 in Continental notes in 1790. It is not known what he owned in 1788. Historians have generally assumed that what was reported in the Treasury Records in 1790 was owned two or three years earlier. But this is a matter of convenience, not fact; the assumption may or may not be correct.

12. Wolcott's essays, "Strictures on the present Mode of Taxation in the State of Connecticut," were published in the *Connecticut Gazette* in September 7, 21, 28, October 5, 1781. They are summarized in Wachtell, "Localism and Nationalism," pp. 116–17, 226–27; Grossbart, "Revolutionary Transition," p. 215n41.

13. Ibid., pp. 359, 360.

14. Wachtell, "Localism and Nationalism," pp. 14–15, 226; Stiles, *Windsor,* I:683; Buel, *Dear Liberty,* pf. 247.

15. *Connecticut Gazette,* September 7, 21, 28, October 5, 1781. Wachtell, "Localism and Nationalism," pp. 116–18. Richard Buel reports that by January 1783, seventy-one Connecticut towns owed back taxes for payment of the Continental requisitions to a total of $3,000,000. *Dear Liberty,* p. 247.

16. Wachtell, "Localism and Nationalism," pp. 227–28; Saladino, "Economic Revolution," pp. 174–76.

17. Loucks, "American Revolution," describes the circle of merchants and politicians surrounding Jonathan Trumbull, pp. 168–70, 228, 97–101. Glenn Weaver's standard biography of Trumbull is subtitled *Connecticut's Merchant Magistrate.* On Trumbull's economic policy, see Saladino, "Economic Revolution," p. 117.

18. Platt, *Wadsworth*, Ch. II: passim, pp. 58–59. In 1784 Wadsworth, Platt says, "was possessed of a great liquid capital equal to virtually any call." Ibid., p. 59.

19. Wachtell, "Localism and Nationalism," pp. 216–17; Saladino, "Economic Revolution," pp. 116–17.

20. Grossbart, "Revolutionary Transition," Chs. VI, VII; Wachtell, "Localism and Nationalism," Ch. VII. That Connecticut's middle course saved it from the political and fiscal strife of its neighbor states is convincingly asserted in both Becker, *Revolution, Reform,* pp. 149–52; and Buel, *Dear Liberty,* pp. 326–27. Roger Brown maintains that the struggle over ratifying the Constitution in 1788 divided the same as the battles over tax policy. Brown applies this thesis to all the states, including Connecticut, where, he says, the debate over tax policy "polarized Connecticut politics into rich and poor." He points out, however, that Connecticut and New York were the only two states that saw no antitax rioting in the Confederation era. Brown, *Redeeming the Republic,* pp. 131–32. I am not sure about the rank and file, but the leading tax reformer was the wealthy Erastus Wolcott, who voted *for* the Constitution; and wealthy Comptroller James Wadsworth, not known to advocate tax reform, led the faction voting against ratification. Though intuitively Brown's categories ought to work for Connecticut, these two major exceptions and our lack of information on this point about other delegates to the convention do not lend support to his thesis. In any event, the gradations of wealth in Connecticut were so gradual that any statement about polarizing the rich and poor has to be viewed with great skepticism.

21. Wachtell, "Localism and Nationalism," pp. 229–30. State fiscal policy and the closely related matter of a congressional impost are thoroughly canvassed in Buel, *Dear Liberty,* Chs. 6 and 7, the most detailed published account. Excusing the poorest landowners from paying taxes—as selectmen were authorized to do—probably reduced Shaysite pressure. *Dear Liberty,* pp. 245–46.

22. Ibid., p. 218; Saladino, "Economic Revolution," p. 174. Estimates of up to 100,000 emigrants from Connecticut in the period 1780 to 1820 seem plausible. The subject of taxation and its relation to emigration from the state is thoroughly explored in Olson, "Economic Aspects," Ch. III.

23. *American Mercury,* October 25, 1784; *Connecticut Journal,* December 17, 1783; both quoted in Wachtell, "Localism and Nationalism," pp. 218, 219. The newspaper writer reported that taxes in Vermont and New York were one-tenth as high as in Connecticut. *Ibid.* I find that hard to believe.

24. Brown, *Redeeming the Republic,* passim; Main, *Antifederalists,* pp. 268–69; Main, *Political Parties,* pp. 65–67, 340–41.

25. Wachtell, "Localism and Nationalism," p. 261; Smith, *Letters,* 24:189.

26. *Norwich Packet,* March 16, 1786, March 2, 1786. Printing paper money was not a mere fiscal measure in the eighteenth century. It had political and moral overtones of which everyone was aware. Inflation undermined creditors and diluted the personal trust upon which so much commerce was based. "Debts," writes Gordon Wood, "were thus thought by many to be more than legal obligations; they were moral bonds tying people together." "Interests and Disinterestedness," in Beeman, ed., *Beyond Confederation,* p. 106. Paper money also undermined status, and demands for printing it "seemed to possess sinister, leveling implications that frightened the genteel part of society." Riesman, "Federalist Political Economy," Ibid., p. 151.

27. Grossbart, "Revolutionary Transition." pp. 252–53; Wachtell, "Localism and

Nationalism," pp. 262–69; Farrand, *Records*, II:439. Sherman had been writing hard-money tracts since 1751. Collier, *Sherman*, p.19.

28. Burnett, *Continental Congress*, pp. 381, 484; Ferguson, "Nationalists of 1781," pf. 245; Kohn, *Eagle and Sword*, pp. 19–39. See above, also, Ch. 1, n53. The impost act passed Congress on February 3, 1781. Burnett, *Continental Congress*, p. 480.

29. *DocHist*, Microfiche 8–13, p. 54.

30. *DocHist*, Microfiche 8–13, p. 58.

31. Quoted in Saladino, "Economic Revolution," p. 196. See also Ibid., pp. 179–81; Wachtell, "Localism and Nationalism," pp. 134–35.

32. Jensen, *New Nation*, pp. 297–99.

33. Ferguson, *Power of the Purse*, pp. 250–53; Burnett, *Continental Congress*, pp. 510–11 and trace index entries, Paper Money.

34. Saladino, "Economic Revolution," pp. 183–96, 201–03; Grossbart, "Revolutionary Transition," pp. 237–38, 272; McDonald, *We the People*, pp. 140–47. McDonald says that in terms of 1787 prices, $650,000 in U.S. securities was held by Connecticuters. Ibid., p. 140.

35. Oliver Ellsworth estimated that New York collected £60,000 to £80,000 in imposts, one-third of which was paid by Connecticut importers directly at their own warehouses in New York and in higher prices charged to their customers in Connecticut. On another occasion he used the figure $50,000, or £15,000. *DocHist*, pp. 544, 549. Noah Webster also gave the figure as £15,000 in impost duties paid to New York. *Connecticut Courant*, March 9, 1784. The antifederalist Hugh Ledlie said £8,000 was paid to New York. *DocHist*, p. 577. From 1785 through 1788 total duties paid in New York averaged $130,000 annually. In 1788 all importers paid $234,000 (£70,200) in duties to New York, one-third of which came from Connecticuters. Saladino, "Economic Revolution," pp. 159–60. See also Buel, *Dear Liberty*, pp. 316–17. A writer to the *Norwich Packet* in January 1788 claimed that the New England states had imported from Maryland 25,000 barrels of flour annually for the previous four years. He warned of the potential tax in Pennsylvania. *DocHist*, microfiche Doc. 73, p. 305; Stiles, *Literary Diary*, II:231.

36. Quoted in Wachtell, "Localism and Nationalism," p. 57 (January 25, 1784).

37. A total of thirty men were elected delegates from Connecticut to the Congress from 1774 to 1789; twenty actually served. Of those, eight were present at various times when the impost was discussed or voted on. They were Oliver Ellsworth, Roger Sherman, Samuel Huntington, Jesse Root, Eliphalet Dyer, William Samuel Johnson, and Stephen Mix Mitchell. Gerlach, "Connecticut Delegates," pp. 123, 124, 133, 136, 139. Gerlach, "Delegation of Steady Habits," pp. 36–37.

38. *SR*, III:314–15; Jordan, "Connecticut Politics," pp. 115–19.

39. Burnett, *Continental Congress*, pp. 530–35, 560, 570. The new proposal for an impost specified rates for certain goods and included the rest at 5 percent ad valorem instead of making them all 5 percent. It limited the impost to twenty-five years; restricted it to payment of the debts of the U.S.; and permitted the states to appoint the collectors, who would be removable by Congress. The act passed Congress April 18, 1783.

40. For a discussion of the Connecticut response to the request for authority to levy the 5 percent impost in 1783, see Buel, *Dear Liberty*, pp. 314–18. See also Wachtell, "Localism and Nationalism," pp. 75–81.

41. *DocHist,* p. 422. Richard Kohn writes that Benjamin Gale was "one of the few men in America to deduce the inner workings of the Newburgh plot, viewed the entire Constitution as the culmination of a conspiracy, first hatched in 1783, to insure commutation for army officers and to enrich financial manipulators." Kohn, *Eagle and Sword,* p. 82.

42. Jordan, "Connecticut Antifederalism," p. 19.

43. The Connecticut act is in *SR,* V:326–27 (May, 1784).

44. *Middlesex Gazette.* November 13, 1786. The speaker was archantifederalist Abraham Granger. Webster writes in *Connecticut Courant,* November 20, 1786.

45. Stiles, *Literary Diary,* III:296; Humphreys, ed., *Humphreys,* I:395 (January 20, 1787). Madison reported to Jefferson that "Connecticut has a great aversion to Conventions and is otherwise habitually disinclined to abridge her State prerogatives." Smith, *Letters of Delegates,* 24:93 (February 11, 1787).

46. Smith, *Letters,* 24:109 (February 21, 1787), 189 (March 31, 1787).

47. Smith, *Letters,* 24:93 (February 15, 1787), 109. Mitchell alludes to his opposition to "Conventions in General and particularly to the Resolve [in Congress] recommending the present one." Burnett, *Letters of Members,* VIII:645 (September 18, 1787). See McCaughey, *Johnson.* pp. 207–08, for a discussion of Johnson's and Mitchell's reluctance to support the call for a convention. Mitchell's action was erroneously perceived by all factions as evidence of antinationalism on his part. It is true that he feared a convention might adopt some nationalizing measures—called, in Connecticut, antirepublican—on the premise that state's autonomy promoted republican government. But Mitchell had written in April of 1786 that "our affairs seem to indicate the Approach of some great Crisis. Our Trade in a very distracted Situation, Britain watching for some opportune season to revenge her smarts, the fickle Indian nations ready to join those, who can best supply their wants." Evidence of Mitchell's nationalism is provided by his support of a congressional resolution in March 1787 declaring that state laws contrary to treaties with foreign nations would be void and could not operate. He hoped for some strengthening of the central government and was sent to the ratifying convention from Wethersfield and voted in favor. Smith, *Letters of Delegates,* 23:227; 24:165. Despite Johnson's reservations in April, and at the end of May just as he arrived in Philadelphia, he told his son that the convention was "an affair of high & agitated Expectation. An arduous Work!" Smith, *Letters,* 24:294

48. Humphreys, *Humphreys,* I:405–06. In the spring of 1787 a majority of the Council were out-and-out localists or moderate-tending localists, or in the case of Mitchell perceived as such. They were Stephen Mix Mitchell, William Hillhouse, Joseph Platt Cook, and Andrew Adams in addition to Erastus Wolcott, William Williams, and James Wadsworth. Adams, Hillhouse, and Cook were not elected delegates to the Connecticut ratifying convention. The others, except Wadsworth, all voted with the federalists. Jensen, "Introduction" to *DocHist,* p. 323, characterizes Sturges as an agrarian; Jordan, "Connecticut Politics," pp. 256–57, says he was a nationalist, a characterization that fits my perception.

49. *Connecticut Courant,* November 20, 1786.

50. "House Journal 1787–1788," pp. 10–11; Jordan, "Connecticut Politics," p. 298; Grossbart, "Revolutionary Transition," pf. 266; Wachtell, "Localism and Nationalism," pp. 279–81; Hutson, ed., *Supplement,* p. 194; Sedgwick, *Sharon,* pp. 80–

84. The view that Shays' Rebellion strengthened federalist forces is summarized in Brown, "Shays' Rebellion," in Beeman, *Beyond Confederation*, pp. 113, 113n1. Unlike the situation in Massachusetts, the repression of Shaysites does not seem to have created an antifederal backlash in Connecticut. Connecticut's merchants were not as numerous, wealthy, or concentrated as were those of Boston. But they no doubt shared Bostonians' edginess about the restlessness of the agrarian natives. Such anxiety would explain Granger's comment that "all men were on tiptoe" and the Assembly's hasty reaction to rumors of rebellious conversations in Sharon. See Patterson, "Federalist Reaction," in Gross, *In Debt to Shays*.

51. "House Journal 1878–1788," p. 1. The debates are carried in the *American Mercury*, May 21 to June 2, 1787, and other Connecticut newspapers for those weeks.

52. Perkins is quoted in the *Middlesex Gazette*, May 28, 1787; Granger in the *Connecticut Journal*, May 27, 1787. Excerpts from these newspaper accounts are printed in Kaminski and Leffler, eds., *Creating the Constitution*, pp. 42–44. These two comments reflect Saul Cornell's division of antifederalists into those who feared the hegemony of a "natural aristocracy" of the well-born and well-bred, and those who feared an artificial aristocracy created by the establishment of civil officers. Cornell, "Aristocracy Assailed." Of course, most antifederalists were not so discriminating about the focus of their animosity and objected to both.

53. Grossbart, "Revolutionary Transition," pp. 249–53.

54. Ibid., pp. 253–54, 256. The General Assembly ignored the good behavior provision and continued to appoint judges annually as it always had.

55. Collier, *Roger Sherman*, p. 228; *SR*, VI:282,399.

56. Hutson, *Supplement*, p. 3. Ellsworth, Johnson, and Wolcott were elected "after a long discussion" on Saturday, May 12. Wolcott resigned on May 14, and Sherman was chosen the next day. Final authorization was concluded on May 16. CSL, "House Journal 1786–1787," pp. 3, 5, 6, 16. Erastus Wolcott had refused to attend the First Continental Congress in 1774 on the same grounds, fear of smallpox. His refusal to go to Philadelphia was criticized in the state's newspapers. *Connecticut Courant*, August 2; CSL, *Arch.* "Revolutionary War," Ser. 1, I:56ab; Loucks, "Reformation and Revolution," p. 765.

3. National Objectives, Local Concerns:
Part 1. Protecting State Governments

1. Collier, *Roger Sherman*, pp. 14, 201, 90. This sketch is drawn almost entirely from the work cited. Citations for biographical facts can be located by reference to the index of that book.

2. Ibid., pp. 93, 185n, 315, 193, 94, 315–16.

3. To Simeon Baldwin (January 21, 1791): "Sherman Collection," Historical Manuscripts Room, Yale University Library.

4. Stiles, *Literary Diary*, III:500; Farrand, *Records*, 3:89.

5. The question of who spoke most at the convention is an open one. Madison has himself speaking most often. After him, Gouverneur Morris and Roger Sherman have the best claims, but it depends on what you count as "speaking." Does, for instance, merely seconding someone else's motion count as speaking? There are several

reliable editions of the debates at the constitutional convention. Every quotation here is accompanied by a date, either in the text or the citations, so readers will find it easy to locate them in any edition. I have provided citations to the standard work by Farrand updated in 1987 by James Hutson.

6. King, *King*, I:221; Massachusetts Historical Society (Hereafter MHS), "Henry Knox Collection," (June 3, 1787).

7. Edwards, *Edwards*, p. 184.

8. The biographical facts in this sketch are taken mostly from McCaughey, *Johnson*, Chs. 1 and 2.

9. The best account of the Stamp Act crisis in Connecticut, and the resultant political changes that brought both Sherman and Johnson to the Council of Assistants, is Zeichner, *Years of Controversy*, Ch. 3.

10. Groce, *Johnson*, p. 94.

11. McCaughey, *Johnson*, p. 37.

12. Ibid., pp. 182, 164; Collier, *Roger Sherman*, p. 89; McCaughey, *Johnson*, p. 168. Johnson was promoted from major to lieutenant colonel in January 1774 and resigned in October 1774. *CR*, XIV:221, 331.

13. Ford, ed., *Correspondence of Webb*, III:44; Groce, *Johnson*, p. 129. On Johnson's slaves, see Groce, *Johnson*, p. 146n43; and Smith, *Letters*, 22:494.

14. Hutson, *Supplement*, p. 303. His fellow congressman, Stephen Mix Mitchell, characterized Johnson as "very diffident & modest in Speaking," except in formal debate. Smith, *Letters*, 23:265.

15. The only full-scale biography of Ellsworth is that published in 1905 by William Brown. An excellent supplement is the pamphlet by Ronald Lettieri. William Casto has dealt very ably with Ellsworth's judicial career and legal thought. Ellsworth was rusticated from Yale for a youthful prank and graduated from Princeton. Ellsworth's wife was the daughter of William, first cousin to Erastus and Oliver Wolcott.

16. Lettieri, *Young Man*, p. 43; Brown, *Ellsworth*, p. 57; Casto, *Ellsworth*, pp. 28, 38, 78.

17. Hutson, *Supplement*, p. 303. Since there were three delegates, the contingent could not divide evenly—there was always a majority on one side or the other. However, on two occasions one member was absent, and during those periods three votes revealed that Sherman differed from Ellsworth twice and Johnson once. Sherman voted against a general grant of power to Congress, favoring a short enumeration; and he voted in favor of election of the members of the House by state legislatures, a stance that makes clear his conviction that the Constitution should be a compact among the states rather than a national system based on the people. Ellsworth at this point favored a general grant of authority and the direct election of representatives. These votes make clear the relative nationalism of Ellsworth. Johnson favored, and Sherman opposed, a ban on religious tests for officeholding under the new government, a natural division between the dissident Anglican and the establishment Congregationalist.

18. William Casto tries to make the case that New England Calvinists' belief in predestination made it feasible for them to compromise with evil in the short term in order to bring about a long-term objective. "Because everything was part of God's plan, a Calvinist politician like Ellsworth could work enthusiastically with people whose principles he reviled. An interim compromise with evil would be acceptable

as long as Ellsworth had faith in the general direction of politics." Casto, *Ellsworth*, p. 12. Casto also explains Ellsworth's self-righteousness as a function of a Manichean division of men into virtuous and evil: Those who agreed with him, of course, were virtuous. Ibid., 113, 122, 123. This ordering of society reflected another characteristic, as well, says Casto: Ellsworth "worshiped system and order." Ibid., p. 114.

19. Saladino, "Economic Revolution," p. 200; McCaughey, *Johnson*, pp. 197, 209.

20. Collier, *Roger Sherman*, p. 229; King, *King*, I:221; MHS, "Henry Knox Collection," (June 3, 1787), *DocHist*, p. 327. For other assessments of the relative nationalism of the Connecticut delegates see also: Saladino, "Economic Revolution," p. 207; Jordan, "Connecticut Politics," p. 327; Collier, *Roger Sherman*, pp. 228–29; Wachtell, "Localism and Nationalism," p. 284.

21. Tansill, ed., *Formation of the Union*, pp. 45–46; *SR*, VI:293. The credentials originally required two delegates to bind the state. "House Journal 1786–1787," pp. 3, 5, 6, 16. Of the Connecticut delegates, Ellsworth was present from May 28 to about August 23; he did not sign the Constitution, though he worked for its ratification in his home state. Sherman took his seat on May 30, and Johnson three days later. Sherman and Johnson made one joint trip together back to Connecticut. They arrived in New Haven in the rain, and a week later the *Courant* reported Sherman's arrival, but was blocked from further news of the convention by the ban of secrecy. Meanwhile the convention had adjourned until August 6, the day that Johnson and Sherman returned. Sherman attended for ninety-six days, Johnson for ninety-four, and Ellsworth ninety. Yale, Beinecke Library, "Sherman Papers"; *Gaines Pocket Almanac for 1787;* Connecticut Historical Society (Hereafter CHS), "Johnson Papers," Diary for 1787; *Courant*, July 30, 1787; Stiles, *Literary Diary*, III:271.

22. Sherry, "Founders' Unwritten Constitution," pf. 1132, develops this Coke/Locke dichotomy in relation to American constitutionalism.

23. Farrand, *Records*, I:48 (May 31).

24. Swift, *System*, I:62.

25. Farrand, *Records*, II:376 (August 22); Sherman to Dear Sir (December 8, 1788), Yale University Library, Historical Manuscripts Room, "Sherman Collection."

26. The Connecticut court system is described by Thomas Day in 1 Day iii–xxx. Farrand, *Records*. II:428 (August 27), 587–88 (September 112). I have discribed Connecticut's common-law judicature, 1639–1791, in "Individual Rights."

27. Max Farrand, who most definitively does not trivialize the work of the framers, enumerates and describes the major compromises in "Compromises of the Constitution." Article III Section 2 of the U.S. Constitution says, "The judicial power shall extend to all cases, in Law and Equity."

28. Farrand, *Records*, I:468 (June 29).

29. See for instance the speech in the Connecticut ratifying convention by Jedediah Huntington, who saw at a future day without the Constitution the time when New York, Rhode Island, and Massachusetts would, by military force, divide Connecticut among them. "What can we promise ourselves from the turbulent spirit of one, the selfishness of another, and the righteousness of a third?" he asked. *DocHist*, Microfiche 8-B, p. 47.

30. Farrand, *Records*, I:133 (June 6).

31. Ibid., II:642. Historians debate the objectives of the fifty-five delegates to the convention, and the historiographic literature is vast. There is, however, a solid con-

sensus among historians of the past half-century on the nationalist-property orientation of the body viewed collectively. An excellent historiographic s summary up to
1984 is Hutson, "Creation of the Constitution."

32. Farrand, "Compromises of the Constitution," p. 480n1. The term was first
given popular currency by the great nineteenth-century historian George Bancroft.
In his monumental work on the creation and establishment of the Constitution published in 1882, Bancroft entitled his chapter on the clash between the large states and
the small states and its resolution, "Connecticut Compromise," Bancroft, *Constitution of the United States*, II:48, 54, 71. The reason for this was not that the United
States' bicameral system replicated Connecticut's—which it didn't—but rather that
it was the Connecticut delegates who formulated the system, first proposed it at the
convention, and worked most doggedly to push it through.

33. Ford, ed., *Journals of the Continental Congress*, VI:1081; Collier, *Roger Sherman*, p. 262.

34. This dual method of voting is included in a proposed form of confederation
drawn up by Silas Deane sometime in late 1775. Deane may have consulted with
Sherman in devising his scheme, but the proposal includes a form of proportional
representation that would undermine the principles involved in Sherman's proposal,
and in other ways grants far more power to Congress than Sherman would delegate
even in 1787, and far less so in 1776. Deane's draft is in Smith, ed., *Letters*, II:418–
19. It is discussed in Rakov, *Beginnings of National Politics*, pf. 136. John Adams
noted Sherman's plan. Smith, ed., *Letters*, IV:592. Thomas Jefferson in May 1777
claimed he put forth such a proposal. He wrote Adams, "The Point of Representation
is what most alarms me, as I fear the great and small colonies are bitterly determined
not to cede. Will you be so good as to recollect the proposition I formerly made you
in private. . . . It was that any proposition might be negatived by the representatives
of a majority of the people of America, or of a majority of the colonies of America.
The former secures the larger and the latter the smaller colonies." Jefferson had been
present at Congress on August 1, when Sherman moved his proposal. Adams responded that he would "endeavour to get [Jefferson's idea] introduced" if he could
not win acceptance of proportional representation. Cappon, ed., *Adams-Jefferson
Letters*, I:4, 5–6. That Jefferson was present on August 1 is confirmed in Smith, *Letters*, IV:xxi.

35. Farrand, *Records*, I:20 (May 29). A side issue was the question of whether or
not to count slaves in states' populations when determining both their quotas of taxes
and their proportion of representatives. This issue was largely a North-South one, and
was resolved by continuing the de facto acceptance of the three-fifths rule that had
been developed in the Confederation Congress. The three-fifths compromise was
debated sporadically through June and July and resolved at last on August 5. It is discussed in detail by Paul Finkelman, who asserts that the three-fifths rule in relation
to representation was not a holdover from the Confederation system. This is hard to accept since the rule was tentatively agreed to as early as June 11 by a vote of nine states
to two in a proposal that explicitly linked the three-fifths rule to the "Act of Congress
agreed to by eleven states." The Confederation rule, of course, related to quotas of
revenue, not representation, since each state was represented equally in the old Congress. Farrand, *Records*, I:201 (June 11). See Finkleman, "Slavery and the Constitutional Convention," in Beeman, et al., eds., *Beyond Confederation*, pp. 194–208.

36. Farrand, *Records*, II:5 (July 14).

37. An official census was taken in 1790, and the percentages of the white population of the United States in each state in that year were:

Va.	16.5	N.Y.	10.1	N.H.	4.5
Mass.	14.8	Conn.	7.5	S.C.	4.5
Penna.	13.9	Md.	6.9	R.I.	2.2
N.C.	10.3	N.J.	5.5	Ga.	1.7
				Del.	1.6

Rank order of territorial size was:

1.	Ga.	6.	Mass.	10.	N.J.
2.	Va.	7.	S.C.	11.	Conn.
3.	N.C.	8.	Md.	12.	Del.
4.	N.Y.	9.	N.H.	13.	R.I.
5.	Pa.	9.	N.H.		

Roll, "We, Some of the People," passim; Wattenberg, ed., *Statistical History*, p. 39. Note that, with the exception of New York, the traditional interpretation of small-state/large-state division over representation follows if small and large refer to area rather than population. When blacks are added, Georgia's population is larger than Rhode Island's. Only Delaware's population is smaller.

38. Farrand, *Records*, I:151 (June 7); I:37 (May 30) (emphasis added); I:180 (June 9).

39. Ibid., I:37 (May 30); I:167 (June 8); I:177 (June 9). I have not seen it asserted that the Connecticut delegates viewed the Paterson Plan as a foil to the Virginia Plan that would open space in which to insert the Connecticut Compromise. But since Sherman was almost certainly involved in the discussions eventuating in the Paterson Plan; and since the Connecticut delegation did not speak during the debate on the plan; and since they ultimately voted against it; the inference that they found the Paterson Plan a convenient stalking horse for their compromise is plausible. Farrand, *Records*, I:241–322, 242n; O'Connor, *William Paterson*, p. 149, uses the "stalking horse" metaphor; and Casto, *Ellsworth*, pp.42–44, implies the foil concept. Perhaps the most accurate metaphor is the "straw man." Collier, *Decision in Philadelphia*, pp. 142–54.

40. Ibid., I:196. John Dickinson of Delaware is sometimes given credit for first introducing the compromise of an equal vote in one house and proportional vote in the other. See, e.g., McDonald, *Requiem*, pp. 97–101. The Connecticut Compromise, McDonald writes, "In fact, . . . was not a compromise, and did not originate with the Connecticut delegation." Ibid., p. 98. What Dickinson suggested (on June 2) was "that each State would retain an equal voice at least in one branch of the National Legislature" and in the other the vote should be based on the relative amount of money paid by each state into the national treasury, which he thought "would form a better ratio . . . than either the number of inhabitants or the quantum of property." On June 6 he said he "considered it as essential that one branch of the Legislature shd. be drawn immediately from the people; and as expedient that the other shd. be chosen by the Legislatures of the States." On June 7 he moved that "the members (of

the 2d. branch ought to be chosen) by the individual Legislatures," but allowed as how he thought that house [the Senate] "ought to be composed of a large number." Sherman thought there should be one member from each state. In neither case does Dickinson suggest the combination of equality and proportions found in the Sherman proposal and in the finished Constitution. Farrand, *Records*, I:87, 136, 150, 153, 52.

41. Ibid., I:196, 201 (June 11).

42. Smith, ed., *Letters*, 24:93.

43. Farrand, *Records*, I:343, 355, 406–07, 450.

44. Ibid., I:461–62.

45. Ibid., I:461–62. For a full discussion of the new basis of bicameralism, see Wood, *Creation of the American Republic*, pp. 214–22, 553–62.

46. Farrand, *Records*, I:468–69.

47. Ibid., I:484, 492 (June 30). A long-standing Connecticut tradition dating to the 1830s, but gaining its greatest strength from the writings of John Fiske in the late nineteenth century, holds that the Connecticut General Assembly was the prototype for the bicameral Congress. The deputies in the lower house—one or two from each town without relation to population—paralleled the Senate; the Council elected at large by "the people" paralleled the House. On this basis, the General Assembly in 1959 decreed that "Connecticut shall be known as the Constitution State." I find no evidence in the debates of 1787 to justify this contention, and the two systems do not parallel each other in several fundamental respects.

In fact, the councilors and deputies were elected by the freemen, a smaller number by about half than town meeting voters. No reference was made by anyone at the Philadelphia convention to any such parallel, nor have I found any relevant contemporaneous analogy. Furthermore, the proponents of this theory claim that Connecticut was a federation of autonomous towns voluntarily uniting like the United States for certain purposes. In fact, the towns were never autonomous, but right from their inception were creations of the colony government and subject to the most fundamental and detailed regulation by it—even to their very dismemberment.

The confederation theory of Connecticut's origins was rejected by the state supreme court in 1864, a decision that has been reiterated without exception in every relevant judicial action since. See Collier, "Why Connecticut Is the Constitution State," and "New England Specter."

48. Farrand, *Records*, I:484, 492, 406 (June 30, 26).

49. Ibid., I:484–85, 510, 511, 526 (July 2, 5). Ellsworth had been elected to serve on this committee but became "indisposed," and Sherman took his place. Madison, who was not there, claims that the proposal as reported out was put forward by Benjamin Franklin. Sherman, Madison says, moved "that each State should have an equal vote in the 2d branch; provided that no decision therein should prevail unless the majority of States concurring should also comprize a majority of the inhabitants of the U. States," a motion "not much deliberated on" in the committee meeting. Ibid., I:526n.

50. Ibid., I:550 (July 7). Sherman and many other delegates were not consistent: Whether by "states" they meant the people of the states or the state governments must be inferred from the context. The confusion over the word "state" was not limited to its application to both the government and the people of a state. The term was also applied indiscriminately to the state as a corporate entity with certain elements

of sovereignty like the power to tax, make treaties, raise and command armies, etc.; and to the collection of individuals who constituted the government, especially executives, whose powers and perquisites such as those of commander-in-chief, of appointment, director of a staff, wielder of influence, etc., might be curtailed by the overlay of a national government.

51. Pinckney had from time to time proposed that the states be classed large, medium, and small with variable numbers of members in the Senate. This time it was one each for Rhode Island and Delaware; two each for Georgia, New Jersey, and New Hampshire; three each for New York, Connecticut, Maryland, North Carolina, and South Carolina; four each for Pennsylvania and Massachusetts; and five for Virginia. Ibid., II:1 (July 14). Pinckney's ratio points up the fact of Connecticut's middling rather than small size.

52. Ibid., II:15.

53. Farrand says, "The important feature of the compromise was that in the upper house of the legislature each state should have an equal vote. The principle of proportional representation in the lower house was not a part of the compromise." Farrand, *Framing of the Constitution*, p. 105. He writes from the nationalist-large state point of view. Obviously, to the states'-rights/small-state delegates, altering the Articles to introduce the practice of proportional representation was a radical alteration of the prevailing system and thus the major compromise. In another place Farrand calls the Connecticut Compromise "the first and greatest compromise of the Constitution." Farrand, "Compromises," p. 488. Charles Warren considers the Connecticut Compromise a "victory for the smaller States," and notes, "Had it failed, the Convention itself would have failed; for it is certain that the delegates of the small States would not have remained longer." Warren, *Making of the Constitution*, pp. 310, 309.

54. For instance, Madison said, "The use of the Senate is to consist in its proceeding with more coolness, with more system, & with more wisdom, than the popular branch." Farrand, *Records*, I:151 (June 7). Madison said as late as July 9 that the Senate "had for one of its primary objects the guardianship of property," and Gouverneur Morris said that the Senate "must have great personal property, it must have the aristocratic spirit; it must love to lord it thro' pride." Farrand, *Records*, I:562, 512. See also statements by Mason, Baldwin, Davy. Ibid., I:428, 469, 542.

55. See, for instance, "Federalist No. 62."

56. Farrand, *Records*, II:5 (July 14); I:373 (June 22).

57. See, for instance, "Federalist No. 51."

58. O'Connor, *Paterson*, pf. 130.

59. This paper is printed in full in Farrand, *Records*, III:615–16. The original is in the "Sherman Papers" at the American Antiquarian Society in Worcester, Mass. It is of uncertain date and could have been written any time between 1784 and 1787. H. L. Boutell believes it to have been written in "the last days of the Confederation." Boutell, *Roger Sherman*, p. 132. J. Franklin Jameson thought that it was Sherman's summary of the resolutions of the Committee of the Whole modified by changes up to July 2. American Antiquarian Society, "Sherman Papers." Jameson to G. F. Hoar (May 6, 1903). Madison spoke on July 17 of a paper from which Sherman read, calling it "an enumeration." Farrand, *Records*, II:26. Sherman's proposed amendments as reported by Madison are nearly verbatim from his paper. Farrand quotes Bancroft as saying that the plan that Sherman presented "in importance stands next to that of

Virginia." Farrand believes the paper to be Sherman's contribution to the New Jersey Plan. Ibid., III:615–16. The paper, it seems to me, represents ideas more nationalist than Sherman would entertain on his own. I think Jameson is probably closest to correct, but suspect it was written later than July 2, probably after July 16, when equality in the Senate had been sealed. An August date is not impossible; see Abraham's Baldwin's discussion of papers written by delegates during the convention in Ibid., III:170.

60. Ibid., I:229, II:25, 21 (July 17). Sherman's concern would be addressed in the Tenth Amendment in 1791.

61. *DocHist.* p. 525. Of course the powers of Congress were not clearly defined; the federal courts today work almost full-time defining them. (On deliberate ambiguities in the Constitution, see Baldwin in Farrand, *Records,* III:369). The Virginia Plan assigned to the new Congress all the authority of the old one and also "power to legislate in all cases to which the separate States are incompetent, or in which the harmony of the United States might be interrupted by the exercise of individual legislation;" Ibid., I:21 (May 29). Roger Sherman, not surprisingly, was the only man present to vote against it, differing with Ellsworth, Johnson not having arrived. Ibid., I:47 (May 31). This broad general grant remained part of the draft until the report of the Committee of Detail on August 6. II:177. This report included Article I, Section 8 with its enumerated powers, altered in debate and reported out of the Committee of Style on September 12 essentially as found in the final draft. This change from a general grant to an enumeration is in principle really quite radical. It would logically be considered a great victory for the states'-rights forces; but it is clear that many, if not most, of the delegates had anticipated such a listing. Edmund Randolph, who had introduced the Virginia Plan with its broad general grant, said that the language there "involves the power of violating all the laws and constitutions of the States, and intermeddling with their police [powers]." Ibid., II:26 (July 17). See also I:53 (May 31). Madison "said that he had brought with him into the Convention a strong bias in favor of an enumeration." Ibid., I:53 (May 31). Other delegates voiced concern about the vagueness of the various words and phrases in the general grant. By August 16, when debate began on the report of the Committee of Detail, it seems clear that there was a palpable consensus on an enumeration. Collier, *Decision in Philadelphia,* pp. 246–54. Thus this fundamental structural element of the Constitution cannot be accounted a states'-rights victory because there was no contest over the question.

62. Farrand, *Records.* II:558; Warren, *Making of the Constitution,* p. 675.

63. Farrand, *Records,* II:629–30.

64. The opinions of Henry and Calhoun are in Boutell, *Sherman,* pp. 290, 165.

65. The clause as drafted by the Committee of the Whole is Farrand, *Records,* II:503; Morris' version is Ibid., II:594. The statement that it was Sherman who caused the change was made by Albert Gallatin, who called Morris' effort "a trick." Ibid., III:379. The intent of the varied punctuation is discussed fully by Madison in a letter of 1830. Ibid., III:483–84. That the general welfare clause was intended merely to qualify the power to lay taxes, duties, etc., is explained in that letter and in Madison's *Federalist 41.* Sherman "thought it necessary to connect with the clause for laying taxes duties &.c. an express provision of the old debts." Ibid., II:414. The rendering in the official Constitution is: "The Congress shall have Power To lay and collect Taxes, Duties, Imposts and Excises, to pay the Debts and provide for the common

Defence and general Welfare of the United States." To achieve the full force of Sherman's intent, he would have also had to remove the comma after "Excises." As a representative in the First Congress Sherman said, "One great object that the States had" in ratifying the Constitution was the "support of the public credit." He declared that the people had sent their representatives to fulfill "the great object of Congress," to raise a revenue and pay the public debt. Collier, *Sherman*, pp. 285–87.

4. National Objectives, Local Concerns:
Part 2. Protecting the Local Economy

1. See especially Lynd, *Class Conflict*, and Robinson, *Slavery in American Politics*. Paul Finkelman, "Slavery and the Constitutional Convention" in Beeman, et al., eds., *Beyond Confederation*, uses the phrase "dirty compromise," p. 214. Finkelman links the compromising of northern concern for controlling navigation acts with southern concern for the slave trade to the North-South compromise relating to the three-fifths formula. Finkelman's interpretation of the convention debate is based on the assumption that slavery and the slave trade were the central concerns of the delegates. While that may well have been the case for some delegates, especially southerners, neither slavery nor the slave trade was a major factor for the Connecticut delegates, who were principally concerned with balancing stability with states' rights. In regard to the navigation acts compromise, Finkelman agrees generally with the one outlined here, which I first put forward in *Decision in Philadelphia*. However, though Finkelman notes that "Roger Sherman . . . virtually always voted with the South on important matters" and "would prove to be the Deep South's most vocal northern ally," and that "Oliver Ellsworth, of Connecticut, came from a state which had consistently supported southern interests in the convention," he does not explain this odd alliance. pp. 209n60, 211. He recognizes the Sherman-Rutledge partnership, but does not separate Connecticut commercial interests from those of the other New England states. Nevertheless he describes the compromise as I do: "The South Carolina delegation would support the [external] commerce clause if New England would support protection for the slave trade and a prohibition on export taxes." pp. 213, 214.

2. The New England-South Carolina axis has always fascinated historians, who have suggested several explanations of the puzzle. See for instance, McDonald, *Formation of the American Republic*, pp. 176–77; Rossiter, *Grand Convention*, pp. 215–18. I have more fully developed my own explanation in Collier, *Decision in Philadelphia*, pp. 146–52.

3. Farrand, *Records*, I:486.

4. By interpretation of the state constitution, the Massachusetts supreme court had declared slavery illegal in 1783, though some individuals continued in bondage for a time. Zilversmit, *First Emancipation*, pp. 113–16. New Hampshire's case concerning slavery is unclear. By some accounts, slavery there was abolished by the state's constitution of 1783; by others, it was not abolished until 1857. Ibid., p. 117. Fewer than eight hundred Negroes, not all of them slaves, resided in New Hampshire in 1787. Greene, *Negro in Colonial New England*, p. 76. Many documents relating to slavery—private letters, speeches, public papers, legislative debate, etc.—generated

by the revolutionary generation after 1777 with a focus on the writing and ratification of the Constitution have been collected by John Kaminski in *A Necessary Evil?*.

5. Petitions against the importation and sale of Africans were presented to the General Assembly as early as 1768. Agitation for the abolition of slavery in Connecticut began during the mid-1770s, and the General Assembly passed legislation making it easier to manumit slaves in 1777. Bills for gradual emancipation were introduced in 1779, and the revised code of 1784 provided that all children born of slave mothers after March 1 of that year would become free on their twenty-fifth birthdays. The code was amended in 1797 to provide freedom on the child's twenty-first birthday. Zilversmit, *First Emancipation*, pp. 122–23; Collier, *Roger Sherman*, p. 194n. A full account of antislavery sentiment and activity in Connecticut during the revolutionary era, a study that reveals much hitherto undiscovered liberalism, is Loucks, "Reformation and Revolution." In 1788 the General Assembly prohibited any Connecticut citizen from having anything to do with the slave trade—an extension of a 1774 statute forbidding the importation of slaves into the state. *SR*, VI:472; *CR*, XIV:329.

6. Slavery remained legal in Delaware until the adoption of the Amendment XIII to the United States Constitution in 1865, but Delaware had "virtually ceased being a slave state" by 1861 and remained loyal to the Union during the Civil War. Genovese, *Roll, Jordan, Roll*, p. 400.

7. Davis, *Problem of Slavery*, pp. 121–23.

8. Farrand, *Records*, II:220, 221–22, 370, 417 [reporting the speeches of King, Morris (August 8), Mason (August 22), and Madison (August 25), respectively]. One should note that these speeches were given in debate over the slave trade, not slavery per se.

9. Ibid., II:222 (August 8).

10. See, for instance, *American Negro Reference Book.* "Down to the War for Independence the slave trade was vital to the economic life of New England and, indeed, the very heart of the highly profitable triangular trade." p. 16.

11. McCusker and Menard, *Economy of British America*, pp. 110–11.

12. *SR*, VI:472; Hedges, *Browns of Providence*, I:82–83; Jordan, *White Over Black*, p. 410.

13. Fogelman and Engerman challenge the widely held view that slavery was dying in the United States only to be revived by the invention of the cotton gin and the consequent expansion of the cotton culture. They show a precipitous drop in slave imports during the Revolution but then a similarly sharp increase beginning in 1780—thirteen years prior to Eli Whitney's invention. Fogel and Engerman, *Time on the Cross*, pp. 24–25; see also Farrand, *Records*, II:373 (Charles Cotesworth Pinckney's speech of August 22).

14. McCusker and Menard, *Economy of British America*, p. 111.

15. Marine lists for the period from January 1786 to January 1787 show only three ships, but 163 smaller vessels not including coasters, arriving in port. Caulkins, *History of New London*, p. 578. A ship was a large sailing vessel, usually of at least three masts. Two-masted brigantines and single-masted sloops were used in the American coastal and Caribbean trade.

16. McCusker and Menard, *Economy of British America*, pp. 109–11.

17. Farrand, *Records,* II:374 (August 22).

18. Daniels, "Economic Developments," passim. Small amounts of European goods were transshipped from foreign West Indies, but they were an inconsiderable part of the trade. Saladino, "Economic Revolution," pp. 151–56. This and the next paragraph summarize chapter 2 above.

19. *DocHist,* pp. 544, 576.

20. Farrand, *Records,* I:286. (June 18); *Norwich Packet,* January 17, 1788. The need to import wheat fluctuated with the depredations of the Hessian fly in Connecticut, which were especially bad in the mid-1780s.

21. Ferguson, *Power of the Purse,* pf. 116.

22. Farrand, *Records,* II:362, 306, 361 (August 21, 16, 21).

23. McCusker and Menard, *Economy of British America,* pp. 174–81.

24. Burnett, *Continental Congress,* pf. 654; Marks, *Independence on Trial,* pp. 26–36.

25. Smith, *Letters,* 23:542,332 (June 4, September 3, 1786).

26. Ibid., 23:465 (August 12, 1786). Concern that westward migration might bring about the dismemberment of the Union was voiced by such leading early nationalists as James Madison. He saw the dominating demographic trend as western and southern, and in the First Congress sought to weld future Kentuckians and Tennesseeans to the national government. A separation, of course, would thwart the expected southern domination. McCoy, "Visions of American Nationality," in Beeman, et al., eds., *Beyond Confederation,* pp. 227–30.

27. Saladino, "Economic Revolution," pp. 151–56.

28. Farrand, *Records,* II:181, 183.

29. Ibid., II:220, 221–22 (August 8).

30. Ibid., II:364 (August 21), 372 (August 22).

31. Ibid., II:364 (August 21), 220 (August 8), 369 (August 22).

32. Ibid., II:370 (August 22). On Mason's slaves, see Rowland, *George Mason,* passim and his will in Appendix VI.

33. Farrand, *Records,* II:370, 370–71, 374 (August 22). Under convention rules, a day must intercede before a decision could be reconsidered.

34. Ibid., II:373, 374, 375 (August 22).

35. Ibid., II:415 (August 25), 375 (August 22).

36. Ibid., II:396–97 (August 24).

37. See, e.g., Luther Martin in Ibid., III:187.

38. Ibid., II:416 (August 25). Roger Sherman had said earlier that "[h]e was opposed to a tax on slaves imported as making the matter worse, because it implied they were *property.*" Ibid., II:374 (August 22).

39. Ibid., II:449–50, 449n (August 29). Sixteen members of the convention were also members of Congress sitting at New York, and there was a good deal of communication between the two bodies. Just as the debate on slavery and trade matters was climaxing in Philadelphia, Congress was completing work on the Northwest Ordinance, which forbade slavery north of the Ohio River; omitted any mention of the area south of the Ohio; and included a fugitive slave clause of virtually the same language as that found in the Constitution. An explicit relationship between the two has been suggested. Lynd, *Class Conflict,* pp. 205–07.

40. Farrand, *Records,* II:451, 453–54 (August 29).

41. Ibid., III:334, 84. See also Ibid., III:210–11, 254, 436. Finkelman agrees that the fugitive slave clause is the dirtiest part of what he has aptly called the "dirty compromise." Beeman, et al, eds., *Beyond Confederation*, pp. 223–25, 214.

42. Farrand, *Records*, I:21–22. The courts would also hear maritime disputes, including piracy; cases involving the national revenue; impeachments of federal officers; and "questions which may involve the national peace and harmony."

43. See generally Onuf, *Origins*. Chs. 3 and 4; Farrand, *Records*, I:22, 121. For expressions of fear that New York and Massachusetts might cut up Connecticut between them, see note 29, ch. 3 above.

44. Ibid., II:170, 171, 183–84, 462. The original version omitted the words "or any of them." II:162. The system established under Article IX of the Articles of Confederation and carried into the draft Constitution was expunged on August 24 on Rutledge's motion with Johnson's second and Sherman's audible approval. Ibid., II:400–01. Johnson for Connecticut had lost the only suit brought to that court.

45. Ibid., II:465 (August 30).

46. Ibid., II:602.

47. The clause also protected another of Sherman's clients—Vermont settlers still disputing jurisdiction with New York and New Hampshire. Of course, the only federal court provided for in the Constitution was the U.S. Supreme Court. Had no inferior courts been established (as Sherman hoped, Farrand, I:125, II, 46), one supposes these cases would bypass the state courts and be tried in the Supreme Court. As it turned out, the Wyoming land claims dispute was finally heard in 1795 in appeal from lower federal courts to the Supreme Court; in the case of *Van Horne's Lessee v. Dorrance*. 2 Dallas 304. It resulted, like the Trenton decision of 1782, in a complete victory for the Pennsylvania claimants. In 1799 the Pennsylvania government gave the Connecticut settlers compensatory lands in other parts of the state.

48. Farrand, *Records*, II:81 (July 21).

49. Ibid., I:65, 68. Within a couple of days Sherman had accepted the single executive. I:97.

50. Ibid., I:97, 99, 85; II:301.

51. Ibid., II:318, 401, 405, 426, 419.

52. Ford, ed., *Pamphlets*, p. 240.

53. The convention forwarded the document to Congress (where thirteen members of the convention—including James Madison—now sat) and it was read on September 20. Discussion began six days later, and on the 28th Congress resolved to send the Constitution to the state legislatures to be put before special conventions. There is no explicit endorsement of it. Burnett, *Continental Congress*, pp. 695–97.

54. Article VI, second paragraph, reads: "The Constitution, and the Laws of the United States . . . shall be the supreme Law of the Land." Article I, Section 8, third paragraph reads: "Congress shall have Power . . . To regulate commerce . . . among the severall states." Paragraph eighteen authorizes Congress "To make all Laws which shall be necessary and proper" to execute all the other provisions of the Constitution.

55. McCaughey, *Johnson*, pp.224–25. Johnson attended the ratifying convention and spoke there. He accepted appointment to a six-year term in the U.S. Senate meeting in New York near Columbia College. When Congress adjourned to Philadelphia he resigned his seat, and the General Assembly appointed Roger Sherman to replace him. Sherman died two years later.

56. The best sympathetic discussion of Ellsworth's work in the convention is Lettieri, *Ellsworth*, pp. 66–76. Lettieri agrees that there were elements of deception in Ellsworth's presentation of the case for the Constitution, but would disagree with my characterization of him as a "closet federalist." He portrays Ellsworth's contradictions—which he terms "inconsistencies"—as a result of a (rapid) evolution. Ibid., pp. 77, 81, 83. See also Collier, "Sovereignty Finessed," in Conley and Kaminski, eds., *The Constitution and the States*.

57. See below Ch. 5 and Ibid.

58. Saladino, "Economic Revolution," pp. 215–23, and Ch. 7 passim describe Connecticut's revival after 1788.

5. Ratification in Connecticut

1. *DocHist*, pp. 364–68, 351–52, 452 (Ashbel Baldwin, November 13, 1787), 355n3; Steiner, "Connecticut's Ratification," p. 97; *SR*, VI:355.

2. Saladino, "Economic Revolution," Chapter 5; pf. 160, pp. 176–77.

3. Ibid. A whole series of acts levying taxes for different purposes, in different amounts, and payable in different ways—produce, specie, and paper—were passed in 1784 and 1785. They can be traced best by referring to the indexes of *SR*, vols. V and VI.

4. Saladino, "Economic Revolution," pp. 178, 180–81.

5. On the influence of Shays' Rebellion on constitution making see Gross, ed., *In Debt to Shays*, Part I.

6. *DocHist*, p. 352; Some observers saw the nationalist implications, but liked them. One former Loyalist joyfully told another one, "We are upon the Eve of another Revolution in the System of Government." The proposed Constitution "leaves but a shadow of power in the States." Dibble to Peters, November 16, 1787, quoted in Brown, *Redeeming the Republic*, p.3. Interestingly, in Pennsylvania, federalists saw adoption of the new Constitution as one way to reform the state government—something many of them had been trying to do since 1776. Thus what in Connecticut the federalists denied was not even a possibility, was in Pennsylvania a desired outcome by what, it became clear, was a majority of the voters. Ireland, *Religion, Ethnicity, and Politics*, Ch. I.

7. *DocHist*, pp. 354, 394; Stiles, *Literary Diary*, III:288; *DocHist*, pp.452–53.

8. *Ibid.*, pp. 352–53, 485, 351.

9. *SR*, VI:355–56.

10. There were three newspapers in New Haven; two in Hartford; one each in Norwich, New London, Middletown, Fairfield, and Litchfield. No papers were published in rural Tolland and Windham Counties. Katz, "Connecticut Newspapers," p. 33.

11. *DocHist*, pp. 354, 577. (Hugh Ledlie, January 15, 1788); Simeon Baldwin to James Kent, March 8, 1788. Baldwin Collection, Yale University Library, Historical Manuscripts Room.

12. The *Documentary History* prints the relevant entries from all the extant town meeting minutes. pp. 405–52. There were ninety-eight towns plus Weston—incorporated in 1787 and voting with Fairfield in these elections. The towns instructing their delegates to ratify were Danbury, Greenwich, and Ridgefield; those instructing

against were Lebanon, Mansfield, Willington, and Simsbury. Preston's instructions were ambiguous. The town told the delegates to ratify if certain alterations could be made to the document, but authorized them to use their best judgment in the end. Bristol, East Windsor, Ridgefield, Southbury, and Woodbury town meetings endorsed the Constitution; Durham, Ellington, Hamden, Lebanon, Mansfield, Simsbury, and Willington meetings rejected it. *DocHist*, pp. 405–52; for Derby, *Ibid.* Fiche 24, p. 123 (*New Haven Gazette*, October 11, 1787). Constant Southworth of Mansfield later said he had been instructed to vote against. *Ibid.*, p. 598. In many towns there was a clear consensus that should have compelled their delegates—but such a consensus was not always compelling, as witness William Williams of Lebanon and others who violated even explicit instructions. Several other towns apparently instructed their delegates, but the record does not make clear which way (I have read all the extant minutes of all the towns).

13. *DocHist*, pp. 354–55; Humphreys, *Humphreys*, I:426; *DocHist*, p. 577. The importance of commanding the press in this crucial debate is emphasized in Cornell, *Other Founders*, Ch. 1.

14. *DocHist*, p. 399. Ellsworth wrote thirteen "Letters of a Landholder." The last five "Letters" were published after Connecticut had ratified the Constitution and were addressed to a national audience. They are all reprinted in *DocHist* and can also be found in Ford, *Essays on the Constitution*. Ronald Lettieri, the most careful modern analyst of these essays, sees them as expressing an unfolding "unified and coherent" political philosophy based on the old republican concept of an integrated organic society, explicitly rejecting Madison's system of competing interest groups. But Lettieri also admits that the "Landholder Letters" were framed in a "bitterly personalized brand of partisanship," characterized by a "vituperative" and "acerbic" style. Lettieri, *Connecticut's 'Publius,'"* pp. 31, 33–34, 25, 26. Ellsworth's essays were aimed particularly at Elbridge Gerry's "Objections," the most widely reprinted antifederalist argument. They are included in *DocHist*, 548–50. For the claim that Gerry's essays were the most reprinted (forty-six times), see Saul Cornell, *Other Founders*, pp. 28–29 and Appendix 1.

15. The statements are found on the back of a broadside in which Governor Samuel Huntington declares a day of Thanksgiving. The document was found among the Benjamin Trumbull papers and is in his handwriting. It is undated and unsigned. There is a photocopy at the North Haven Historical Society. The original is thought to have been at Yale University in 1987, but cannot be located at this writing (2002). Trumbull also noted as suggestions he had heard that the president's salary should be fixed by Congress and that soldiers' notes now in the hands of speculators should be paid in full. William Riker has noted that of all the rights antifederalists thought were threatened by the new Constitution, trial by jury was by far the most discussed. Riker, *Strategy of Rhetroic*, pp. 265–66. Trumbull's list of objections typified those heard in all the states. There was nothing unique in the Connecticut antifederalists' protests. For a convenient summary of those protests throughout the states, see Cornell, *Other Founders*, pf. 26, esp. 30–31.

16. *DocHist*, p. 491. "Landholder Letter VI." Robert Rutland has characterized Ellsworth's "Letters" as "slashing attacks on the motives and personalities of the Antifederalists. Reckless of fact and given to exaggeration." Ellsworth had a "facile pen and loose regard for the niceties of fact." Rutland, *Ordeal*, pp. 75, 74.

17. *DocHist,* p. 472. "Countryman Letter II." Also, see below, Ch. 4.

18. Ibid., pp. 489, 479. "Landholder Letters" VI and IV. That the delegates knew changes would have to be made in state governments, see Rakov, *Original Meanings,* pf. 105.

19. *DocHist,* p. 524

20. Ibid., p. 525. At the convention Sherman had protested that "it would be difficult to draw the line between the powers of the Genl. Legislatures [*sic*], and those to be left with the states." Farrand, *Records,* II:25 (July 17), I:34–35 (May 30). *DocHist,* p. 525. On what the antifederalists would accept, see Storing. *What the Anti-Federalists Were For,* pp. 32–33, 38.

21. Farrand, *Records,* I:65, 68 (June 1), 85 (June 2). *DocHist,* p. 526. Emphasis in original.

22. See above in Ch. 2.

23. *DocHist,* p. 527.

24. Ibid., pp. 329–30. The dearth of antifederal prints in Connecticut was unusual. In most states, though there were fewer newspapers proportionate to population, at least one was antifederal or willing to publish antifederal arguments, and three-quarters of all newspapers published some antifederal material. In Connecticut, the suppression was virtually total. Cornell, *Other Founders,* pp. 1–26, 46, 122.

25. Boyd, *Politics of Opposition,* pp. 22, 24–25, 34, 56, 60.

26. *DocHist,* p. 563; Smith, *Letters,* 21:346; Riggs, ed., *Anarchiad,* p. 29; Howard, *Connecticut Wits,* p. 190. Wadsworth faced injury as well as insult; his replacement, Oliver Wolcott, Jr., was paid £200 instead of Wadsworth's £150. *SR,* VI:412, 413. Wadsworth's refusal to swear a new oath to the United States might much better be seen as a politically fatal, but heroic, act of conscience. He, like all other Connecticut officeholders, had sworn an oath proclaiming that "by the Name of the Everliving God, . . . you will be true and faithful to the State of *Connecticut,* as a free and independent State, and in all things do your Duty as a good and faithful Subject of the State, in supporting the Rights, Liberties and Priviledges of the same." In January 1789—perhaps just to snare Wadsworth—the General Assembly prescribed an additional oath for all officeholders: "You Swear by the Name of the everliving God . . . that you will support the Constitution agreed upon by the Convention of the United States and ratified by the Convention of this State." The contradiction between the two oaths was stark; but among Connecticut officeholders, James Wadsworth was alone in getting out of its way. Cushing, *First Laws,* p. 182; *SR,* VI:500. For a discussion of the potential for conflict between state and U.S. oaths, see Duncan, *Anti-Federalists,* pp. 144–45.

27. *DocHist,* pp. 486n1, 577, 580, 576, 421.

28. Ibid., p. 580; Stiles, *Literary Diary,* III:298. On Huntington, see Gerlach, *Huntington,* pp. 60–67, 84–85, 98–99. These were, of course, the very men who as state officeholders might be supposed to have the most to lose under the overweening national government, a logical problem not addressed by the antifederalists. A list of delegates showing their vote to the convention by towns is at *SR* VI, 549–52.

29. *DocHist,* p. 576.

30. Delaware 30–0, Dec. 7, 1787; New Jersey 38–0, Dec. 18, 1787; Georgia 26–0, Jan. 2, 1788; Pennsylvania 46–23, Dec. 12, 1787.

31. *DocHist,* p. 586.

32. Ibid., p. 586. Mandating a single up or down vote on the entire document was the standard tactic among federalist politicians in every state. Challenges in other states are discussed in Rakov, *Original Meanings*, pf. 113.

33. *DocHist*, p. 544. Estimates ranged from £100,000 to the antifederalists' £8000. Ibid., p. 576. Ellsworth's estimates in pounds translate into $60,000 to $88,600.

34. In 1783 the Continental Loan Office estimated that of $11.5 million, $1,265,000 (over 11 percent) was owed to Connecticut creditors of the U.S. *DocHist*, p. 320. Connecticut's population was 7.5 percent of that of the thirteen states.

35. Ibid., pp. 543–45.

36. Ibid., p. 547–48. Our understanding of the Connecticut antifederalists' rationale is severely limited, not only by newspapers' refusal to publish their materials, but also by the extreme bias of the man reporting the convention debate, Enoch Perkins. He revealed himself, not only by omitting the opposition speeches, but also in his private correspondence. "General Wadsworth attacked the Constitution pugnis and calcibus, conquibusm & rosto. Colonel Dyer, to show his wisdom and importance, & to show that other men did not know so much as I, made a great many objections against it. He talked till, I believe, he disgusted every single soul who heard him. Mr. Hopkins was afraid lest the liberties of the people should be infringed." Perkins reported none of these speeches. *DocHist*, p. 584. Earlier he had written to a friend that the antinationalists were "acting a part that is unreasonable, dishonest and injurious to the public; They are likewise ridiculous objects." Baldwin, *Baldwin*, p. 395.

37. *DocHist*, pp. 548–54, 558.

38. Ibid., p. 554.

39. Ibid., pp. 576, 580.

40. Ibid., p. 559.

41. Ibid., pp. 559–60.

42. Ibid., pp. 575–83, 420–29, 486. Ledlie was an old militia captain who had survived the worst campaigns of the Seven Years' War, serving among other places in the lethal Havana expedition, Crown Point, and other battles. He did not rise above the rank of captain. He was from Windham, but from about 1770 to 1777 he ran a shop in Hartford. He was a delegate to the Middletown anticommutation convention. Noah Webster referred to him as "a *noted wild Irishman.*" He was a Son of Liberty as early as 1765, but never held statewide civil office. Ibid., p. 486n1

43. *DocHist*, pp. 576–77, 423, 579, 428, 429, 547.

44. Ibid., pp. 580–81. In an exhaustive analysis of the Connecticut opposition to parliamentary measures between 1765 and 1775, Rupert Charles Loucks has described an antiaristocratic and antiauthoritarian character type. He calls these people "diffusionists" who were "hypersensitive to the dangers of moral corruption, conspiracies against liberty and abuse of power, conditions that invariably appeared when authority was concentrated into a few hands." Loucks, "Reformation and Revolution," pp. 17–18. This describes those antifederalists whose sentiments we know.

45. *DocHist*, Microfiche 3. *Connecticut Courant*, November 20, 1786; Benjamin Gale in *DocHist*, pp. 426, 459, 421; Jordan, "Connecticut Politics," p. 283.

46. "Landholder II" in *DocHist*, p. 402; Perkins in ibid., Microfiche 8-B, p. 52; Ibid., p. 576.

47. *DocHist*, p. 595. Anonymous in the *Massachusetts Gazette*, February 5, 1788.

6. Constitutional Crosswinds

1. *DocHist,* Fiche #77, p. 320. Anonymous letter from New York, January 2, 1788, printed in the *Connecticut Courant,* January 21, 1788.

2. See, for example, Ledlie in *DocHist,* pp. 577, 598n3.

3. Hall, *Life and Letters of Parsons,* p. 502.

4. In some other states the antiaristocracy rhetoric was spelled out fully enough to constitute an ideology. See e.g., Onuf, *Origins,* p. 189; Yarbrough and Eubanks in Gillespie and Lienesch, *Ratifying the Constitution;* and especially Wood, who says, "Nothing was more characteristic of Antifederalist thinking than this obsession with aristocracy." *Creation,* p. 488. The fear of establishing a distant government and a heterogeneous nation was also articulated as an ideology in other states. See, e.g., Eubanks in Gillespie and Lienesch, *Ratifying the Constitution;* Rakov, *Original Meanings,* pp. 181–84; Wood, *Creation,* e.g., pp. 499–500.

5. Jordan, "Connecticut Politics," pp. 296–97, 309; Wachtell, "Localism and Nationalism," p. 282; *DocHist,* p.325.

6. Jordan, "Connecticut Politics," p. 350; Grossbart, "Revolutionary Transition," p. 362. Oliver Wolcott hoped that events in Massachusetts would bring "our visionary politicians" down to earth; and indeed, such a one as Benjamin Gale expressed concern that the Shays "disease wil [*sic*] become Epidemical." Quoted in Wachtell, "Localism and Nationalism," p. 282.

7. The *New Haven Gazette,* August 2, 1787, quoted in Jordan, "Connecticut Politics," p. 309; Grossbart, "Revolutionary Transition," pp. 266–67; *Susquehannah Papers,* IX:21. Timothy Hosmer to Paull Schott, February 3, 1787.

8. *Hampshire Herald,* November 6, 1786, quoted in Buel, *Dear Liberty,* p. 327.

9. September 23, 1787. *DocHist,* p. 351.

10. *DocHist,* p. 598. Throughout this analysis I have treated the men who voted against ratification as a distinct group opposed to those who voted for. The presence among the antifederalists of men like Constant Southworth who wanted to vote in favor, and men among the federalists like Hopkins who only voted to ratify under the most extreme pressure, makes the division somewhat artificial. To assign men to antifederal and federal factions on any other basis, however, would require a significant number of judgment calls that would be hard to justify on any objective grounds. The problem of classifying men as antifederalists is discussed by Herbert Storing in *What The Anti-Federalists Were For,* pp. 4–5.

11. The ten men who represented the five incorporated cities were all nationalists (in the Connecticut context, anyway) and would have voted to ratify no matter what town sent them to the convention.

12. The term "commercial orientation" means that a town included a number of merchants who engaged in the interstate and West Indies trade. These towns also had newspapers and a proportionately greater share of lawyers. But all Connecticut towns were populated predominately by farmers. Benjamin Gale was speaking hyperbolically, perhaps, but more or less correctly when he wrote in 1782, "It would be needless to attempt to prove, not one in a hundred on the sea shore are concerned in trade, directly or indirectly, it is clear and evident as the shining of the sun." *Brief, Decent but Free,* pp. 51–2.

13. Though lacking idealogical coherence, a number of issues dealt with by the General Assembly in the mid-1780s drew many deputies into voting blocs. These blocs have been identified by Stephen Grossbart, "Revolutionary Transition," passim.

14. I discovered the birth dates coincidentally of 82.5 percent of each group. Historians have made much of the fact that many federalist leaders were relatively young—especially those whose first public service took place during the Revolution, a national cause. See especially Elkins, "Founding Fathers." Main, *Antifederalists*, does not believe age was a significant factor. He found that in Massachusetts antifederalists were fifty-two years old on average, and federalists fifty-one. p. 259. In another work, Main's analysis of hundreds of state legislators yields a *median* age of forty-four for localists and forty-two for cosmopolitans. *Political Parties*, p. 377. See also Wood, *Creation*, p. 484. Wood does not think age was very significant.

15. Of sectarian affiliation, I found 65 percent (28) of antifederalists and 66.4 percent (85) of federalists. That Anglicans [Episcopalians] were well integrated into Connecticut society is demonstrated in Steiner, "Anglican Officeholding," and his *Connecticut Anglicans*. Episcopalians were concentrated in unanimously federalist Fairfield County, but only three of the nine Episcopal delegates came from there.

16. There were three physicians among the antifederalists, two of whom were college graduates; among the federalists eight, four of whom were college graduates.

17. Henry Ward Beecher recalled that at the beginning of the nineteenth century "the nearest approach to a line drawn between the common people and an aristocratic class in New England is that which education furnishes. And there is almost a superstitious reverence for a '*college education.*' If a man has been to college, he has a title." Beecher, *Norwood*, p. 181. The novel was published in 1868, but Beecher drew from his early nineteenth-century childhood in Litchfield for his sketch.

18. Between 1774 and 1788, thirty men were elected at one time or another to represent Connecticut in Congress. Ten of those never attended. Of those ten, three were elected delegates to the ratifying convention, but one of those, William Pitkin, was absent when the vote was taken. Short biographies of these congressmen are conveniently provided in Gerlach, "Connecticut Delegates," pp. 182–90. The four not at the convention were Joseph Trumbull, Joseph Spencer, Silas Deane, and J. P. Cooke.

19. Thirty-four nonmilitia officers among the 174 delegates elected to the ratifying convention is surprisingly few: only 20 percent of the delegates. Hundreds of Connecticut men served as Continental or Line officers and many must have been prominent leaders in their towns.

20. A list of the members of the Connecticut Society of the Cincinnati is in Johnston, *Military Record*, pp. 373–76. Trumbull's comment is in *DocHist*, p. 568. Trumbull in 1788 was a deputy from Lebanon and Speaker of the House. It must have chagrined him to be passed over in favor of his brother-in-law Williams and to see his town instruct against ratification. All men who had served as Continental officers after 1778 were clouded with commutation. But not only did such service strengthen their national spirit, it also bound them together. Hezekiah Rogers of Norwalk, for instance, was aide de camp to Brigadier General Jedediah Huntington when Huntington was serving under Samuel H. Parsons. Rogers also was adjutant in Philip B. Bradley's regiment when Conelius Higgins was a fellow lieutenant there, and Rogers served in the same company in which Jeremiah West was surgeon. Johnston, *Military*

Record, pp. 312, 330, 193, 194. These six men constitute half of the members of the Society of Cincinnati elected as delegates to the convention.

21. The members of the Connecticut Society of Arts and Sciences are listed in Stiles, *Literary Diary,* III:277.

22. I include farm laborers—mostly farmers' sons—along with the actual farmers to arrive at the figure of about 80 percent. Main says about 20 percent of the adult males were artisans; a small number were merchants and professionals. Main, *Society and Economy,* pp. 369–70.

23. The vote of each delegate at the ratifying convention is given in *SR,* VI:549–52.

24. Bronson, *Waterbury,* pp. 411–12, 364–66; Anderson, *Waterbury,* pp. 625, 257; Genealogical chart compiled by Judith Plummer in author's possession. (Hereafter "Plummer chart".) John Hopkins was Joseph's grandfather and Lemuel's greatgrandfather.

25. Bronson, *Waterbury,* p. 365; Grossbart, "Revolutionary Transition," pp. 252, 363, 359; *DocHist,* fiche 8-B, p. 57; McDonald, *We the People,* p. 143, says Hopkins was a lawyer and a state creditor. He provides no evidence for the latter statement, and he is wrong about the first. Hopkins was not and never had been a lawyer.

26. *DocHist,* pp. 369, 370, 547, 598, 584, 577.

27. Bronson, *Waterbury,* p. 412. Hopkins fits Jackson T. Main's description of artisan/manufacturers as federalists. Main, *Antifederalists,* p. 274.

28. For a brief account of Williams' political career see Stark, *Williams.*

29. *SR,* III–VI, passim. Carpenter, *Carpenter Family,* pp. 94–95. Buel, *Dear Liberty,* p. 312. "The Crank" is now the town of Columbia.

30. *DocHist,* pp. 430–32.

31. *CR,* X:4, XV:43; *SR,* I:135; Stark, *Williams,* pp. 15, 16; Shipton, *Sibley's,* XV:409. Trumbull's other daughter married high nationalist Jedediah Huntington, delegate from Norwich. But she died in 1775, so Williams and Huntington were not connected in 1788.

32. Stark, *Williams,* pp. 68–70. The most complete account of Williams closing the courts is in Wachtell, "Localism and Nationalism," pp. 279–80. Stark, *Williams,* p. 71, says that the charge that Williams closed the court due to the influence of Shaysites is "absurd." It doesn't seem so to me.

33. Ibid., p. 71; Jordan, "Connecticut Politics," pp. 281–82; Jedediah Huntington to Andrew Huntington, May 1787, in "Jedediah Huntington Papers," CHS.

34. *DocHist,* pp. 536, 325. A diagramatic sketch of this cartoon is in the *DocHist,* microfiche section, p. 39–C. There is an original at the Connecticut Historical Society. Photographic reproductions appeared in a Sotheby's auction house catalog dated New York, April 16, 1988, when a second original came up for sale; and in *Life,* "Special Issue: The Constitution," Fall 1987, pp. 22–23. See Appendix E.

35. Riggs, *Anarchiad,* p. 44; Baldwin, *Baldwin,* p. 398. (Enoch Perkins to Simeon Baldwin, April 30, 1787).

36. *DocHist,* pp. 589, 584, 453. Williams wished that "the first introductory words" of the Constitution read: "We the people of the United States, in a firm belief of the being and perfections of the one living and true God, the creator and supreme Governor of the world, in His universal providence and the authority of His laws, that He will require of all moral agents an account of their conduct, that all rightful powers

among men are ordained of, and mediately derived from God, therefore in a dependence on His blessing and acknowledgment of His efficient protection in establishing our Independence, whereby it is become necessary to agree upon and settle a Constitution of federal government for ourselves. . . ." *DocHist,* p. 589. On the context of conservative calls for such religious oaths during the ratification process see Storing, *Anti-Federalists,* pp. 22–23. Support for religious oaths was typical of elite antifederalists. Cornell, *Other Founders,* p. 57. Sherman's support for and Johnson's opposition to such an oath in the Philadelphia convention is noted above, Ch. 3, note 17.

37. Since Williams was a participant in the most bitter and personal acrimony at the convention, it is possible that this comment is intended as irony; but I doubt it. It is more like a penance paid to regain acceptance by the political establishment.

38. Stark, *Williams,* p. 72. By Stark's account, Williams was defeated by populist, almost Shaysite, forces in town. A somewhat fuller appraisal of Williams' defection is in Stark's dissertation, "Lebanon, Connecticut," pp. 464–66. I agree that Williams changed his mind at the convention, and was not a closet federalist as suggested by Forrest McDonald in *We the People,* p. 142; and Jordan, "Connecticut Politics," pp. 348–49.

39. Stark, *Williams.* pf. 72. Williams, however, appears to have continued a closet *anti*nationalist. As late as October 1788 he wrote Benjamin Huntington, then at Congress in New York, requesting a copy of Luther Martin's polemic against the Constitution, adding, "you will be kind enou not to mention to any, this request &c. for I suppose it is treason with the hot Constitutionalists." *DocHist,* Microfiche, 100, p. 364.

40. Wolcott's nephew, Oliver, would serve as governor 1817–27. His wife's nephew was governor 1811–12. At the time he was appointed county surveyor, his father was lieutenant governor. *CR,* VIII:509. On Wolcott's absentee landholding, see *SR,* VI:220.

41. Stiles, *Windsor.* II:810–11; *CR,* XI:338, 422; *SR,* I:134, III:326.

42. Ibid., I:88; Johnston, *Military Record,* pp. 429, 613; *SR,* III:326, I:88.

43. Buel, *Dear Liberty,* p. 40.

44. Grossbart, "Revolutionary Transition," p. 143. The test oath was passed in October, repealed in December 1776 and repassed in May 1777. *SR,* I:4, 100, 226. Wolcott was among the first in his town to take the oath. Of 239 doing so, only Erastus, his cousin William Wolcott, and a Daniel Ellsworth are listed as squires. Daniel was an uncle and William was father-in-law of Oliver Ellsworth. Stiles, *Windsor,* I:653.

45. *SR,* VI:282, 355, 293.

46. He may have attended a price-fixing convention in Providence in 1782. *SR,* III:322.

47. Stiles, *Windsor,* I:414, 766.

48. See, e.g., Stiles, *Windsor,* I:640; Trumbull, *Memorial History,* I:119.

49. Wolcott's proposals for tax reforms were published in the *Connecticut Gazette* in September and October of 1781 and the *Connecticut Courant* in March 1787. They are discussed in Wachtell, "Localism and Nationalism," pp. 116–17, pf. 225. It is significant that all of his plans would have continued to pay the civil list—which included himself and many family and friends—in hard currency.

50. Grossbart, "Revolutionary Transition," p. 359, 360.

51. McDonald, *We the People*, p. 144.

52. *SR*, VI:293; Hutson, *Supplement*, p. 3; CHS, *Collections*, II:138n. See note 45 above.

53. *DocHist*, p. 413.

54. Ellington town meeting instructed its delegate, Ebenezer Nash, to vote against ratification—which he did. CSL, *Arch.* "Towns and Lands," ser. I, X:66; Stiles, *Windsor*. I:817, 711, 516. Nash was rewarded with election to selectman. Ellington, "Minutes" of town meeting, April 9, 1788, in town clerk's office.

55. Agrarian dominance of the legislature in the mid-1780s is documented in Saladino, "Economic Revolution," pf. 175; Grossbart, "Revolutionary Transition," Ch. 7; Wachtell, "Localism and Nationalism," Ch. 7.

56. Hugh Ledlie in *DocHist*, p. 579.

7. Those Who Voted No

1. *DocHist*, p. 358 (October 8, 1787).

2. Thaddeus Leavitt, January 10, 1788; *DocHist*, p. 567.

3. Cornell, *Other Founders*, pp. 10–11. "Except for the common world of print, there was little, if anything, to unite the diverse groups who opposed the Constitution." p. 10.

4. Simeon Baldwin to James Kent, March 8, 1788. *DocHist*, fiche 89:341.

5. *DocHist*, p. 411; Fowler, *Durham*, p. 148; *DocHist*, pp. 454. Durham was transferred from New Haven County to Middlesex County in 1799.

6. Dexter, *Biographical Sketches*, II:192; Fowler, *Durham*, pp. 229, 233–37; Dexter, *Biographical Sketches*, II:192; *CR*. X:75, 200, 315; *SR*, V:207, 318, VI:4, 5, 143, 145, 146.

7. Fowler, *Durham*, p. 186; Gerlach, "More Perfect," p. 77, and "Delegation of Steady Habits," passim.

8. *CR*, XIV:84, VIII:281, X:75, XIV:332; *SR*, I:134–35, 262, II:294; *DocHist*, fiche. 41. p. 198; Ward, *War of the Revolution*, p. 247. Appointed to brigadier general at the same time as Wadsworth, in this order, next after him: Oliver Ellsworth, Gurdon Saltonstall, Gold S. Silliman, Eliphalet Dyer, and Oliver Wolcott.

9. Ward, *Revolution*, p. 242; Riggs, *Anarchiad*, p. 36; *New Haven Gazette*, November 22, 1787, in *DocHist*, p. 476, 476n4, Microfiche 41; Buel, *Dear Liberty*, pp. 209–10.

10. Fowler, *Durham*, pp. 233–37, 199; Dexter, *Biographical Sketches*, II:192–93; Durham tax list for 1791 in town clerk's office. McDonald, *We the People*, p. 146, says he was a lawyer. He was not. This large sum of money out at interest puts Wadsworth squarely in that class of men Gordon Wood has so insightfully characterized as the bulwark of federalist opposition to democratizing and equalizing tendencies. "Interests and Disinterestedness," passim., esp. pf. 85. The only problem here is that Wadsworth was Connecticut's leading and most stalwart *anti*federalist.

11. *SR*, VI:174. On Wadsworth's ouster from the comptrollership see: Wachtell, "Localism and Nationalism," p. 224; Jordan, "Connecticut Politics," p. 310; *DocHist*, pp. 395, 402, 454, 474–76. On Lawrence's tangled affairs see Bland, "Tangled Af-

fairs." Bland inexplicably does not mention Wadsworth, but focuses on his successor as comptroller, Oliver Wolcott, Jr., who laid bare Lawrence's frauds and favoritism. One of the beneficiaries of this favoritism was William Pitkin of Windsor, a potential antifederal delegate who absented himself on the day of the vote. Lawrence had been appointed in 1769 to straighten out the tangled affairs of Joseph Talcott. In 1770 Wadsworth's Durham town meeting had been at the center of the movement to replace Talcott. Loucks, "Reform and Revolution," pp. 353–58. Wadsworth's salary of £150 per year compares with £300 for the governor; £100 for the lieutenant governor; £200 for superior court judges. Of course, all of the men holding these offices were paid for others as well. *SR*, VI: 174, 347, 289. In the winter of 1785, the authors of *The Anarchiad* listed Wadsworth's offices as "Judge, General, Delegate [to Congress], Registrar, Comptroller, and Councillor," where he could "catch some new salary from each opening job." Riggs, *Anarchiad*, pp. 35–36.

12. *Connecticut Journal*, June 29, 1785.

13. *SR*, VI:134, 146, 283, 398.

14. Riggs, *Anarchiad*, pp. 29, 25, 36. The Wits also charged Wadsworth with cowardice during the raid on Danbury in the April 1777. At the time he was brigadier general of the Second Brigade, which was not involved. In May he was promoted to major general. There is no evidence to support the Wits' charge. *Anarchiad*, p.36.

15. Fowler, *Durham*, prints the anticommutation resolution in its entirety, pp. 144–45; *Connecticut Courant* (November 26, 1787). Philip Jordan makes the case that James Wadsworth's rise was related directly to the anticommutation and debtor sentiment that affected a majority of the voters only from the fall of 1784 to the fall of 1786; his reliable political base was otherwise a minority. "A political leader alienated from the majority party, Wadsworth had no choice but to cling to his following and to oppose the Constitution." "Connecticut Politics," p. 360. But the same analysis applies to Wolcott, Hopkins, Williams, and several other agrarian leaders who voted to ratify. The difference, at least in part, lay in the fact that unlike the others, Wadsworth was not part of the establishment family network and had no family relations whose political progress required his support.

16. *SR*, I:134; *CR*, XV:93, 225.

17. Ward, *Ward*, p. 488; *CR*, XI:227, XIV:393, XV:237, 253, 300, 480, 128; *SR*, I;363, 262; *CR*, XIV:242; Steiner, *Guilford*, pp. 473, 515–16, 426; *SR*, I-VII, passim, I:478; Steiner, *Guilford*, p. 473; Grossbart, "Revolutionary Transition," pp. 359–63; Daniels, *Connecticut Town*, p. 152; *SR*, VI:221–23; *Town Record Book* II and tax list in folder in Guilford town clerk's office; Ward, *Ward*, p. 491. Ward's daughter, Roxane became the grandmother of Harriet Beecher Stowe. Roxane's daughter of the same name grew up in Ward's household, and her memories of Nutplain in North Guilford are described in Cross, ed., *Lyman Beecher*, I:35f; Hendrick, *Stowe*, pp. 10–15. "Plummer chart." (See above Ch. 6, note 24.)

18. Davis, *Wallingford*, pp. 767, 756; *CR*, X:346, 394, XV:93, 125.

19. *CR*, XIV: 331, 393; Thoms, *Jared Elliot*, pp. 117–18; Emerson, *Descendants of John Elliot*, pp. 69, 45–46; "Plummer Chart"; tax folder in Guilford clerk's office.

20. "Plummer chart"; Trowbridge, *Descendants of William Hoadley*, pp. 27–28; *SR*, II:420, VI:279; Trowbridge, *Hoadley*, p. 28; Johnston, *Military Record*, p. 625.

21. "Plummer chart"; *CR*, XIV:162; Carr, *Old Branford*, p. 33; *SR*, IX:397; *Branford Town Records*, vol. III in town clerk's office.

22. Photostat list in Daniel Basset folder at North Haven Historical Society; Cutler, *Manasseh Cutler,* I:216; *SR,* VI:350; Jacobus, *New Haven Families,* pp. 701, 1710; Brusic, *North Haven,* p. 74; *CR,* XIV:341, 162.

23. Hughes, *East Haven,* "Appendix," pp. 19, 311; "Minutes" of town meetings, 1786, town clerk's office, East Haven, pp. 174, 178; Davis, *Wallingford,* pp. 904–05; CSL, *Arch.,* "Towns and Lands," ser. 1. IX:325.

24. Dexter, *Biographical Sketches,* III:272; "Minutes" of town meetings (Photostat) vol. I in Cheshire town clerk's office; *SR,* I:410; Davis, *Wallingford,* p. 362; Johnston, *Military Record,* pp. 155, 232, 329, 496. I have gone back three generations looking for connections.

25. Dexter, *Biographical Sketches,* II:449–50; *SR,* VI:532 (petition of creditors); Beach, *Cheshire,* Ch. VI; *CR,* XV:2; *SR,* III:169; *Minutes of Town Meetings* (Photostat) vol. I in Cheshire town clerk's office; Davis, *Wallingford,* p. 361n. His uncle John Beach was stepfather to John Holbrook, federalist from Derby, west of New Haven.

25. Dexter, *Biographical Sketches,* III:272; *Minutes of Town Meetings* (Photostat) vol. I in Cheshire town clerk's office; *SR,* I:410; Davis, *Wallingford.* p. 362; Johnston, *Record,* pp. 155, 232, 329, 496. I have gone back three generations looking for connections.

26. See Chapter 1. On family recruitment see Seleski, *War and Society,* pp. 170–71, 200. That the militia was seen more as a political vehicle than a military one in peacetime is attested to by the very large number of men who resigned their commissions in 1775 and 1776.

27. This tally is based on officer appointments as given in *CR,* and *SR,* Johnston, *Military Record,* and CHS, *Collections,* vols. VIII, IX, X, "French and Indian Rolls" and "Revolutionary War Rolls."

28. Dexter, *Biographical Sketches,* III:493; *SR,* III:passim; Grossbart, "Revolutionary Transition," p. 359; Marvin owed the state £32, which he would pay, apparently, if he was granted bankruptcy protection for his private debts. The comptroller—James Wadsworth—would have to approve the deal. Eben Bushnell to James Wadsworth, April 3, 1787, in "Connecticut Comptroller's Papers," CHS, *SR,* III:167–68; Marvin, *Marvin,* p. 97; *SR,* II:421; Ingham, *Ingham,* p. 16; *CR,* XII:418.

29. *SR,* V:224; *CR,* XV:300; Vibert, *Simsbury,* p. 86; Stiles, *Windsor,* II:570; Grossbart, "Revolutionary Transition," pp. 361, 363. Delegates Noah Phelps, Charles Phelps of Stonington, and John Phelps of Stafford were all third cousins. "Plummer chart."

30. Humphreys, *Humphreys,* p. 141; *SR,* II—VIII:passim, XII:294, 472; *DocHist,* p. 486; Grossbart, "Revolutionary Transition," p. 361; Wachtell, "Localism and Nationalism," p. 211; *DocHist,* p. 486; Daniel Humphrey was not a minister as reported by McDonald, *We the People,* p. 147; Crissey, *Norfolk,* p. 564; *CR,* XI:303. One historian of Simsbury believes that Humphrey voted in opposition to the Constitution despite his personal inclinations in favor. Barber, *Simsbury,* p. 330. Barber presents no evidence; there is plenty on the other side.

31. Humphreys, *Humphreys,* p. 144; *DocHist,* Microfiche 8-B; Jordan, "Connecticut Politics," pp. 283, 290; *SR,* VI:281, 351; Humphreys, *Humphreys,* p. 144. The Humphrey family owned land in Norfolk and migrated back and forth to Simsbury, a long day's ride away. Daniel's father, Michael, moved to Norfolk from Simsbury in 1760 and was immediately chosen town clerk, a position he held until his

death in 1778. He had been a deputy from Simsbury and a justice of the peace, an appointment he continued to receive annually till the end of his life. Crissey, *Norfolk*, p. 564; *CR*, XI:303.

32. *SR*, II:124, 172, VI:141, 228, 351, 397, VII:475; Humphreys, *Humphreys*, p. 143; Grossbart, "Revolutionary Transition," p. 363; *DocHist*, p. 437. Hosea and Daniel were Norfolk's deputies in October 1787. *SR*, VI:351.

33. Militia connections no doubt also influenced some men to vote in favor of the Constitution. The Hartford County colonelcies were passed around among leading families and a series of appointments to major general focused on Wolcotts and their marital and blood kin.

34. Bowen, *Boundary Disputes*, Chs. II and III. passim, p. 109, 109n2; Taylor, *Colonial Connecticut*, pp. 54–55; Bowen, *Woodstock*, pp. 109, 207. The Massachusetts perspective on this dispute is in Ammidown, *Historical Collections*, I:293–97. For suggestions that the border towns operated jointly, see ibid., I:296–97. Granby was taken from Simsbury in 1786. The territory constituting the new town consisted largely of previously disputed lands which had been attached to Simsbury in 1739 and 1749, and parts of Suffield. Grossbart, "Revolutionary Transition," pp. 359–64; Williams, *Granby*, Ch. VI.

35. CSL, *Arch.*, "Towns and Lands," ser. 1. VIII:3331, X:104. "Minutes" of town meetings, April 9, 1788, in town clerk's office.

36. Wachtell, "Localism and Nationalism," p. 279.

37. Starr, *Cornwall*, pp. 343, 25; Johnston, *Military Record*, pp. 61, 110, 111, 112; CHS, *Collections*, vol. VIII, "Revolutionary Rolls," p. 35; p. 35; Grossbart, "Revolutionary Transition," p. 363; *SR*, III–VI:passim; Starr, *Cornwall*, p. 47; CHS, *Collections*, vol. IX, "French and Indian Rolls," II:46.

38. Starr, *Cornwall*, p. 355; "Minutes" of town meetings in Cornwall town clerk's office, September 16, 1783; Starr, *Cornwall*, p. 47; *CR*, XI:99, 227; CHS, *Collections*, vol. IX, "French and Indian Rolls," II:47; *CR*, XV:426; *SR*, I:255.

39. Starr, *Cornwall*, p. 96; Gold, *Cornwall*, p. 54–59, 205, 263.

40. By 1787 Sedgwick had also turned against Gold. Sedgwick, whose brother, Theodore, was a major figure among Massachusetts federalists, was elected to the General Assembly in 1785 and 1786. When, in May 1787, Theodore warned him of Shaysite activity in Sharon, Sedgwick alerted his militia company to be ready to march into the neighboring town. "A national Revolution is approaching in America," he wrote at the time, "for want of the necessary powers of Government." He was not reelected to the General Assembly that year or the next two. Instead, in an effort to reconcile the parish division, the citizens sent as their civil representatives to that political body their two pastors, Gold and John Cornwell. It was almost certainly a unique event in the entire history of Connecticut, a state where religious professionals very rarely held political offices, to have both deputies parish ministers. The attempt at reconciliation did not work. The ministers were elected in September; Cornwell was reelected in April 1788, but neither were in September 1788. Welch, *Sedgwick*, passim; *SR*, VI:351, 396, 471; Gold, *Cornwall*, pp. 54–59.

41. Foster, "Connecticut Separate," pp. 318, 322–23, 328. Grossbart, "Revolutionary Transition," p. 363 shows Patterson to evince a localist voting pattern. Rogers' leanings must be inferred; they are not necessarily localist, but rather anti-Sedgwick.

42. Torrington *Records* in town clerk's office. July 7, 15, 1783; *SR*, VI:464–68; Orcott, *Torrington*, pp. 31–35.

43. Orcutt, Torrington, p. 28; *SR*, I:264, V:284.

44. Torrington *Records*, July 7, September 1, 1783; Orcutt, *Torrington*, pp. 762, 27–28, 65–66, 28; Hodges, *Hodges*, p. 15; *CR*, XIV:265; *SR*, VI:23; to Jeremiah Wadsworth, January 28, 1788, CHS, "Jeremiah Wadsworth Papers."

45. Orcott, *Torrington*, pp. 688, 265, 447; Stiles, *Windsor*, II:242–43, 291.

46. Torrington Congregational Church, *Notice*, p. 17; Hodges, *Hodges*, pp. 18–19; Orcutt, *Torrington*, pp. 28, 66; Sheldon to Wadsworth (January 28, 1788), CHS, "Jeremiah Wadsworth Papers."

47. *SR*, VI:464–66, VII:60; Chipman, *Harwinton*, pp. 114, 118; Hinman, *Historical Collection*, p. 411; *SR*, VI–VII:passim.

48. Johnston, *Military Record*, p. 396; *SR*, VI–VII:passim; Chipman, *Harwinton*, pp. 119–21; Goodenough, *Litchfield Clergy*, pp. 215, 119. Harwinton had no settled Congregational minister from 1787 to 1790. The Episcopal Church was organized there in 1787. Wilson is referred to as deacon in Harwinton *Town Records*, Vol. III in town clerk's office, September 1, 1783, when he moderated the meeting at which delegates to the anticommutation convention were elected.

49. *SR*, III:426; Johnston, *Military Record*, p. 110; *SR*, I–VI:passim, X:2n; Purcell, *Connecticut in Transition*, p. 250; Trumbull, *Hartford County*, II:411; *SR*, II:529, III:110; Saladino, "Economic Revolution," p. 403.

Conclusions

1. Banning, "Virginia," p. 262. Madison may not have been an exception. Banning writes, "Throughout the Constitutional Convention, Madison's Virginia background and perspective strongly influenced his positions." p. 273.

2. See, generally, Jensen, *Articles of Confederation*, Chs. IV, I, XI.

3. Brown, *Mirror*, p. 15. Brown's description of the eastern seaboard is as of 1810; but the elements of physical geography, topography, and climate would have been the same during the eighteenth century.

4. Onuf, "Maryland," P. 174; Stiverson, "Necessity, The Mother," p. 133.

5. Watson, "States' Rights," p. 253.

6. Banning, "Virginia," p. 263. Emphasis in the original. Farrand, *Records*, I:567 (July 10), and see Bedford's diatribe attacking the special interests of the large and Deep South states at ibid., I:500 (July 30).

7. Farrand, *Records*, I:529 (July 5).

8. Ibid., I:315 (June 12). See also Wilson, I:253, 261, 266 (June 16), II:287 (August 14).

9. Ibid., II:371 (August 22); II:329 (August 18); I:178 (June 9); I:125 (June 5).

10. DePauw, *Eleventh Pillar*, pp. 27,169.

11. Ireland, *Religion, Ethnicity*, passim; Doutrich, "Revolution to Constitution," passim; Graham, "Pennsylvania," pp. 59, 63, 69.

12. Banning, "Virginia," pp. 262, 268. Emphasis in original. Banning says, "Virginia's close division on the Constitution does not lend itself convincingly to any of the

most familiar explanations of the ratification contest. It was not essentially a function of conflicting economic interests, class divisions, or contrasting localist and cosmopolitan perspectives. It did not pit radicals against conservatives or younger men against their seniors. Among the state's most influential men, it pitted unionists against particularists only in a complicated sense, and one that only partly overrode their shared commitments and agreements." p. 287. The vote was 79 to 89 in favor of ratification.

13. Quoted in Onuf, "Maryland," p. 191.

Appendix C

1. CSL, *Arch.*, "Towns and Lands," ser. 1, IX:245. (October 1780); *SR*, III:203–04, VIII:379; Wilder, *Book of Wilders*, p. 203; CSL, *Arch.*, "Towns and Lands," ser. 1 IX:245.

2. *SR*, V:152, VI:393, 220; Lee, Barkhamsted, p. 29.

3. *SR*, VI:464–67; Ransom, *Hartland*, p. 129; "Hartland Town Records, 1761–1833" (in town clerk's vault). September 16, 1783, p. 124; Ransom, *Hartland*, p. 129, 171–72; "Town Records," 1763, p. 27; Hartland, "Land Records" (in town clerk's vault), I:21, 73, 388; Ransom, *Hartland*, pp. 41, 65, and back cover map; Wheeler, *Barkhamsted*, p. 260, map, "Homesteads and Other Sites."

4. It is unique in my experience to find a deputy who did not live in the town he represented. No deputy from Barkhamsted is recorded as attending the General Assembly until 1796. Part of Barkhamsted was in a Hartland parish. It is likely that Joseph Wilder lived in that area; he owned land in both towns. Barkhamsted could escape state taxes as long as it remained unrepresented in the Assembly. Perhaps Wilder's official listing as a deputy from Hartland was a subterfuge to avoid those taxes—though one easily seen through if anyone took the trouble to look. In 1796 the General Assembly decided that the town had "now become opulent and wealthy, and well able to pay public Taxes." *SR*, VII:379.

5. Correll Tiffany, "Copy of Church Records of First and Second Churches of Hartland," "Copy of Church Records of West Hartland" manuscripts at the Connecticut State Library; *SR*, III:3, 62, 90; Wheeler, ed., *Barkhamsted Heritage*. Map in back pocket.

6. Cole, *Tolland History*, pp. 197–98, 249; Webber, *Genealogy*, pp. 205–07; *CR*, XIII–XV; *SR*, I–XI:passim; Loucks, "Reformation and Revolution," p. 998; Grossbart, "Revolutionary Transition," p. 359. Southworth's father migrated to Mansfield some time before 1730, when Constant was born. His father died at sea about the same time. Apparently Southworth's mother—a descendant of Thomas Hooker—did not remarry, and the boy grew up not only fatherless, but poor as well. Thrice cursed, he also lost the use of one hand in an accident. He was unfit for manual labor and never served in the military. Webber, *Southworths Genealogy*, pp. 205–07; *CR*, III–XV:passim; *SR*, I–XII, passim.

7. *DocHist*, pp. 598–598n2; Smith, *Constant Years*, pp. 28–29; "Minutes" of town meetings, town clerk's office, Mansfield. September 8, 1789, p. 322.

8. *CR*, XV:3, 92; *SR*, III–VI:passim Grossbart, "Revolutionary Transition." That he owned a large farm is attested to by Isabel Atwood in an interview in Mansfield on

January 31, 1994. Her great-uncles sold the farm about 1915; it was then three hundred acres, but may hve been added to during the nineteenth century.

9. It is known that they both owned large property; that they were not millers, taverners, physicians, lawyers, or merchants. Interview with Isabel Weigold at Willington, February 1, 1994; Demers, *Willington,* pp. 132–33; I find no record of any service during the years 1754 to 1783. A man by the same name—and he had a son who shared his name—served briefly as a private in 1776. Johnston, *Military Record,* p. 401; "Record of Willington Cemeteries," typescript in Willington town clerk's vault.

10. *SR,* II, II, VI:passim; III:192; Demers, *Willington,* pp. 132–33.

11. *DocHist,* pp. 434, 450, 598.

Sources Cited

Adams, Charles Francis, ed. *The Works of John Adams*. 10 vols. Boston: Little, Brown & Company, 1856.

American Negro Reference Book. John P. Davis, ed. New York: Prentice-Hall, 1966.

Ammidown, Holmes. *Historical Collections*. 2 vols. New York: the Author, 1874.

Andrews, Charles M. *The Connecticut Intestacy Law*. New Haven: Yale University Press, 1933.

Baldwin, Simeon E. *Life and Letters of Simeon Baldwin*. New Haven: Tuttle, Morehouse and Taylor, 1919.

Bancroft, George. *History of the Formation of the Constitution of the United States*. 2 vols. Boston: D. Appleton and Co., 1882.

Banning, Lance. "Virginia: Sectionalism and the General Good," in Gillespie and Lienesch, eds. *Ratifying the Constitution*. Lawrence: University Press of Kansas, 1989.

Barber, Louis I. *A Record and Documentary History of Simsbury*. Simsbury, Conn.: Phelps Chapter, D.A.R., 1931.

Beach, Joseph Perkins. *History of Cheshire, Connecticut, from 1694 to 1840*. Cheshire, Conn.: Lady Fenwick Chapter, D.A.R., 1912.

Beard, Charles A. *An Economic Interpretation of the Constitution of the United States*. New York: Macmillan Company, 1961 [1913]. This is a reprint of the 1935 edition.

Becker, Robert A. *Revolution, Reform, and the Politics of American Taxation, 1768–1783*. Baton Rouge: Louisiana State University Press, 1980.

Beecher, Henry Ward. *Norwood, or Village Life in New England*. New York: Charles Scribner & Company, 1868.

Beeman, Richard, et al., eds. *Beyond Confederation: Origins of the Constitution and American National Identity*. Chapel Hill: University of North Carolina Press, 1987.

Bellesiles, Michael A. *Revolutionary Outlaws: Ethan Allen and the Struggle for Independence on the Early American Frontier*. Charlottesville: University Press of Virginia, 1993.

Bender, Thomas. *Community and Social Change in America*. Baltimore, Md.: Johns Hopkins University Press, 1978.

Bland, James E. "The Tangled Affairs of Treasurer John Lawrence." *Bulletin* of the CHS, 36(January, 1971)1:1–7.

Boutell, Lewis Henry. *The Life of Roger Sherman*. Chicago: A. C. McClurg, 1896.

Bowen, Clarence Winthrop. *The Boundary Disputes of Connecticut*. Boston: James Good and Company, 1882.

————. *History of Woodstock, Connecticut.* Woodstock, Conn.: Priv. pr., 1928.

Boyd, Steven R. *The Politics of Opposition: Antifederalists and the Acceptance of the Constitution.* Millwood, N.Y.: KTO Press, 1979.

Brady, James Edward. "Wyoming: A Study of John Franklin and the Connecticut Settlement in Pennsylvania." Unpublished dissertation. Syracuse University, 1973.

Bronson, Henry. *History of Waterbury, Connecticut . . . .* Waterbury, Conn.: Bronson Brothers, 1858.

Brooke, John L. *The Heart of the Commonwealth: Society and Political Culture in Worcester County, Massachusetts, 1713–1861.* Cambridge: Cambridge University Press, 1989.

Brown, Ralph H. *Mirror for Americans: Likeness of the Eastern Seaboard, 1810.* New York: American Geographical Society, 1943.

Brown, Richard D., "Shays' Rebellion," in Beeman, Richard, et al., eds. *Beyond Confederation: Origins of the Constitution and American National Identity.* Chapel Hill: University of North Carolina Press, 1987.

Brown, Roger H. *Redeeming the Republic: Federalists, Taxation and the Origins of the Constitution.* Baltimore, Md.: Johns Hopkins University Press, 1993.

Brown, William Garrott. *The Life of Oliver Ellsworth.* New York: Macmillan Company, 1905.

Brusic, Lucy McTeer. *Amidst Cultivated and Pleasant Fields: A Bicentennial History of North Haven, Connecticut.* Canaan, N.H.: Phoenix Publishing, 1986.

Buel, Richard, Jr. *Dear Liberty: Connecticut's Mobilization for the Revolutionary War.* Middletown, Conn.: Wesleyan University Press, 1980.

Burnett, Edmund Cody. *The Continental Congress,* New York: Macmillan Company, 1941.

————. *Letters of Members of the Continental Congress.* 8 vols. Washington: Carnegie Institute, 1921–36.

Bushman, Richard J. *From Puritan to Yankee: Character and the Social Order in Connecticut, 1690–1765.* Cambridge: Harvard University Press, 1968.

————. *King and People in Provincial Massachusetts.* Chapel Hill: University of North Carolina Press, 1985.

Butterfield, L. H., ed. *The Adams Papers.* Cambridge, Mass.: Harvard University Press, 1961–.

Cameron, Kenneth W., ed. *The Works of Samuel Peters of Hebron, Connecticut.* Hartford, Conn.: Transcendental Press, 1967.

Cappon, Lester J., ed. *The Adams-Jefferson Letters: The Complete Correspondence Between Thomas Jefferson and Abigail and John Adams.* 2 vols. Chapel Hill: University of North Carolina Press, 1959.

Carpenter, Amos B. *A Genealogical History of the Rehoboth Branch of the Carpenter Family in America.* Amherst, Mass.: Carpenter & Morehouse, 1898.

Carr, John C. *Old Branford.* Branford, Conn.: Tercentenary Committee, 1935.

Casto, William R. *Oliver Ellsworth and the Creation of the Federal Republic.* New York: Second Circuit Committee on History and Commemorative Events, 1997.

————. *The Supreme Court in the Early Republic: The Chief Justiceships of John Jay and Oliver Ellsworth.* Columbia: University of South Carolina Press, 1995.

Caulkins, Frances Manwarning. *History of New London, Connecticut.* New London, Conn.: the author, 1852.

————. *History of Norwich, Connecticut, From Its Settlement in 1660, to January 1845.* Norwich, Conn.: Thomas Robinson, 1845.

Chipman, R. Manning. *The History of Harwinton . . . .* Hartford, Conn.: Williams, Wiley & Turner, 1860.

Cole, J. R. *History of Tolland County, Connecticut . . . .* New York: W.W. Preston & Co., 1888.

Collier, Christopher. "New England Specter: Town and State in Connecticut History, Law and Myth." *Bulletin* of the CHS. 60 (Summer/Fall 1995) 3–4:137–92.

————. "The Common Law and Individual Rights in Connecticut before the Federal Bill of Rights," *Connecticut Bar Journal.* 76 (2003) 1–70.

————. *Roger Sherman's Connecticut: Yankee Politics and the American Revolution.* Middletown, Conn.: Wesleyan University Press, 1971.

Collier, Christopher, and James Lincoln Collier. *Decision in Philadelphia: The Constitutional Convention of 1787.* New York: Random House, 1986.

Collier, Christopher, and Bonnie Collier. *The Literature of Connecticut History.* Occasional papers of the Connecticut Humanities Council #6. Middletown, Conn.: Connecticut Humanities Council, 1983.

Conley, Patrick T., and John P. Kaminski, eds. *The Constitution and the States: The Role of the Original Thirteen in the Framing and Adoption of the Federal Constitution.* Madison, Wisc.: Madison House, 1988.

Connecticut. *Public Records of the Colony of Connecticut.* 15 vols. J. Hammond Trumbull and Charles J. Hoadley, eds. Hartford, Conn.: various publishers, 1851–1890.

————. *Public Records of the State of Connecticut.* 17 vols. to date. Charles J. Hoadley, et al., eds. Hartford, Conn.: various publishers, 1894–.

Connecticut Historical Society. "Correspondence of Silas Deane, 1774–1762," *Collections* of the CHS. vol. II. Hartford, Conn.: CHS, 1870.

————. "Rolls of Connecticut Men in the French and Indian War, 1755–1762," *Collections* of the CHS. vols. IX and X. Hartford: CHS, 1903, 1905.

————. "Sketch of Roger Wolcott," *Collections* of the CHS. vol. XVI. Hartford, Conn.: CHS, 1916.

Cornell, Saul. "Aristocracy Assailed: The Ideology of Backcounty Anti-Federalism," *Journal of American History.* 76 (March 1990) 4:1148–1172.

————. *The Other Founders: Anti-Federalism and the Dissenting Tradition in America, 1788–1838.* Chapel Hill: University of North Carolina Press, 1999.

————. "The Changing Fortunes of the Anti-Federalists," *Northwestern University Law Review.* 84 (Fall 1989) 1:39–74.

Corner, G.W., ed. *The Autobiography of Benjamin Rush: His "Travels Through Life" Together with His Commonplace Books for 1789–1813,* Princeton, N.J.: Princeton University Press, 1948.

Crissey, Theron W. *History of Norfolk, Litchfield County, Connecticut, 1744–1900.* Everett: Massachusetts Publishing Company, 1900.

Cross, Barbara M., ed. *The Autobiography of Lyman Beecher.* 2 vols. Cambridge, Mass.: Harvard University Press, 1961.

Cushing, John D., comp. *The First Laws of the State of Connecticut.* Wilmington, Del.: Michael Glazier, 1982.

Cutler, William P. and Julia P. Cutler. *Life, Journals, and Correspondence of Rev. Manesseh Cutler.* 2 vols. Cincinnati, Ohio: Robert Clarke, 1888.

Daggett, David. *An Oration Pronounced in the Brick Meetinghouse . . . Fourth of July, 1787 . . . .* New Haven, Conn.: T. and S. Green, 1787.

Daniell, Jere R. *Experiment in Republicanism: New Hampshire Politics and the American Revolution, 1741–1794.* Cambridge: Harvard University Press, 1970.

Daniels, Bruce C. *The Connecticut Town: Growth and Development, 1635–1790.* Middletown, Conn.: Wesleyan University Press, 1979.

————. *Connecticut's First Family: William Pitkin and His Connections.* Chester, Conn.: Pequot Press, 1975.

————. *Dissent and Conformity on Narragansett Bay: The Colonial Rhode Island Town.* Middletown, Conn.: Wesleyan University Press, 1983.

————. "Economic Developments in Colonial and Revolutionary Connecticut: An Overview," *William and Mary Quarterly,* 3rd series 37(July, 1980)3:429–50.

————. "Large Town Power Structures in Eighteenth Century Connecticut: An Analysis of Political Leadership in Hartford, Norwich, and Fairfield." Unpublished dissertation, University of Connecticut, 1970.

Davenport, Robert Ralsey. *Davenport Geneology.* N. p., priv. pr., 1982.

Davis, Charles H.S. *History of Wallingford . . . .* Meriden, Conn.: the author, 1870.

Davis, David B. *The Problem of Slavery in Western Culture.* Ithaca, N.Y.: Cornell University Press, 1966.

Demers, Ronald F. *Modernization in a New England Town: A History of Willington, Connecticut.* Willington, Conn.: Willington Historical Society, 1983.

DePauw, Linda Grant. *The Eleventh Pillar: New York State and the Federal Constitution.* Ithaca, N.Y.: Cornell University Press, 1966

Dexter, Franklin B. *Biographical Sketches of the Graduates of Yale College . . . .* 6 vols. New Haven, Conn.: Yale University Press, 1885–1912.

Doutrich, Paul. "From Revolution to Constitution: Pennsylvania's Path to Federalism" in Gillespie and Lienesch, eds. *Ratifying the Constitution.* Lawrence: University of Kansas Press, 1989.

Duncan, Christopher M. *The Anti-Federalists and Early American Political Thought.* DeKalb: Northern Illinois University Press, 1995.

Edwards, Jonathan, Jr. *The Works of Jonathan Edwards, Jr.,* Tyron Edwards, 2 vols. ed. Andover, Mass.: Allen, Morrill and Warwell, 1842.

Elkins, Stanley, and Eric McKitrick. "The Founding Fathers," *Politican Science Quarterly.* 76 (1961).

Emerson, Wilhelmina H. *Genealogy of the Descendants of John Elliot . . . 1598–1905.* New Haven, Conn.: Committee of Descendants, 1905.

Fane, Francis. *Reports on the Laws of Connecticut,* Charles M. Andrews, ed. Hartford, Conn.: Acorn Club, 1915.

Farrand, Max. "Compromises of the Constitution," *American Historical Review,* 9(April, 1904)479–89.

————. *The Framing of the Constitution of the United States.* New Haven, Conn.: Yale University Press, 1962 [1913].

————, ed. *The Records of the Federal Convention of 1787.* Revised ed. in 4 vols. New Haven, Conn.: Yale University Press, 1986 [1936].

Ferguson, E. James. "The Nationalists of 1781–1783 and the Economic Interpretation of the Constitution," *Journal of American History.* 56(September, 1969) 2: 241–61.

————. *The Power of the Purse: A History of American Public Finance, 1776–1790*. Chapel Hill: University of North Carolina Press, 1961.

Fischer, David Hackett. *The Revolution of American Conservatism: The Federalist Party in the Era of Jeffersonian Democracy*. New York: Harper and Row, 1965.

Fogelman, Robert W., and Stanley L. Engerman. *Time on the Cross: The Economics of American Negro Slavery*. Boston: Little, Brown and Co., 1974.

Ford, Paul Leicester, ed. *Essays on the Constitution of the United States* . . . . New York: Burt Franklin, 1970 [1892].

————. *Pamphlets on the Constitution of the United States Published During its Discussion by the People, 1787–1788*. New York: Burt Franklin, 1971 [1888].

Ford, Worthington C. et al., eds. *Journals of the Continental Congress, 1774–1789*. 34 vols. Washington, D.C.: U.S.G.P.O., 1904–1937.

————. *Correspondence and Journals of Samuel Blachley Webb*. 3 vols. New York: Arno Press, 1969 [1894].

Foster, Stephen. "A Connecticut Separate Church: Strict Congregationalism in Cornwall, 1780–1809," *New England Quarterly*. 39(September, 1966)3:309–33.

Fowler, William Chauncey. *History of Durham, Connecticut* . . . Hartford, Conn.: Wiley, Waterman & Eaton, 1866.

Gale, Benjamin. *Brief, Decent but Free Remarks and Observations on Several Laws Passed . . . Since the Year 1775*. By a Friend to His Country. Hartford, Conn.: Hudson & Goodwin, 1782.

Gates, Stewart L. "Disorder and Social Organization: The Militia in Connecticut Public Life, 1660–1860." Unpublished dissertation, University of Connecticut, 1975.

Genovese, Eugene D. *Roll, Jordan, Roll: The World the Slaves Made*. New York: Random House, 1972.

Gerlach, Larry R. "Connecticut Delegates and the Continental Congress." Unpublished M.A. thesis, University of Nebraska, 1965.

————. *"Connecticut and Commutation, 1778–1784,"* Bulletin of the CHS. 33(April, 1968)2:51–58.

————. *Connecticut Congressman: Samuel Huntington, 1731–1796*. Hartford: American Revolution Bicentennial Commission of Connecticut, 1976.

————. "A Delegation of Steady Habits: The Connecticut Representatives to the Continental Congress," Bulletin of the CHS. 32 (April 1967) 2:33–39.

————. "Firmness and Prudence: Connecticut, the Continental Congress and the National Domain, 1776–1786," Bulletin of the CHS. 31(July, 1966)3:65–75.

————. "Toward 'A More Perfect Union': Connecticut, the Continental Congress and the Constitutional Convention," Bulletin of the CHS. 34(July, 1969)3:65–78.

Gillespie, Michael Allen, and Michael Lienesch. *Ratifying the Constitution*. Lawrence: University Press of Kansas, 1989.

Gipson, Lawrence H. *American Loyalist: Jared Ingersoll*. New Haven, Conn. Yale University Press, 1971 [1920].

————. *The British Isles and the American Colonies: The Northern Plantations, 1748–1754*. New York: Alfred A. Knopf, 1960 [1936].

Gilsdorf, Joy B., and Robert R. Gilsdorf. "Elites and Electorates: Some Plain Truths for Historians of Early America," in David Hall et al., eds. *Saints and Revolutionaries: Essays on Early American History*. New York: W.W. Norton, 1984.

Gold, Theodore S. *Historical Records of the Town of Cornwall, Litchfield County, Connecticut.* Hartford, Conn.: Case, Lockwood & Brainard, 1904.

Goodenough, Arthur. *The Clergy of Litchfield County.* Litchfield, Conn.: Litchfield County University Club, 1909.

Goodwin, Joseph O. *East Hartford* . . . . Hartford, Conn.: Case, Lockwood & Brainard, 1879.

Graham, George T. "Pennsylvania: Representation and the Meaning of Republicanism," in Michael Gillespie and Michael Lienesch, eds., *Ratifying the Constitution.* Lawrence: University Press of Kansas, 1989.

Grant, Charles. *Democracy in the Frontier Town of Kent.* New York: Columbia University Press, 1961.

Grant, Ellsworth S. *Yankee Dreamers and Doers.* Hartford, Conn.: Pequot Press, 1973.

Greene, Lorenzo J. *The Negro in Colonial New England.* New York: Atheneum, 1971 [1942].

Groce, George C., Jr. *William Samuel Johnson: A Maker of the Constitution.* New York: Columbia University Press, 1937.

Gross, Robert A, ed. *In Debt to Shays: The Bicentennial of an Agrarian Rebellion.* Publications of the Colonial Society of Massachusetts. Vol. VI (1993).

Grossbart, Stephen R. "The Revolutionary Transition: Politics, Religion, and Economy in Eastern Connecticut." Unpublished dissertation, University of Michigan, 1989.

Hall, Charles S. *Life and Letters of Samuel Holden Parsons.* New York: James Pugliese, 1968.

Hedges, James B. *The Browns of Providence Plantations: The Colonial Years.* Providence, R.I.: Brown University Press, 1968.

Hendrick, Joan D. *Harriet Beecher Stowe: A Life.* New York: Oxford University Press, 1994.

Hinman, Royal R. *A Historical Collection from Official Records, Files, Etc., of the Part Sustained by Connecticut During the War of the Revolution.* Hartford, Conn.: E. Gleason, 1842.

Hodges, Theodore B., *Erastus Hodges, 1781–1847: Connecticut Manufacturer, Merchant, Entrepreneur.* Torrington, Conn.: Torrington Historical Society, 1994.

Howard, Leon. *The Connecticut Wits.* Chicago: University of Chicago Press, 1943.

Hughes, Sarah E. *History of East Haven.* New Haven, Conn.: Tuttle, Morehouse & Taylor Press, 1908.

Humphreys, Frank L. *Life and Times of David Humphreys.* 2 vols. New York: G.P. Putnam's Sons, 1917.

Humphreys, Frederick. *The Humphreys Family in America.* New York: Humphreys Print., 1883.

Hutson, James H. "The Creation of the Constitution: Scholarship at a Standstill," *Reviews in American History* 12 (December 1989).

———, ed. *Supplement to Max Farrand's The Records of the Federal Convention of 1787.* New Haven, Conn.: Yale University Press, 1987.

Ingham, Samuel. *John Ingham and His Descendants, 1639–1948.* Essex, Conn.: priv. pr., 1948.

Ireland, Owen S. *Religion, Ethnicity, and Politics: Ratifying the Constitution in Pennsylvania*. University Park: Pennsylvania State Press, 1996.

Jacobus, Donald L. *Families of Ancient New Haven*. New Haven, Conn.: the author, 1931.

Jensen, Merrill, John R. Kaminski, and Gaspare J. Saladino, eds. *Documentary History of the Ratification of the Constitution: Volume III, Ratification of the Constitution by the States: Delaware, New Jersey, Georgia, Connecticut*. Madison: State Historical Society of Wisconsin, 1978.

Jensen, Merrill, *The Articles of Confederation: An Interpretation of the Social-Constitutional History of the American Revolution, 1774–1781*. Madison: University of Wisconsin Press, 1940.

———. The New Nation. *New York: Alfred A. Knopf, 1950*

Jodziewicz, Thomas. "Dual Localism in Seventeenth Century Connecticut: Relations between the General Courts and the Towns, 1635–1691." Unpublished dissertation, College of William and Mary, 1974.

Johnston, Henry P., ed. *Connecticut Military Record, 1775–1848: The Record of Connecticut Men in the Revolution*. Hartford, Conn.: Adjutant-General of Connecticut, 1889.

Jones, Frederick R. *History of Taxation in Connecticut, 1636–1776*. Baltimore, Md.: Johns Hopkins University Press, 1896.

Jordan, Philip H., Jr. "Connecticut Antifederalism on the Eve of the Constitutional Convention: A Letter from Benjamin Gale to Erastus Wolcott, February 10, 1787," *Bulletin* of the CHS. 28 (January, 1963) 1:14–21.

———. "Connecticut Politics During the Revolution and Confederation, 1776–1789." Unpublished dissertation, Yale University, 1962.

Jordan, Winthrop P. *White Over Black: American Attitudes Toward the Negro, 1550–1812*. Chapel Hill: University of North Carolina Press, 1968.

Kaminski, John P. "Antifederalism and the Perils of Homogenized History: A Review Esssay," *Rhode Island History*. 42 (February 1983) 1:30–37.

———. *A Necessary Evil?: Slavery and the Debate Over the Constitution*. Madison, Wisc.: Madison House, 1995.

———. "New York, The Reluctant Pillar" in Stephen L. Schechter, ed., *The Reluctant Pillar: New York and the Adoption of the Constitution*. Troy, N.Y.: Russell Sage College, 1985.

———, and Richard Leffler, eds. *Creating the Constitution*. Acton, Mass.: Copley Publishing Group, 1999.

Katz, Judith M. "Connecticut Newspapers and the Constitution, 1786–1788," *Bulletin* of the CHS. 30 (April, 1965) 2:33–44.

Kenyon, Cecilia M. "Men of Little Faith: The Anti-Federalists on the Nature of Representative Government," *William and Mary Quarterly*. 3rd ser. 12 (January, 1955) 1:3–43.

King, C. L., ed. *Life and Correspondence of Rufus King*. 6 vols. New York: G.P. Putnam's Sons, 1894–1900.

Kirby, John B. "Early American Politics—The Search for Ideology: An Historical Analysis and Critique of the Concept of Deference," *Journal of Politics*. 32 (November 1970) 4:808–38.

Kohn, Richard H. *Eagle and Sword: The Federalists and the Creation of the Military Establishment in America, 1783–1802.* New York: The Free Press, 1975.

——. "The Inside History of the Newburgh Conspiracy: America and the Coup D'Etat," *William and Mary Quarterly* 27 (April 1970) 187–220.

Lamb, Robert K. "The Entrepreneur and the Community," in William Miller, ed. *Men in Business: Essays in the History of Entrepreneurship.* Cambridge: Harvard University Press, 1952.

Lee, William W. *Barkhamsted and its Centennial, 1889 . . . .* Meriden, Conn.: Republican Steam Press, 1881.

Lettieri, Ronald J. "Connecticut's 'Publius': Oliver Ellsworth, *The Landholder Series,* and the Fabric of Connecticut Republicanism," *Connecticut History.* 23 (April, 1982) 24–45.

——. *Connecticut's Young Man of the Revolution: Oliver Ellsworth.* Chester, Conn.: Pequot Press, 1978.

Libby, Orin G. "The Geographical Distribution of the Vote of the Thirteen States on the Federal Constitution, 1787–8," *Bulletin* of the University of Wisconsin, Economics, Political Science, and History Series. 1 June, 1894)1:1–116. Reprinted in facsimile in *NDQ: North Dakota Quarterly.* 37(Summer, 1969)3 with a biographical introduction by Robert P. Wilkins. The page numbers are the same in both editions.

Loucks, Rupert Charles. "Connecticut in the American Revolution." Unpublished M.A. thesis, University of Wisconsin, 1959.

——. "'Let the Oppressed Go Free': Reformation and Revolution in English Connecticut, 1764–1775." Unpublished dissertation, University of Wisconsin, 1995.

Lovejoy, David S. *Rhode Island Politics and the American Revolution, 1760–1796.* Providence, R.I.: Brown University Press, 1958.

Lynd, Staughton. *Class Conflict, Slavery & The United States Constitution.* Indianapolis, Ind.: The Bobbs-Merrill Company, Inc., 1967.

Madison, James. The Papers of, Robert A. Rutland, ed., Vol. X. Chicago: University of Chicago Press, 1977.

Main, Jackson T. *The Antifederalists: Critics of the Constitution, 1781–1788.* Chicago: Quadrangle Paperbacks, 1964 [1961].

——. *Connecticut Society in the Era of the American Revolution.* Hartford, Conn.: The American Revolutionary Bicentennial Commission of Connecticut, 1977.

——. *Political Parties Before the Constitution.* Chapel Hill: University of North Carolina Press, 1973.

——. *Society and Economy in Colonial Connecticut.* Princeton, N.J.: Princeton University Press, 1985.

Marcus, Richard H. "The Militia of Colonial Connecticut, 1639–1775: An Institutional Study." Unpublished dissertation, University of Colorado, 1965.

Marks, Frederick W., III. *Independence on Trial: Foreign Affairs and the Making of the Constitution.* Baton Rouge: Louisiana State University Press, 1973.

Martin, James Kirby. *Men in Rebellion.* New Brunswick, N.J.: Rutgers University Press, 1973.

Marvin, George F., and William T.R. Marvin. *Descendants of Reinold and Matthew Marvin . . . .* Boston: T.R. Marvin and Sons, 1904.

McCaughey, Elizabeth P. *From Loyalist to Founding Father: The Political Odyssey of William Samuel Johnson.* New York: Columbia University Press, 1980.

McCusker, John J., and Russell R. Menard. *The Economy of British America, 1607–1789.* Chapel Hill: University of North Carolina Press, 1985.

McDonald, Forrest. *The Formation of the American Republic, 1776–1790.* Baltimore, Md.: Penguin Books, 1965.

———. *We the People: Economic Origins of the Constitution.* Chicago: University of Chicago Press, 1958.

——— and Ellen S. McDonald. *Requiem: Variations on Eighteenth-Century Themes.* Lawrence: University Press of Kansas, 1988.

McDonald, Terrence J., ed. *Plunkitt of Tammany Hall.* Boston: Bedford Books, 1994.

Morris, Richard B. *The Forging of the Union, 1781–1789.* New York: Harper and Row, 1987.

Moyer, Paul Benjamin. "Wild Yankees: Settlement, Conflict, and Localism Along Pennsylvania's Northwest Frontier, 1760–1820." Unpublished dissertation, College of William and Mary, 1999.

Nutting, Parker B. "Charter and Crown: Relations of Connecticut with the British Government, 1662–1776." Unpublished dissertation, University of North Carolina, Chapel Hill, 1972.

O'Connor, John E. *William Paterson, Lawyer and Statesman, 1745–1806.* New Brunswick, N.J.: Rutgers University Press, 1979.

Olson, Albert L. "Economic Aspects of the Migration from Connecticut, Particularly in the Late Eighteenth Century." Unpublished dissertation, Yale University, 1934.

O'Neill, Tip. *Man of the House: The Life and Political Memoirs of Speaker Tip O'Neill.* New York: Random House, 1987.

Onuf, Peter S. "Maryland: The Small Republic in a New Nation" in Gillespie and Lienesch, eds. *Ratifying the Constitution.* Lawrence: University of Kansas Press, 1989.

———. *The Origins of the Federal Republic: Judicial Controversies in the United States, 1775–1787.* Philadelphia: University of Pennsylvania Press, 1983.

Orcutt, Samuel. *History of Torrington . . . Biographies and Genealogies.* Albany, N.Y.: J. Munsell, 1878.

Platt, John D.R. *Jeremiah Wadsworth: Federalist Entrepreneur.* New York: Arno Press, 1982.

Purcell, Richard J. *Connecticut in Transition: 1775–1818.* Middletown, Conn.: Wesleyan University Press, 1963 [1918].

Rakov, Jack M., *The Beginnings of National Politics: An Interpretive History of the Continental Congress.* New York: Alfred A. Knopf, 1979.

———. *Original Meanings: Politics and Ideas in the Making of the Constitution.* New York: Random House, 1996.

Ransom, Stanley A. *History of Hartland . . . .* Hartland, Conn.: Hartland Bicentennial Committee, 1961.

Reisman, Janet A. "Money, Credit, and Federalist Political Economy," in Richard Beeman, et al. eds. *Beyond Confederation: Origins of the Constitution and American National Identity.* Chapel Hill: University of North Carolina Press, 1987.

Riker, William H. *The Strategy of Rhetoric: Campaigning for the American Constitution.* New Haven, Conn.: Yale University Press, 1996.

Riggs, Luther G., ed. *The Anarchiad: A New England Poem (1786–1787).* Gainesville, Fla.: Scholars' Facsimiles, 1967.

Robinson, Donald L. *Slavery in the Structure of American Politics, 1765–1820.* New York: Harcourt, Brace, Jovanovich, 1971.

Roeber, A. G. *Faithful Magistrates and Republican Lawyers: Creators of Virginia Legal Culture, 1680–1810.* Chapel Hill: University of North Carolina Press, 1981.

Roll, Charles W., Jr. "We, Some of the People: Apportionment in the Thirteen State Conventions Ratifying the Constitution." *Journal of American History.* 56 (June, 1969)1:21–40.

Rossiter, Clinton. *1787: The Grand Convention.* New York: Macmillan Company, 1966.

Rowland, Kate Mason. *The Life of George Mason, 1725–1792.* 2 vols. New York: G.P. Putnam's Sons, 1892.

Royster, Charles. *A Revolutionary People at War: The Continental Army and the American Character, 1775–1783.* New York: W.W. Norton & Company, 1981 [1979].

Rush, Benjamin. *The Autobiography of Benjamin Rush; His "Travels Through Life" Together with His Commonplace Book for 1789–1813.* G. Corner, ed. Princeton, N.J.: Princeton University Press, 1948.

Rutland, Robert A. *The Ordeal of the Constitution: The Antifederalists and the Ratification Struggle of 1787–1788.* Norman: University of Oklahoma Press, 1965.

Saladino, Gaspare J. "The Economic Revolution in Late Eighteenth Century Connecticut." Unpublished dissertation, University of Wisconsin, 1964.

Sedgwick, Charles F. *General History of the Town of Sharon, Litchfield County, Connecticut . . . .* Amenia, N.Y.: Charles Walsh Printer, 1898.

———. *A History of the Town of Sharon, Litchfield County.* Hartford, Conn.: Case, Tiffany & Co., 1842.

Selesky, Harold E. "Military Leadership in American Colonial Society." Unpublished dissertation, Yale University, 1984.

———. "Patterns of Officeholding in the Connecticut General Assembly: 1725–1774," in George J. Willauer, Jr., ed. *A Lyme Miscellany, 1776–1976.* Middletown, Conn.: Wesleyan University Press, 1977.

———. *War and Society in Colonial Connecticut.* New Haven, Conn.: Yale University Press, 1990.

Selleck, Charles M. *Norwalk.* Norwalk, Conn.: pub. by the author, 1896.

Sheehan, Colleen A., and Gary L. McDowell. *Friends of the Constitution: Writings of the "Other" Federalists, 1787–1788.* Indianapolis, Ind.: Liberty Fund, 1998.

Sherry, Suzanna. "The Founders' Unwritten Constitution," *University of Chicago Law Review.* 54 (Fall, 1987) 4:1127–77.

Shipton, Clifford, ed. *Sibley's Biographical Sketches of Those Who Attended Harvard College.* 6 vols. Worcester, Mass.: American Antiquarian Society, 1933–1968.

Shy, John. *A People Numerous and Armed: Reflections on the Military Struggle for American Independence.* New York: Oxford University Press, 1976.

Slonim, Shlomo. "Securing States' Interests at the 1787 Constitutional Convention: A Reassessment," *Studies in American Political Development.* 14(Spring 2000) 1:1–19.

Smith, Paul H., ed. *Letters of Delegates to Congress, 1774 to 1789.* 25 vols. Washington, D.C.: Library of Congress, 1976–98.

Smith, Roberta K. *The Constant Years: The Life of Constant Southworth (1730–1813)*. Mansfield, Conn.: Mansfield Historical Society, 1990.

Stark, Bruce P. *Connecticut Signer: William Williams*. Chester, Conn.: Pequot Press, 1975.

———. "Lebanon, Connecticut: A Study of Society and Politics in the Eighteenth Century." Unpublished dissertation, University of Connecticut, 1970.

———. "The Upper House in Early Connecticut History" in George Willauer, Jr., ed. *A Lyme Miscellany, 1776–1976*. Middletown, Conn.: Wesleyan University Press, 1977.

Starr, Edward C. *A History of Cornwall, Connecticut: A Typical New England Town*. New Haven, Conn.: Tuttle, Morehouse, 1926.

Steiner, Bernard C. "Connecticut's Ratification of the Federal Constitution," *Proceedings* of the American Antiquarian Society. 25(October 1915)2:70–127.

———. *History of Guilford and Madison, Connecticut*. Guilford, Conn.: Guilford Free Library, 1975 [1897].

Steiner, Bruce E. "Anglican Officeholding in Pre-Revolutionary Connecticut: The Parameters of New England Community," *William and Mary Quarterly*. 3rd ser. 31(July, 1974)3:369–406.

———. *Connecticut Anglicans in the Revolutionary Era: A Study in Community Tensions*. Hartford, Conn.: The Pequot Press for the Connecticut Bicentennial Commission, 1978.

Stiles, Ezra. *Extracts from the Itineraries and Other Miscellanies of Ezra Stiles, . . . with Correspondence*. Franklin Bowditch Dexter, ed. New Haven, Conn.: Yale University Press, 1916.

———. *The Literary Diary of Ezra Stiles*, Vol. III., Franklin Bowdich Dexter, ed. New York: Charles Scribner's Sons, 1901.

Stiles, Henry R. *The History of Ancient Windsor*. Somersworth, N.H.: New Hampshire Publishing Company, 1976 [1892].

Stiverson, Gregory. "Necessity, The Mother of Union: Maryland and the Constitution" in Conley and Kaminski, eds. *The Constitution and the States*. Madison, Wisc.: Madison House, 1988.

Storing, Herbert J. *The Complete Anti-Federalist*. 7 vols. Chicago: University of Chicago Press, 1981.

———. *What the Anti-Federalists Were For: The Political Thought of the Opponents of the Constitution*. Chicago: University of Chicago Press, 1981.

Susquehannah Company Papers. Julian P. Boyd and Robert J. Taylor, eds. II vols. Wilkes-Barre, Penna.: Wyoming Historical Society, 1930–1971.

Swift, Zephaniah. *A System of the Laws of the State of Connecticut*. 2 vols. Windham: printed by John Byrne, 1795.

Tansill, Charles C., ed. *Documents Illustrative of the Formation of the Union of the American States*. Washington, D.C.: U.S. Government Printing Office, 1927.

Taylor, Robert J. *Colonial Connecticut: A History*. Millwood, N.Y.: KTO Press, 1979.

———. "Trial at Trenton," *William and Mary Quarterly*. 26(October 1969)4:502–47.

Thoms, Herbert. *Jared Eliot, Minister, Doctor, Scientist, and His Connecticut*. Hamden, Conn.: The Shoe String Press, 1967.

Tocqueville, Alexis de. *Democracy in America.* 2 vols. Phillips Bradley, ed. New York: Random House, 1945.

Torrington Congregational Church. *Historical Notice of the Congregational Church in Torrington, Conn. . . .* Hartford, Conn.: Elihu Geer Stationers, 1852.

Trowbridge, Francis B. *A History of the Descendants of William Hoadley.* New Haven, Conn.: the author, 1894.

Trumbull, Benjamin. *Complete History of Connecticut Civil and Ecclesiastical.* 2 vols. New London: H.D. Utley, 1898. [1797, 1818].

Trumbull, J. Hammond, ed. *Memorial History of Hartford County, Connecticut, 1633–1884.* 2 vols. Boston: Edward L. Osgood, 1886.

Turner, Sylvie, ed. *Journal Kept by William Williams . . . May 1757.* Hartford, Conn.: CHS, 1975.

Vibert, William M. *Three Centuries of Simsbury.* Simsbury, Conn.: Simsbury Tercentenary Committee, Inc., 1970.

Wachtell, Harvey M. "The Conflict Between Localism and Nationalism in Connecticut, 1783–1788." Unpublished dissertation, University of Missouri, 1971.

Waldstreicher, David and Stephen R. Grossbart. "Abraham Bishop's Vocation; or the Mediation of Jeffersonian Politics," *Journal of the Early American Republic.* 18 (Winter 1998)4:617–58.

Walradt, Henry F. *The Financial History of Connecticut from 1789 to 1861.* New Haven, Conn.: Yale University, 1912.

Ward, Christopher. *The War of the Revolution.* 2 vols. New York: Macmillan Company, 1952.

Ward, George K. *Andrew Ward and His Descendants, 1597–1910.* New York: Association of the Descendants of Andrew Ward, 1910.

Warfel, Harry R., ed. *Letters of Noah Webster.* New York: Library Publishers, 1953.

Warfle, Richard T. "Connecticut's Critical Period: The Response to the Susquehannah Affair, 1769–1774." Unpublished dissertation, University of Connecticut, 1972.

Warren, Charles. *The Making of the Constitution.* New York: Barnes & Noble, Inc., 1967. [1928].

Warren-Adams Letters. Collections of the Massachusetts Historical Society. 2. vols. Boston: MHS, 1917, 1925.

Watson, Alan D. "States' Rights and Agrarianism Ascendant" in Conley and Kaminski, eds. *The Constitution and the States.* Madison, Wisc.: Madison House, 1988.

Wattenberg, Ben J., ed. *The Statistical History of the United States from Colonial Times to the Present.* New York: Basic Books, 1976.

Weaver, Glenn. *Jonathan Trumbull, Connecticut's Merchant Magistrate, 1710–1785.* Hartford: CHS, 1956.

———. Book review of J.T. Main's *Society and Economy of Colonial Connecticut, Bulletin* of the CHS 50(Spring, 1985)2:105–07.

Webber, Samuel G. *A Genealogy of the Southworths . . . .* Boston: The Fort Mill Press, 1905.

Webster, Noah. *A Collection of Essays and Fugitive Writings, on Moral, Historical, Political and Literary Subjects.* Boston: Thomas and Andrews, 1790.

Weitenkampf, Frank. *Political Caricature in the United States.* New York: 1953.

Welch, Richard E., Jr. *Theodore Sedgwick, Federalist: A Political Portrait.* Middletown, Conn.: Wesleyan University Press, 1965.

Wheeler, Richard G., and George Hilton, eds. *Barkhamsted Heritage.* Barkhamsted, Conn.: Barkhamsted Historical Society, 1975.

Wiebe, Robert H. *The Search for Order, 1877–1920.* New York: Hill and Wang, 1967.

Wilder, Moses H. *Book of the Wilders: A Contribution to the History of the Wilders.* New York: Edward O. Jenkins, 1878.

Williams, Mark. *A Tempest in a Small Town: The Myth and Reality of Country Life, Granby, Connecticut, 1680–1940.* Granby, Conn.: Salmon Brook Historical Society, 1996.

Williams, Chilton. "The Connecticut Property Test and the East Guilford Voter," Connecticut Historical Society *Bulletin* 19 (October 1954) 10–4.

Willingham, William F. *Connecticut Revolutionary: Eliphalet Dyer.* Chester, Conn.: Pequot Press, 1976.

Wood, Frederic J. *The Turnpikes of New England.* Boston: Marshall Jones Company, 1919.

Wood, Gordon S. *The Creation of the American Republic, 1776–1787.* Chapel Hill: University of North Carolina Press, 1969.

———. "Interests and Disinterestedness in the Making of the Constitution," in Richard Beeman et al., eds., *Beyond Confederation: Origins of the Constitution and American National Identity.* Chapel Hill: University of North Carolina Press, 1987.

———. *The Radicalism of the American Revolution.* New York: Alfred A. Knopf, 1992. I used the Random House Vintage paperback edition.

Zeichner, Oscar. *Connecticut Years of Controversy, 1750–1776.* Hamden, Conn.: Archon Books, 1970 [1949].

Zilversmit, Arthur. *The First Emancipation: The Abolition of Slavery in the North.* Chicago: University of Chicago Press, 1967.

Index

Abolition, in Conn., 65, 69, 184n5; in the north, 64–65

Adams, Andrew, 174n48; as depicted in cartoon, 158

Adams, John, 178n34; on Conn. aristocracy, 17; on Conn. government, 18; on Ellsworth and Sherman, 48; on Sherman, 45

Africa, as source of slaves, 65

African Americans, suffrage in Conn., 164n12

Age, at Convention of 1787, 44; on the Conn. frontier, 149; of militia, 19, 166n34, 167n40; of ratifiers, 99, 192n14

Agriculture, in Conn., 29–30

Alabama, 68

Algerines, as extortionists, 27

Allen, Ethan, 26

Amending Process, 61

American Revolution, and slavery, 184n10, n13

Anarchiad, 94, 116, 157–59, 196n11

Anglicans, 46, 47, 99, 117, 130, 192n15

Annapolis Meeting, 3, 40

Antifederalists, 40, 84, 110–31 *passim;* collective portrait, 99–100; in Conn., 6, 7, 40, 81–82, 94, 99–100, 136, 158, 190n44, 191n10; ideology of, 191n4; in other states, 162n12; social attitudes, 92–93; stereotype, 94

Antifederal publications, kept out of Conn., 88

Antinationalists, in Conn., 42–43, 53, 101–09, 158–59, 110–31 *passim;* at Convention of 1787, 137

Articles of Confederation, 29, 86; as bad for Conn., 37; courts, 186n44; equal representation in, 58; fear of altering, 40; as federation, 52; first president, 16; and national debt, 61; similarities to Constitution, 81; as state rights, 61; and Trenton Decision, 26; violated, 39

Atwood, Nathaniel, 101, 151

Baldwin, Abraham, 57, 71, 81; on slave trade, 70

Baltimore, 133

Banning, Lance, 4

Barlow, Joel, 159

Basset, Daniel, 118, 119

Barkhamsted, 200n4; antifederal, 127, 149–50

Beach, John, 119, 197n25

Beach, Samuel, 119

Bedford, Gunning, 53, 54

Beecher, Henry Ward, 192n17

Berkshire County, Mass., deputies, 14

Bills of Rights, 5, 6, 50, 83, 85, 135

Black Rock, 30

Board of Trade, 12

Boston, 13, 30, 31, 66, 107, 133; dominates Mass. government, 14, 31; merchants, 175n84; and West Indian trade, 69

Bradley, Philip B., 192n20

Branford, 113, 127; antifederalists, 118

Bristol, endorses Constitution, 188n12

Brooks, David, 119

Buel, Richard, 107

Bulkeley, Gershom, 12

Burnham, Isaac, 150

Burrall, Charles, 98, 101, 130, 131

Burr Family, 16

Butler, Pierce, 134; at convention, 72

Calhoun, John C., 61

Calvinism, 50, 176n18; of Sherman, 44–45

Canaan, federal, 131